Pope John Paul II

A FESTIVE PROFILE

Pope John Paul II

A FESTIVE PROFILE

BY

LUDVIK NEMEC, Ph.D., S.T.D.

with a Foreword by

JOHN CARDINAL KROL
Archbishop of Philadelphia

CATHOLIC BOOK PUBLISHING CO.
NEW YORK

NIHIL OBSTAT: Daniel V. Flynn, J.C.D.
Censor Librorum

IMPRIMATUR: Joseph T. O'Keefe
Vicar General, Archdiocese of New York

The nihil obstat and imprimatur are official declarations that a book or pamphlet is free of doctrinal or moral error. No implication is contained therein that those who have granted the nihil obstat and imprimatur agree with the contents, opinions or statements expressed.

ACKNOWLEDGMENTS

The author and publisher are grateful for permission to quote from the following copyrighted works:

Francine Cardman, "A Lightning Look at the History of Christian Spirituality," *The Wind Is Rising*, ed. William R. Callahan, SJ, and Francine Cardman, 2nd ed. (Mount Rainier, Md: Quixote Center, 1979), pp. 37-40.

Peter Hebblethwaite, *The Year of Three Popes* (Cleveland: William Collins, 1979).

Leszek Kolakowski, "Pomyslne Proroctwa i Pobozne Zyczenia laika na progu Nowego Pontyfikatu w wiecznej Sprawie Praw Cesarskich i Boskich," *Kultura* (Paris, Dec. 1978), pp. 5-13.

Karol Wojtyla (Andrjez Jawien), *Easter Vigil and Other Poems*, trans. Jerzy Peterkiewicz (New York: Random House, 1979).

NOTE: If through inadvertence a copyright has failed to be acknowledged, sincere apologies are offered together with the assurance that this omission will be remedied in future editions.

PHOTO CREDITS: Libreria Editrice Redenzione: 2*; NC News Service: 1*, 3* (bottom), 4* (top), 5* (bottom), 6*, 7* (top), 12* (bottom); Ludvik Nemec: 7* (bottom); *Osservatore Romano*: cover; Religious News Service: 3* (top), 5* (top), 9*, 10*, 11*, 12* (top); Leo Rudnytsky: 6* (bottom).

(T-800)

ISBN: 0-89942-000-1

Humbly dedicated
to
His Excellency
the Most Reverend John L. Morkovsky, S.T.D.
Bishop of Galveston-Houston and
Chairman of Trustees of St. John Neumann Chapel
in the National Shrine of the Immaculate Conception
in Washington, D.C.

and

the Reverend Sister Alice Anita Murphy, SSJ
Superior General of the Sisters of St. Joseph of Philadelphia
and Chairman of Trustees of Chestnut Hill College
in appreciation and admiration
by the author

FOREWORD

THE annals of the Catholic Church will mark the year 1978 as the year of two conclaves in 7 weeks and three Popes in 71 days; as the year of two conclaves with the largest number of electors—111 from five continents and 50 countries; as the year of the election of the youngest Pope in 125 years; the first non-Italian Pope in 455 years; the first Pope from Poland since it became Christian in 966; the first Pope from a Communist governed country; the first author and lecturer in philosophy to be elected Pope in over 700 years, and as the first Pope to speak English, Polish, and the many other languages used by Pope John Paul II in his solemn inaugural homily.

Seldom had there been more interest of the genéral public in the election of a Pope than there was in the two 1978 conclaves. The first conclave was covered by representatives of the press which had a potential readership of over one billion, and representatives of the electronic media which had a potential of 750 million viewers and listeners. At the second conclave both the printed and electronic media respectively directed their reports to over a billion people. Before the conclaves there was a great deal of speculation, and real and near experts—some using computers—discussed the favorites and predicted the results of the election. Seldom were predictions as wide of the mark as they were in the two 1978 conclaves. The attempts of some of the forecasters to explain the surprising results of the election demanded more faith than is required to believe Our Lord's promise: "The Holy Spirit, whom the Father will send in my name, will teach you everything. . . . He will guide you in all truth, . . . He will confute the world" (John 14:26; 16:13).

Seldom too has there been such an overwhelming response to and acceptance of a Supreme Pontiff by the Catholic and non-Catholic world, as there has been of Pope John Paul II. The general audiences could not be ac-

commodated in the Audience Hall, so an additional audience was scheduled for the Basilica. Then two audiences were held in the Hall and one in the Basilica. Finally, to accommodate the 50 to 70,000 requests, the general audience was transferred to—and is now held in—Saint Peter's Square.

There has been a great deal of curiosity about the person and background of Pope John Paul II. What is his charism? It is easy to say that he was born in a small Polish village, one of two sons of a family of modest means. A rugged man of the people, who studied diligently, who worked in a quarry, and a chemical factory, who was involved in the many problems created by the Nazi invasion and subsequent Communist control of Poland. He is a poet, playwright, and author of books and many articles, a philosopher and theologian, a professor, lecturer, retreat master, a linguist and world traveler, He is perfectly at ease with the poor people of the land, and with brilliant scholars. A bare-bone statistical biography does not provide the answers that people seek.

The Reverend Doctor Ludvik Nemec, a scholar and author, in his "Pope John Paul II" endeavors to provide information that will satisfy those who seek to know something of the man, his origins, his work, and his office. This book is well documented, and reflects the author's own knowledge and experiences with the circumstances and situations which helped to form and develop the person who was elected by his confreres to be the Supreme Pontiff.

This "Festive Profile" is not just another biography. It is a history of the many factors which influenced and helped to form the character of our Holy Father. My best recommendation of this volume cannot possibly match the merits of its contents. It is a treasure of information about the Papacy, Poland, and Pope John Paul II.

John Cardinal Krol

April 12, 1979. *Archbishop of Philadelphia*

INTRODUCTION

TO WRITE about the Pope, the head of the Catholic Church, is no small task because of the complex nature, conditioning, and mission of his office as well as the difficulties of getting proper and adequate information. To write a pope's biography is especially difficult because of the many secrets inherent in his office, but since every biography is something like a detective story—a few clues are handled, a few witnesses examined, and from these a complicated series of events reconstructed—in it is the pleasure of the chase.

Contrary to Voltaire's saying that "no man that ever lived deserved a quarto to himself," the Pope does seem to deserve it because of the vital importance of the mission of the Vicar of Christ, especially responsible to continue the salvific action of Jesus Christ in the framework of historical dimensions. To write the biography of the still living Pope implies, moreover, a great responsibility in the writer's precision to convey pertinent data and events because of the ever-impending check board for immediate verification. Notwithstanding, such a work is demanded when the holder of the papacy is one certain to play a decisive role against a background of difficulties, such as the present Pope must confront.

Faced with the request of the publisher, I was hesitant at first to undertake this task, but later I felt it my special privilege to have an opportunity to write about the first Slavic Pope. I followed then my interest and found in it as well a great pleasure.

At this point I wish to express gratitude to all the understanding persons who have helped me in this: first to His Eminence John Cardinal Krol, for his kindness in writing a Foreword to this biography. I thank also Sister Margaret

Rose, SSJ, English scholar of Chestnut Hill College, for ameliorating my style in the English idiom and reading the whole of the manuscript. I thank also the Very Reverend Tomas Špidlik, SJ, professor of the Oriental Institute and the Gregorian University (Rome); the Reverend Peter Ovečka, SJ, editor-in-chief of *Nový Život* (Rome) for providing Italian, German, and Spanish materials; Dr. Leo D. Rudnytsky, professor of La Salle College (Philadelphia), for providing some Polish material; and Monsignor Peter Lekavy of Cavalier, North Dakota, for some in German. I thank Mrs. Jeanne Brady who read critically and typed the entire manuscript.

Not least am I grateful for acceptance of my dedication by His Excellency, the Most Reverend Bishop John L. Morkovsky of Galveston-Houston, and Reverend Sister Alice Anita Murphy, SSJ, Superior General of the Sisters of St. Joseph of Philadelphia, whose motherhouse is in Chestnut Hill.

For the pictures which add much meaning to the text, I express thanks to Monsignor John P. Foley, Reverend Bernard Witkowski, and Reverend Leo J. McKenzie, all of Philadelphia; to Dr. Barbara Klaczynska Schmidt of Temple University; Janice Kubiak of the Northwest Regional Library of the Free Library of Philadelphia; as well as to Dr. Carmen Mayer of Mount Airy Community College. Special acknowledgment is likewise expressed to all the authors and writers, the reporters and interpreters, the prognosticators and analysts, as they are quoted in my notes, on the basis of which resources was written my festive profile of *Pope John Paul II*, which is hereby presented to the public.

Ludvik Nemec

Feast of St. Joseph, March 19, 1979

CONTENTS

CHART OF KAROL WOJTYLA'S LIFE IN PERSPECTIVE

Parents	Karol Wojtyla and Emilia Kaczorowska .
May 18, 1920	Their son, Karol, born in Wadowice in the Beskidi Mountains, Poland.
1926-1931	Elementary School in Wadowice.
1932-1938	Studied at gymnasium in Wadowice, outstanding student in humanities, a linguist; as student he edited a Catalogue of Historical Monuments in his native city.
June 1938	Graduated from gymnasium with diploma of maturity.
1938-1942	Matriculated at the Faculty of Philosophy, Department of Philology at the Jagiellon University at Krakow. He developed a love for poetry, wrote poems, and became a member of the Rhapsody Theater in Krakow.
1941-1942	Worked as a miner in the quarry at Zakozowek, and then as a worker in the chemical plant of Solvey in Krakow.
1942-1945	Initiated his course of theological studies in a clandestinely arranged seminary in Cardinal Sapieha's palace, while politically involved in underground activities against the Nazis.
1945-1946	Accepted into Major Theological Seminary; opened after the War, in 1945.
Nov. 1, 1946	Ordained priest for the Archdiocese of Krakow.
1946-1948	Advanced studies at the graduate school of philosophy of the University of St. Thomas Aquinas (Angelicum) in Rome; earned doctorate degree in philosophy (Ph.D.) with a defense of his disseration, "The Virtue of Faith in the Works of St. John of the Cross."
Fall of 1948	Returned to Poland and matriculated at the Faculty of Theology at the Jagiellon University in Krakow.
June 1949	Presented his extended doctoral dissertation on "The Problem of Faith in the Works of St. John of the Cross," and was awarded a degree in sacred theology (S.T.D.) maxima cum laude.

1948-1951	Chaplain to two parishes in Krakow and simultaneously chaplain to university students.
1951-1953	Pursued his academic career by presenting his habilitationis thesis: "Evaluation as to the Possibility of Founding a Catholic Ethics on the Basis of the System of Max Scheler," at the Jagiellon University, as the requirement to become docent.
1953	Assistant professor of moral theology at Major Seminary at Krakow, then on Faculty of Theology.
1954	Accepted also the post of professor of ethics at the Catholic University at Lublin, where he became also chairman of the department of philosophy.
July 24, 1958	Appointed titular bishop of Osubi and auxiliary bishop to the apostolic administrator, Eugene Baziak, in Krakow.
1959	Became an established scholar and prolific writer and was named a member of the Polish Academy of Sciences.
June 1962	Appointed capitular vicar for Archdiocese of Krakow.
June 13, 1964	Appointed archbishop of Archdiocese of Krakow and de facto chancellor of the Catholic University at Lublin.
June 26, 1967	Created cardinal by Pope Paul VI.
Sept. 1974	Participated in reconciliation services with Cardinal Döpfner, archbishop of Munich, in the infamous concentration camp in Dachau.
June 1977	Awarded honorary doctoral degree from the Johannes-Gutenberg University in Mainz.
Sept. 20-24, 1978	Companion of the Polish primate, Stefan Cardinal Wyszynski on official visit of reconciliation in Federal Republic of Germany.
Oct. 16, 1978	Elected pope, took the name of John Paul II; became the first non-Italian pope since Pope Hadrian VI (1522-23)
Oct. 22, 1978	Solemn inauguration into papal ministry at St. Peter's Square.

Chapter 1

THE ELECTION OF JOHN PAUL II AS A SIGN OF THE TIMES

A Non-Italian Pope

THE election of a non-Italian pope was a great surprise to the world, especially after the lapse of 455 years, for Hadrian VI (1522-23) of Holland was the last non-Italian pontiff.[1] One must wonder why there was a general assumption that the pope should be an Italian, if one kept in mind that the Church is universal and that canon law eliminates any kind of national or racial preference for this office.[2]

The most acceptable explanation seems to be the fact that the head of the universal Church is concomitantly the bishop of Rome. As long as Rome was the capital of the world and the Roman Empire in existence, the combination of the office as "head of the Church and bishop of Rome" was well substantiated. After the division and disintegration of the Roman Empire, however, the title of bishop of Rome lost in subsequent centuries some of its meaning of universality, although it was always believed and recognized as such even in time of rivalry among the patriarchs[3] charged with the administration of the universal Church.

In the later Middle Ages, Rome succeeded in keeping this position and survived in it during all political struggles until the beginning of the 19th century when the struggle for the independence of Italy emerged (1831) and was successful in 1870 with Garibaldi's seizure of Rome. Thus ended the Papal States, a symbol of the pope's sovereignty.

Here the notion of Italian nationality came really to the front. With the creation of Vatican City,[4] a sovereign state governed by the pope, by the Lateran Treaty of February 11, 1929, the universality of the Church and the primacy of the pope were reaffirmed also in a public and international forum despite the circumstance that Rome became Italian. This, nonetheless, made it difficult for any non-Italian to aspire to the position of pope.

In spite of all this, among the 264 popes some 15 nationalities are so far represented, although in early centuries one could hardly speak of nationalities in the modern sense of the word. The Christian world was divided for a long time into but two cultural spheres, Greek and Latin. Until the second century, Greek was also a liturgical language in Rome. Every Western cleric had until the 13th century a Latin education, and Latin was, so to speak, the "maternal language." Furthermore, instead of nationalities in the international forum, states were important.

One is, therefore, hard put to state precisely how many non-Italians were on the papal throne. Approximately, in the last 1000 years, when the nationality of the first-millennium popes was often unknown, only 21 of the 125 popes were non-Italian. Twelve were French, four German, two Spanish, one Portuguese, and one Dutch. Including popes of the present millennium, at least 52 of the 264 are known to have been non-Italian. Among the early pontiffs were three Africans, six Syrians, and eleven Greeks.

Previous Non-Italian Popes

A short review reveals that two popes were Jewish, namely, St. Peter and his third successor St. Clement, six were Syrians, and eleven were Greeks—the last of whom was Zacharias (741-752) who anointed Pepin as ruler of the Franks—who were also partly responsible for the fact that in 1054 a great schism was effected between the East and the West.[5]

Three popes were Africans, namely Victor I (189-199), Miltiades (312-313), and Gelasius I (492-499), who prohibited the last pagan feast of the Lupercalia to be celebrated in Rome. There were only three Spaniards: Damasus I (366-384), Calixtus III (1455-58), and his nephew Alexander VI (1492-1503). Damasus was an important pope in the 4th century, for he commissioned St. Jerome to translate the Bible into Latin (the Vulgate). Calixtus was of the famous Borgia family, as was Alexander VI who is generally depicted as the bad Pope.

The French have the most representatives among the non-Italian popes, a total of twelve in all: Sylvester II (999-1003), who crowned the first Hungarian ruler, St. Stephen; Urban II (1088-99), who called the First Crusade and was proclaimed blessed in 1881; Urban IV (1261-64), son of a shoemaker, who introduced in 1264 the Feast of Corpus Christi; Clement IV (1265-68); Martin IV (1281-85); Clement V (1305-14), a Dominican priest, who in 1305 was crowned in Lyons and resided in Avignon; John XXII (1316-34), one of the most influential popes of Avignon; Benedict XII (1334-42), a Cistercian, who built a papal palace in Avignon; Clement VI (1342-52), a Benedictine; Innocent VI (1352-62); Urban V (1362-70), who was beatified in 1870; and Gregory XI (1370-78), who returned to Rome on January 17, 1377, and was the last French pope.

German popes were five: Gregory V (996-999), Clement II (1046-47), Damasus II (1048), Leo IX (1049-54), and Victor II (1055-57), all zealous supporters of moral reform of the Church.

There was one English pope, namely Hadrian IV (1154-59); one Portuguese, John XXI (1276-77); and one Dutch, Hadrian VI (1522-23), who was a saintly man.

Possible Reasons for Choice of John Paul II

In an historical perspective of the popes, one can see that a call for a non-Italian pope was usually conditioned by certain crises or exigencies of political pressure or reform.

This can perhaps be applied to the circumstances under which Karol Cardinal Wojtyla was elected on October 16, 1978, as Pope John Paul II. The Pope acknowledged his election as "an act of trust and great courage"[6] in an audience on October 18 with the College of Cardinals. The circumstance that he comes from Poland, a country behind the Iron Curtain, had a great influence certainly—in addition to his good personal qualities of integrity, piety, learning, knowledge of several languages, skill in political maneuvering and diplomacy—so that the vast majority of the 111 cardinals in the conclave gave their votes in his favor.

One of the most probable reasons for their choice of this Polish prelate may well have been not alone their calculation to tear down the Iron Curtain or their thought as to the effect it might have on Pope Paul VI's policy of detente with Eastern European nations, but their consideration of its influence on many other issues, chiefly concerning human rights. Cardinal Krol contradicts all these speculations by insisting that "the Polish Pope's experience in dealing with Communism was not definitive in his election, however. The first consideration was his role as spiritual head of the Church. There was only one objective, to choose a religious leader, a man of deep piety; the rest was secondary."[7]

The cardinals' choice evidently met with the enthusiastic approval of the general public, as is seen in the tremendous popularity this Polish Pope enjoys. Crowds of people gather wherever he appears.

Recent Shift in Policies toward Communism

Most significant and peculiar to this election is that it reflects also a shift of Vatican policies toward Communism. Just ten years ago, the election of a pope from a Communist country in Eastern Europe would have been almost unthinkable.

During the early 1960s, the Vatican was caught in a cold war with the Soviet Union and its Eastern European satellites—the choice of a pope from the area would have but worsened relations between Church and State.[8]

A rapprochement with Eastern Europe had been initiated cautiously by Pope John XXIII and pursued by his successor, Paul VI. It led to some improvement in relations between the Vatican and Communist-ruled countries.

In 1966, Pope Paul received the first of several visits from Soviet Foreign Minister Andrei Gromyko. This marked the beginning of Pope Paul's policy of improving relations with the Communist block, to secure an easing of restrictions on the tens of millions of Roman Catholics behind the Iron Curtain; but it was and is uneasy dialogue in view of the bitter historical background of Soviet hostility toward religion and of Roman Catholic opposition to materialistic atheism.

The policy of rapprochement paid some dividends, however, and other Communist visitors to the Vatican followed, including the then Soviet President Nikolai Podgorny, President Josip Broz Tito of Yugoslavia, and others.

A major breakthrough came in 1971, when Archbishop Agostino Casaroli, Pope Paul's foreign minister, made an historic visit to Moscow—the first papal envoy to confer with the Soviet officials since the Bolshevik Revolution overthrew the Czar in 1917.

A price had nonetheless to be paid for the Vatican's new policy of improved relations with the Eastern bloc. In 1974 Jozsef Cardinal Mindzenty, who had spent 15 years in defiant self-exile in the United States Embassy in Budapest, was advised by the Vatican to relinquish the Embassy and to go into exile as he was brought back to Rome.[9] It was a symbolic gesture by the Vatican—decried by Pope Paul's critics at the time—which indicated that the Catholic Church was prepared to modify its old stand in its search for common ground with the Communists.

Loss of Momentum in Detente

When Pope Paul died in August of 1978, there were signs that the Vatican's Eastern European approach had lost some momentum. Only one Communist State in Eastern Europe—Yugoslavia[10]—had established full diplomatic relations with the Vatican, and visits to Rome by the leaders of Hungary, Czechoslovakia, and Poland had failed to lead to any breakthrough in East-West relations.

The last part of Pope Paul's reign marked a state of mutual tolerance, but one soured by continuing tensions. Consequently, the Pope took the initiatives.

Pope Paul VI himself raised the issue when Polish Communist party leader Eduard Gierek visited Rome in December 1977. He told Gierek that the Vatican was interested in the full application of the human rights accords signed at the Conference, and that the Church sought only freedom to develop without obstacles.[11] The Pontiff did not specify the obstacles, but Catholic leaders in Eastern European countries have complained of lack of media coverage, of problems of providing adequate Christian education, and of subjection to military service of seminarians training for the priesthood.

Still serious problems for Catholics and others—for all Christians—remain in Czechoslovakia, the Soviet Ukraine, Lithuania, Romania, and elsewhere, according to Vatican sources. Pope John Paul I, who reigned for just 33 days, probably had not time even to consider these problems.[12]

In the light of all these facts, it is no wonder that the election of John Paul II created unusual excitement and met with such surprise as was seldom experienced in papal elections. By expressing their spontaneous joy at this election, the people demonstrated immediately that they sensed the meaning of the act, in that drastic changes in the relations of the Church to Communistic regimes may be forthcoming.[13] "On the problem of detente, I expect great things of the Pope," said Andrew Young, United States Ambassador to the United Nations, in a press interview in Rome shortly after he had met privately with the Pope.[14] This and similar hopes in regard to other concerns are being expressed.

Papal Choice—An Accurate Reading of Signs of the Times

The totally unexpected papal election of Cardinal Wojtyla was an event that gives a startling new twist to the future of the Church not only in Poland but also in the entire Communist world. In retrospect, the election of this Pope, so outspoken a critic of Marxism, might force Poland's Communist rulers, as well as those of other countries behind the Iron Curtain, to start rethinking their entire strategy toward the Vatican.

It is against this background that, if it be true that "at all times, the Church carries the responsibility of reading the signs of the times and of interpreting them in the light of the Gospel,"[15] John Paul's election surely represents an unusually accurate reading by the College of Cardinals of the signs of the times. In itself, this surprising but so very apt choice for pope is a sign of the times, an election fraught with significance for the Church's future.

From all accounts, the new Pope is a man steeped in the practice of regular prayer, of disciplined study, and of orderly pastoral activity. Moreover, he has been tested in perhaps the toughest school in the whole Church today, governance of the huge Archdiocese of Krakow that lies behind the Iron Curtain. The new Pope knows what it is like to try to hand on the Catholic faith to the next generation in a country where the hostile government, officially and openly, does everything possible to prevent practice of the faith and its teaching and which even aggressively promotes a totally atheistic ideology.

The West, which fails also to do and to teach, although it is free, should ponder the further mysterious way in which

God, for the salvation of mankind that he has promised, is working through the fervent Christianity that still flourishes behind the Iron Curtain. Some of the vitality and conviction of the Christian faith in Eastern Europe, where Christians are suffering persecution, can and might be infused by the new Vicar of Christ into members of the Church in other lands, where the faith so often seems to have grown tepid and so many hearts grown cold. We, certainly, are entitled to believe and to rejoice that this is one of the things the Holy Spirit had in mind in this election.

A Man of the Second Vatican Council

The new Pope is very much a man of the Second Vatican Council in his authentic interpretation of the Church's magisterium. A strong proponent of the Council's *Declaration on Religious Freedom*,[16] he sees it as in no way changing Church teaching of the past. Rather he views it as addressing itself to a new situation in which governments, especially Communist, deny the existence of any religious truth at all and vigorously seek to prevent their people from following the true religion or for that matter any religion.

On this basis also the ecumenism of the new Pope may take a new shape and emphasis as he indicated by a peculiar gesture during his speech from the balcony:[17] three times crossing his hands on his chest with fists closed, an action endlessly repeated in Eastern Orthodoxy, revealing through this historical symbolic language where lies the heart of Christian Europe, while the ecumenism of Western countries is seen as a dead end, in the opinion of one sharp critic,[18] whose views are vehemently contradicted by another.[19]

Not the least significant sign coming from the election of the new Pope is that this took place on October 16th, the feast of the Polish Queen St. Hedwig, a saint much venerated in Krakow. Not a bad patroness for a new pontificate! Surely the election of a son of her own city on her own feast day owed something to her intercession. Proving himself always a "seasoned oak," John Paul II is a sign of the times indeed, as the Pope himself acknowledged at his inauguration:

> To the See of Peter in Rome, there succeeds today a bishop who is not a Roman, a bishop who is a son of Poland. But from this moment he too becomes a Roman. Yes—a Roman. He is also a Roman because he is the son of a nation whose history, from its first dawning, and whose thousand-year-old traditions are marked by a living, strong, unbroken, and deeply felt link with the See of Peter, a nation which has ever remained faithful to this See of Rome. Inscrutable is the design of Divine Providence.[20]

A festive profile of this "sign of the times" may prove to be helpful toward an understanding of the providential mission of pastoral ministry of the present Pope as "harbinger of the new era, exorcising the demons of history and recreating a better world for a spiritual and free person."[21]

Chapter 2

AN HISTORIC CHOICE

Popular with the People

THE present Pope is furthermore not only the sign of the times, but he represents an historic choice for these times. He is not only the reflection of, but a hope to confront, the challenges to the problems. Although the whole act of election of the successor to the Vicar of Christ is under special guidance of the Holy Spirit, the fitness of the person to the office is premandated—humanly speaking—by a concomitant divine assistance in a choice. This is particularly evident by the comparison of an unusually popular acceptance of this Pope not from Italy with the unpopular reception accorded previous ones, including the last, when the reign of the non-Italian Pope Hadrian VI of The Netherlands, the son of a poor carpenter and a saintly humble man, was as brief as it was unpopular.[22] In fact, his death in 1523 after little more than one year on the throne of Peter was celebrated with a "great festival" by the Romans.[23]

On the other hand, while Karol Cardinal Wojtyla's selection as the new Pope startled most prognosticators, it represents a masterful move for the Roman Catholic Church, addressing contemporary challenges not only in Communist lands, but also throughout the developing world.[24] The cardinals saw in him an opportunity to advance the Catholic Church in today's world and conveniently took it.

"What a sign for us all," one writer says, "of the vitality of our Church! A fully catholic, that is universal Church, which can permit herself to call to the See of Rome a bishop from a distant country, from a country under the Communist regime."[25]

The circumstance that this Pope is no Italian, the breaking of the apparent Italian monopoly of the Church's highest office, and the choice of a man young enough to be pope at the end of this century was a statement incapable of misinterpretation: It is an historic choice[26] for several reasons.

To Fulfill Hopes for a New Aggiornamento

In view of the fact that the long succession of Italian popes in the past weakened the concept of the universality of the Church and that the change in the situation could be, and was made, reaffirmed strongly Church universality. The Church's need for vigorous, fresh leadership in time of crisis had been recognized and met.

The selection of a non-Italian should help also to diminish the papacy's entanglement in numerous no-win Italian political controversies, thus completing the spiritual liberation of the papacy which had begun with the loss of the Papal States over a century ago. Moreover, since generally all societies grant to foreigners liberties frequently not conceded to natives, this Pope should find it easier than his Italian predecessors to do so.

Even more significant, perhaps, is this new Pope's immediate and unequivocal commitment to a fuller implementation of Vatican Council II than we have yet seen. John Paul has emphasized the primary importance of what is the Council's most successful document, the *Constitution on the Church,* calling it "the Magna Carta of the Council." He has pledged to expand collegiality, mentioning in this connection the Synod of Bishops, at the last two of which he played a prominent role. And he has been equally firm in working to end "the tragedy of division among Christians, this ground for perplexity and possibly even scandal." Assurances of all of this were seen in his previous endeavors and these helped to make possible this historic choice.

As his predecessor John Paul I sparked many hopes by heralding a new *aggiornamento,*[27] this Pope is almost bound to fulfill them as expected, the more probably since the former was a mixture of compassion and gentleness, the latter of compassion and strength; the appeal of John Paul I can be matched by that of the now reigning Pontiff.

A Member of a Faithful Loyal People

The Pope from Poland is an historic choice in many other ways. He comes from a suffering country, and is one who has lived through the tensions of Christian life in the face of adverse political, social, and cultural pressures. He comes from a people staunch in the faith, but suffering often in recent years from the feeling that their faith and loyalty have never been fully understood or appreciated. The circumstance that John Paul II not only is the first Polish, but also (contrary to some expressed views[28]) the first Slavic pope has made a great impact on the subdued, and for centuries underestimated, basically candid souls of the Slavs who begin to feel themselves taken into confidence and considered seriously by others.

The best testimony, perhaps, that a new pope is truly an historic choice in various ways is summed up by the new Pope's long-time friend, Jerzy Turowicz, respected editor-in-chief of the archdiocesan paper of Krakow, *Tygodnik Powszechny*[29] [Universal Weekly], which was founded by Cardinal Sapieha in 1945. This editor experienced many clashes with the Communist government because he refused to publish Communist-ordered propaganda, nor was he for several years allowed to publish the paper. For a while the paper was taken over by a liberal group of fellow travelers, till the Church had to put a ban on it.

Turowicz was also a member of group Znak, and it was then that Father Wojtyla defended him and managed to make peace between him and Cardinal Wyszynski, so that the rather liberal group Znak was allowed to continue to work. With the coming of Wladyslav Gomulka into power in 1956, Turowicz continued to publish his paper under the eyes of, and not without battles with the government censors. Turowicz was in St. Peter's Square in Rome when his friend Cardinal Wojtyla was elected the new Pope, filing copy for a special issue. Here is his convincing prognosis of who Karol Wojtyla really is, synthesizing him as "a witness to the gospel in the changing world."[30]

A Man of God and of Wide Culture

Wojtyla is, in the first place, a man of God, a man of intrepid faith, of deep spirituality, a man of prayer and contemplation. He is a pastor strongly committed to the evangelization of his beloved Church of Krakow, of the whole Polish Church. For this, he shared responsibility together with all the Polish bishops, but under the guidance of a great friend of his, the Primate Stefan Wyszynski.

The new Pope is an intellectual, a scholar of great philosophical and theological culture, bound to the traditional doctrine of the Church, to the magisterium of the Church, but also open to the historical development of theological thought, and in fact himself a promoter of this development. He is a man of great culture, in the widest sense, sensitive to arts and letters, with an excellent knowledge of modern ideological movement, one open to dialogue. He is a man of the Second Vatican Council, committed to the implementation of this great work.

The choice of the name John Paul II must certainly be interpreted as a commitment for the continuation of the line of his three great predecessors. This means that he intends to continue to develop ecumenical dialogue, with a continual effort for the unity of Christians. Deeply concerned with the real participation of the laity in his Diocese of Krakow, he has succeeded in involving a large part of the lay world in the diocesan synod.

Wojtyla knows the world of today and its problems; above all, he knows the problems of the Church in her world dimensions. His participation in the Second Vatican Council and in all the Synods of Bishops since the Council has enabled him to forge direct ties with the heads of all the local Churches, and this knowledge has been further deepened by his journeys. He has visited a large area of the countries of Western Europe, has been twice to the United States and Canada, and has journeyed in the Far East, to the Philippines, to Australia, and to New Guinea.

He is neither a conversative nor a progressive; these classifications do not fit him. He knows the modern mentality and he is sensitive to the sufferings, miseries, and anguish of people today. He believes in the responsibility of the Church, not only in the Church as an institution, but in the Church as communion. He is a man attached, as are all Poles, to the riches of the cultural tradition of Italy. He is a Roman in the sense of being faithful to the Church of Rome, the cornerstone of the universal Church.

A Man of Goodness and Easy Human Contact

He is in short a modest, simple, sincere, kind man of great goodness and of easy human contact. He has not, perhaps, the spontaneity of Pope John XXIII nor the smile of Pope John Paul I. But all individuals express their love for God and their brothers and sisters in a different way.

> I do not think that it will be easy for the Polish Cardinal, metropolitan Archbishop of Krakow, to be Pope. But a man of such staunchness, faith, charity and hope, with the help of God, the inspiration of the Holy Spirit and the protection of the Blessed Virgin, with the brotherly and collegial help of the world episcopate, and sustained by the prayers of the faithful all over the world, will be able to overcome the difficulties. I think that John Paul II, like his predecessors, will be able to be a great Pope, a real witness to Christ and his Gospel in the changing world.[31]

This description is greatly assuring in the light of this truly historic choice, despite the fact that some scattered criticism[32] of his views on some issues or of his openness of expression occasionally may be found.

The hope and the expectations invested in this Pope are perhaps the basic reasons for his popular acceptance. Many of the unsolved problems of the past, the persistent tensions, and the variety of cultural-political confrontations were certainly additional motivations toward such expectations. The circumstance that the new Pope is from behind the Iron Curtain was also instrumental in building all these hopes on him.

Archbishop John R. Quinn of San Francisco heralded this election as "a springtime for the Church," for the reason that "it is particularly important that this Pope is a man who has suffered under the Communist regime, who has been firm and intrepid in the face of obstacles, who has borne oppression,[33] whose convictions stem from the abuses of religious freedom he had seen in his native country and elsewhere under Nazi occupation during World War II and under postwar Communist rule. Such views and similar ones were the general reflection of the people's reaction to the new Pope.

Without doubt, his experience in dealing with the accompanying problems corroborated strongly his undisputed intellectual ability and easy versatility in challenging difficulties, and all this added to the fact that the election of the present Pope is seen and felt as an historic choice. Such expectations were accentuated even more by a comparison with his predecessor, John Paul I,[34] whose goodness has been generally accepted but whose effectiveness could not be tested because of his sudden and untimely death. As a result, the youth, health, and sportsmanship of Pope John Paul II should take away certain fears and should add force to the fulfillment of the hopes put on this historic choice.

Chapter 3

A POPE FOR MODERN TIMES

Elimination of the Tiara

UPDATING the Church with the changing times is the principal legacy of Vatican II.[35] This had necessarily to affect outward expression of the Pope himself. The call for simplicity became part of this mode in a changing world. An appropriate accommodation in this regard was the Pope's decision to bypass the customary coronation ceremony and to eliminate a tiara[36] from the solemnization of the Pope's enthronement. This change was in fact initiated by his predecessor, John Paul I, but really was already championed by Paul VI, who although he was crowned with a tiara when he began his papacy (1963) gave the tiara to Francis Cardinal Spellman[37] for the poor, and it is on display now in the National Shrine of the Immaculate Conception in Washington, D.C. Pope John Paul II himself assesses the appropriateness of wearing the tiara:

> In past centuries, when the Successor of Peter took possession of his See, the *triregnum* or tiara was placed on his head. The last Pope to be crowned was Paul VI in 1963, but after the solemn coronation ceremony he never used the tiara again and left his Successors free to decide in this regard.
>
> Pope John Paul I, whose memory is so vivid in our hearts, did not wish to have the tiara; nor does his Successor wish it today. This is not the time to return to a ceremony and an object considered, wrongly, to be a symbol of the temporal power of the Popes.

Our time calls us, urges us, obliges us to gaze on the Lord and immerse ourselves in humble and devout meditation on the mystery of the supreme power of Christ himself.

He who was born of the Virgin Mary, the carpenter's Son (as he was thought to be), the Son of the living God (confessed by Peter), came to make us all "a kingdom of priests."[38]

Symbolism of the Tiara

The tiara is the papal crown, a beehive-shaped and somewhat bulging head covering, ornamented with three crowns and hence called a *triregnum* or triple crown. It has no sacral character, being solely the ensign of sovereign power,[39] and for this reason is never worn at liturgical functions, for which the pope always wears the miter. The tiara was worn by the pope at his coronation and on such other solemn occasions as processions and public dogmatic pronouncements, as an emblem of his princely power to teach, to rule, and to sanctify.

Its origin is uncertain and its significance varied, as, for example, a symbol of the Church militant, suffering, and triumphant; or of the spiritual powers of teaching, ruling, sanctifying. It was imposed at the coronation with a formula: "Receive this tiara adorned with three crowns and know that you are the father of princes and of kings, guide of the world and vicar upon earth of Christ Jesus our Savior."[40]

The tiara proper developed out of the simple white Phrygian cap adopted during the 7th and 8th centuries; in the 10th or 11th century, the headpiece was stiffened and a single diadem placed around it; the two lappets (or *pendenta)* attached to the rear probably appeared in the 13th century under Boniface VIII (1294-1303) and a second coronet was added; by 1315, still a third was added by Popes Benedict XI (1303-04) and Clement V (1304-14) and formed part of the vestment. The tiara assumed its final shape and costly jewel-encrusted character during the Renaissance.[41] Pope Innocent III indicated that the miter symbolized the *sacerdotium*, while the tiara indicated the *imperium*.[42]

Replaced by Miter to Stress Spiritual Mission

The significance of the tiara[43] can be best understood against the background of the historical struggle between the secular and spiritual power, especially in the era of Roman emperors and in the Middle Ages when the spiritual power of the popes *(sacerdotium)* had a difficult time emerging from the shadow of the protective ruling of emperors *(imperium)*.[44] In the modern world, when separation between the sacred and the profane has become more distinct and the secular strives to take the upper hand of the spiritual, the tiara's significance has lost momentum in favor of emphasis on the spiritual mission of the pope rather than the temporal.

As a result, the new Pope replaced the coronation with a simple inauguration by wearing a miter as a proper insignia of his spiritual mission. It is true that since the pope is not only the vicar of Christ in his pastoral primacy[45] of the world, but is also head of the sovereign Vatican State,[46] the tiara could still hold meaning without its becoming an anachronism. In the follow-up of priority of values, however, and in emphasis on the spiritual before the secular, the Pope's tendency toward simplicity is understandable. It is also a welcome indication of his awareness of the spirit of the rapidly changing times, in which a modern pope is expected to serve as head of the Church in the contemporary world and to succeed, as is his destiny, as a true pope for modern times.

SCENES FROM THE LIFE OF POPE JOHN PAUL II

Coat of arms of Pope John Paul II. The "M" accents his devotion to Mary, the virginal mother of Jesus.

HIS NATIVE LAND. Note the Vistula, or Visla River, that from mountain heights flows through Cracow (or Krakow as the Pope knows it best), pays its respects to the royal and archiepiscopal city, and then reports to the capital at Warsaw before it makes its way to the Baltic Sea.

Karol Wojt mother, E Kaczorowska, father, Serg Karol Woj both natives o Polish villag Kety. They buried at W wice.

The Wojtyla home in Wadowice, which town cannot be found on the map (page 1*), is south-west of Krakow.

First Communion — a tall candle to feed a long-lasting flame.

Karol Wojtyla when he was twelve years old.

Find the future Pope — at this time a good step below his fellows.

The Cathedral, Krakow.

Archbishop Karol Wojtyla with Primate Stefan Wyszynski behind him.

Synod steersman — learning the ropes on Peter's Bark.

Is this Cardinal Wojtyla's script of "The Foundations of Renewal" that he gave at Vatican Council II?

It's another ball game — nine good men meet in Rome: the Cardinals who greet us, from left field to right: 1. Terence J. Cook of New York; 2. John F. Dearden of Detroit; 3. Karol Wojtyla of Krakow; 4. John Krol of Philadelphia; 5. Timothy Manning of Los Angeles; 6. Primate Stefan Wyszynski of Warsaw; 7. John J. Carberry of St. Louis; 8. William W. Baum of Baltimore-Washington; 9. Humberto S. Medeiros of Boston.

Two friends meet — in red zucchetto and white, John Cardinal Krol and the new Pope.

The Shepherd Wojtyla in 1976 at the Pennsylvania Shrine of Our Lady of Czestochowa near Doylestown, flanked by the Rev. Gregory Kotnis, OSP and the Rt. Rev. Jakub Biernak, OSP.

Genin Stach of St. Ladislaus parish, Philadelphia, at the Offertory of the Mass at the Shrine, gives to Cardinal Wojtyla a gift of wheat.

The black Madonna venerated at Jasna Gora, Czestochowa in Poland.

"Drink to the Cardinal once . . ." — the near-Pope at Harvard University, July 1976, with professor O. Putsak who heads there the Ukrainian Research Institute, Professor Ihor Savcenka and his wife.

"Where there's smoke there's fire," but not this time. The photo was taken from the roof above the Bernini columns at Sunday noon, after the second ballot.

A Flame in white appears at the window.

The Pope clenches his hand as he acknowledges the plaudits of the crowd at St. Peter's Square at his inauguration, October 22, 1978.

Cardinal Felice places the snowy sheep's wool pallium on the shoulders of the new Pontiff, symbol of the spiritual authority he now bears. ↓

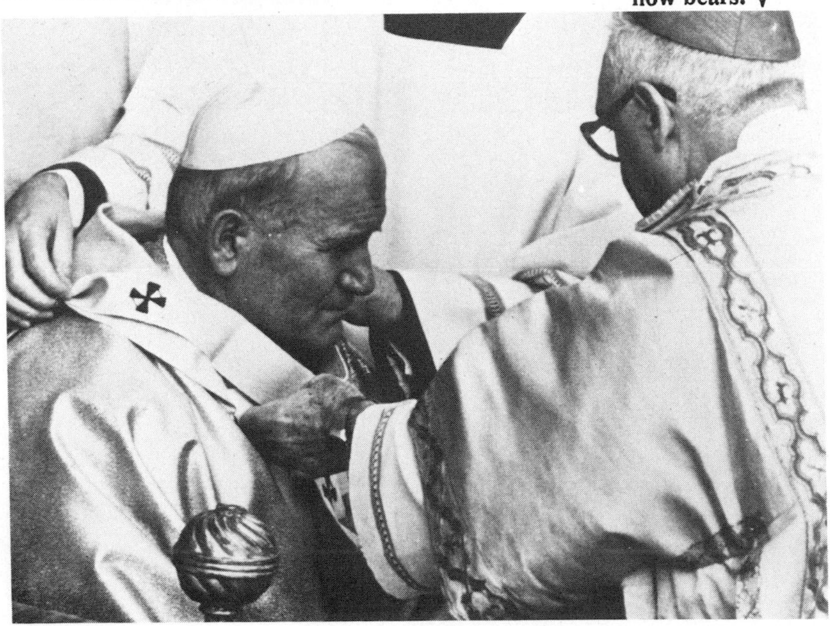

The sombrero-hatted man of peace, in Mexico for the Puebla Conference, clasps a beruffled Hispanic youngster whose father hovers behind her.

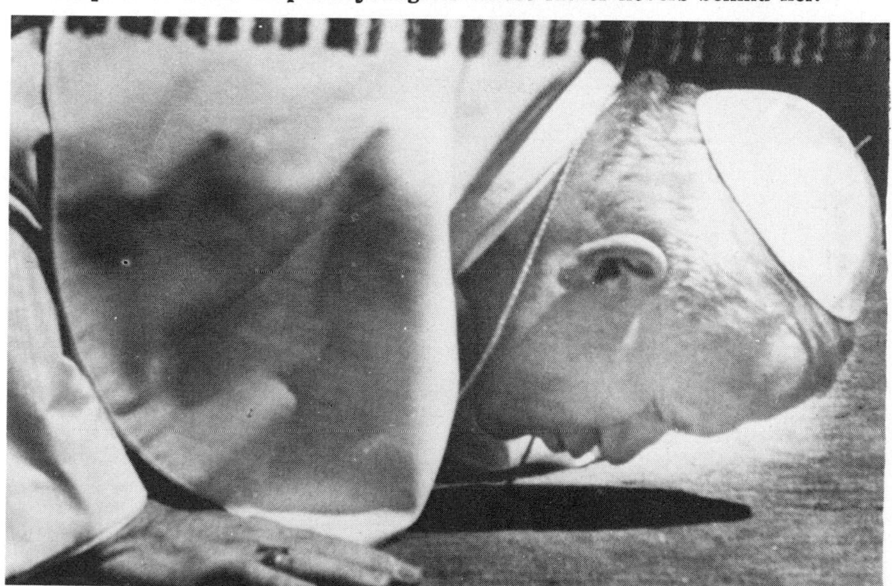

Pope John Paul in the New World at Santo Domingo, D.R. — "He must increase, and I must decrease."

The new Pope stops to give his autograph, a St. Nicholas Day gift, to a jubilant lad at the December 6th audience.

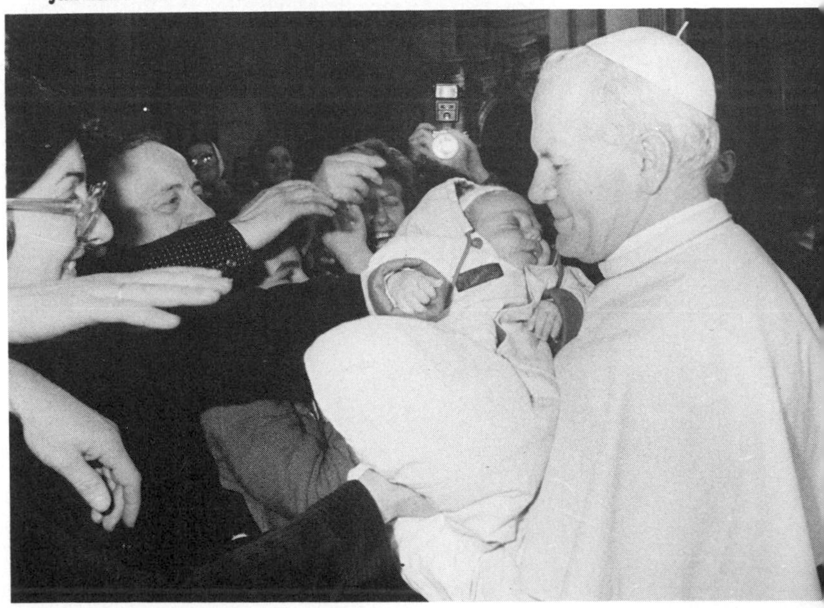

A bundle of Joy! May it be ever the Father of Christendom's burden.

Chapter 4

JOHN PAUL II'S NATIVE LAND

Early History

THE new Pope is from Poland, a country rich in historical events, home of early Christianity and of a high culture, but rife with political encounters and tragedies. Geographically located east of Germany, north of Bohemia, west of Kiev, northwest of Lithuania, it has remained pro-Western in orientation, with some later Eastern influences.

When the first Polish duke attested by history appeared on the political scene, he was about to annex the Pomeranian Slavs to his own State, Mieszko of the dynasty of Piasts. Observing that the Germans had their eyes upon this region, he made a rather clever deal with Gero in 963, promising to hold it as a fief of the Empire. Later, counter to Otto's plans for Magdeburg in regard to the Christianization of the Polabian and Baltic Slavs, he turned to Boleslav I, the Christian duke of Bohemia, who gave Mieszko (960-92) his daughter Dubravka in marriage and sent to him the first missionaries.

Subsequently, the Czech and Polish dukes went even further and, probably in 966, addressed to Pope John XIII (965-972) a request that they might establish bishoprics in their countries. So it came about that the Polish bishopric of Poznan (Posen) was founded about 968 and was made directly subject to Rome, not to Magdeburg.

Another change of great consequence was effected by Mieszko in the East, for he began to annex the Slavic tribes of ancient White Croatia. He seems to have occupied first, after the defeat of the Magyars, what is today Galicia, several cities including the city of Premysl. His growing power attracted the Slavs of Silesia, land of the Krakow region, and impressed even the Slavniks, whose country had long ago belonged to White Croatia. To ensure for himself the protection of the papacy, then the greatest spiritual power in Europe, Mieszko I dedicated to the Holy See the whole of his kingdom, from Stettin to Gdansk and from Gnesen to Krakow, before his death in 992. The move was clever and Mieszko thereby initiated a tradition which Poland followed for many centuries to come.[47]

The Struggle between Empire and Papacy

It was inevitable that the Slavs should become entangled in the struggle between two powers, the empire and the papacy (the *imperium* and the *sacerdotium*[48]), which from the 11th century onward directed the destiny of the Western Christian world. The contest, called by historians the Investiture struggle, had arisen as a result of the introduction of a Germanic principle into Church practice.[49]

It was to be expected that when the papacy of the 11th century threw out the challenge, not to the German Church but to the Emperor, Pope Gregory VII and his successors would take a special notice of the new States in Central and Eastern Europe, looking upon them as a providential means of checkmating Germany's expansion and of bringing the Emperor to heel. The example of Poland at that time indicated that these States would welcome the opportunity to side with the spiritual power against Germany. Such an attitude on the part of these States seemed to be dictated by the instincts of self-preservation, of self-defense, and of independence.

Poland was also the first country to which the new papal claims were fully applied. In 1076 Boleslav II received the royal dignity and title at the hands of the Pope and was crowned by the archbishop of Gniezno (Gnesen) in the

Pope's name. This was an unmistakable challenge to the old theory that the imperial dignity was the one and only source of all political power in Christendom.

Henry IV, chief protagonist of the old order, was determined to proclaim that the papacy was not the sole source of spiritual and temporal power, but that temporal power issued from the *imperium,* which God had predestined to govern the world. Therefore, the right to confer the title upon the prince belonged, he argued, to the emperor. Subsequently, in 1085 he conferred upon the Bohemian Prince Vratislav II the title of King of Bohemia and Poland, and the situation in Poland changed completely. Boleslav II had been displaced on the throne by his brother Wladyslaw (Ladislas) Herman (1079-1102).

One of the main reasons which had led to Boleslav's downfall was his conflict with Stanislas,[50] bishop of Krakow (1072-79). The story of this quarrel was embellished later and made Stanislas grow to the stature of a martyr for Church reform and protagonist of Gregorian ideology against an impious king. The Bishop was canonized in 1253 by Pope Innocent IV and became the first Polish Saint and the national hero. By this time, the city of Krakow had long outstripped Gniezno in the political sphere, and the canonization of its Bishop naturally raised it to further prominence in the religious and cultural life of Poland.[51]

Division into Duchies

Setting his face against such imperial interference in Poland's domestic affairs, Boleslav III Wrymouth (1102-38) divided his realm among his four sons, stipulating that the senior member of the Piast dynasty should occupy the rank of premier duke and ruler of Poland with Krakow as his capital. Unintentionally, he opened the door to the political division of Poland into duchies,[52] a factor whose intricacies are still a nightmare to every student of Poland's past. Great harm was done to the ideal of Polish unity since every duchy had its own interests to look after, to the detriment of the country as a whole. All this also weakened Poland's resistance to the penetration of German influences into the country.

The ecclesiastical organization of all Polish duchies under the jurisdiction of the archbishop of Gniezno as well as the Peter's Pence, a special tax Poland had paid the Apostolic See since the rule of Casimir I, served to remind every Pole, irrespective of the duchy to which he belonged, of his country's common purpose, interests, and unity. The clergy was instrumental in keeping this spirit alive. The clergy was also first to secure important privileges and guarantees against encroachments by the State. In consideration of the privileges he then granted (1180), Casimir the Just carried his point that the duchy of Krakow and its seniority should henceforth be hereditary in his dynasty. It was the beneficial influence which the Church exercised in Poland as main defender of national unity that earned the ecclesiastical loyalty of the Poles.

Divided into several principalities, Poland had been badly hurt by the Mongol invasion of 1241 and was unable to organize a common defense against them on the one side, and of the Baltic Prussians and Lithuanians on the other. Only the intervention of Czech King Przemysl II[53] was of any help. With the subsequent liquidation of this Czech dynasty (1306), Polish political development[54] was on the decline. Again, Pope John XXII helped Lokietek to achieve his coronation at Krakow in 1320, and the idea of Polish unity under a national king was revived.

Unity under Casimir the Great

King Casimir the Great[55] was successful in uniting most of the country in 1355. His greatest achievement was perhaps the foundation of the University of Krakow in 1364 and the introduction of several religious orders into the country. The foundation of the Charles IV University in Prague (1348) contributed considerably to the spread of Western culture in Poland, for many Polish youths obtained their education there. The foundation of a university, or rather a law school (though it had also two chairs of medicine and one of liberal arts) in Krakow in 1364, with three chairs of canon and five of Roman law, gave fresh impetus to the progress of learning in Poland.

Casimir modeled his foundation not on Paris, but rather on Bologna and Padua, a circumstance which testifies to closer relations between Poland and Italy. Despite, however, a promising start the institution had a short life; but it was reconstituted in 1400 with faculties of theology and philosophy. This foundation brought Poles into greater prominence in contemporary Europe.

Casimir is also responsible for the first international congress held at Krakow (1364) for political maneuvering against Ottoman Turks. In all, the King laid the foundations in very many areas for Poland's future greatness.

The idea of the unity of the Polish State found expression also in the coat of arms of the kingdom, the figure of an eagle, which under Casimir began to appear on the national flag and on great state seals. The actual coronation of the king became important in the Polish constitution. Although the coronation ceremony had to be performed in Krakow, it continued nonetheless to be the prerogative of the archbishop of Gniezno. After the revival of the kingdom, the Polish crown remained hereditary[56] though later, because of political changes, it was transformed into an electoral kingdom.

Cultural Progress

Culturally, Poland also made great progress from the 11th century onward, especially after the definitive reestablishment of the national kingdom in the 14th century. From earliest times, the Poles entertained vivid cultural relations with the West, especially with France. Even their first historian is believed to have been a Frenchman, an anonymous priest called Gallus,[57] an important source for Polish history.

His work was continued by a bishop of Krakow, Vincent Kadlubek, who was popular.

Religious writings in Latin testified to the integration of Poland into the framework of Western Latin culture. Profane Latin writings in verse were likewise numerous. The establishment of the University of Krakow gave fresh impetus to the progress of learning. Under the influence of the clergy, the knowledge of Latin was more widespread than elsewhere and, as a result, formation of the Polish literary language slowed down.[58] First were religious translations from Latin or from Czech; the fine arts and architecture of all styles reached their highest level only in the 16th century, accepting patterns and incentives not only from her German and Czech neighbors but also from France and Italy.

Challenging the constant German threat, especially on the part of the Teutonic Order in the Baltic, the Poles made a deal with the Lithuanians when the Polish Queen Jadwiga married Jagiello of Lithuania (1386) and the Polish-Lithuanian[59] union (1386-1572) came into existence, with great impact in enhancing the prestige of the dynasty that had effected it. The Jagiellonians became the most important after the Habsburgs, and the eyes of Poland's neighbors were directed toward Krakow and Wilno whenever a political crisis arose or a new ruler had to be selected.

Unfortunately, the death of Sigismund II (August 1572) marked the end of this dynasty, and the throne was once again open to competition. At one time (1375) even the possibility of a union of Poland, Lithuania, and Russia appeared with the candidacy of Ivan IV as king of Poland-Lithuania, but it ended in complete failure.

Influence of the Renaissance

The influence of the Renaissance was particularly remarkable in Poland.[60] Among the clergy were several protagonists such as the head of the Polish delegation to the Council of Constance (1414-18), archbishop of Gniezno, Nicholas of Traba, advisor to King Wladyslaw Jagiello, who was also one of the candidates for the papacy; Andrew Laskarz, bishop of Poznan; Dean Nicholas Lasocki, zealous promoter of a conciliar theory; the rector of Krakow University, Paulus Vladimir of Brudzen, who in his tractate *De potestate papae et imperatoris respectu confidelium* ["On the Power of the Pope and the Emperor over the Faithful"] condemned all conversion of pagans by force. Through this work he involved himself in the diplomatic battle that was fought, after the defeat of the Teutonic Order at Tannenberg (1410), between Poland and the Order's State.

Further, humanism penetrated Polish minds of such as the eminent statesmen Zbigniew Cardinal Olesnick, bishop of Krakow (1423-55); Gregory of Sanok, archbishop of Lwow; Canon John Dlugosz (1415-80), who wrote a history of Poland, the best work of its kind.[61] The University of Krakow contributed much toward learning; among its alumni appear also the well-known Nicholas Copernicus (d. 1543), who has made Poland famed by his epoch-making astronomical works.

Furthermore, some Polish bishops and professors who had participated in the reform councils spread humanism in Poland-Lithuania and in the 15th century the *Devotio moderna*[62] also made its influence felt. Worthy of particular note were Bishop Jakob Strepa of Halicz-Lvov (d. 1404) and Jan Kanty (d. 1473), who was well known as professor at the University of Krakow and as friend and helper of poor students.

The influence of the Italian Renaissance reached its peak about 1518 after King Sigismund I (1506-48) married the Italian princess Bona Sforza. During the reign of Stephen Batory (1576-86), the prominent protagonist of humanism was his chancellor John Zameyski (d 1605), who cherished the idea of making Krakow a kind of international center of humanistic studies, and who founded also a university in Zanosc, while the King established still another at Wilno (1579).

Polish National Literature and Art

These ideas opened the way for Polish national literature. This was championed by the first poet of importance, Nicolas Rey[63] (1505-64), who was followed by John Kochanowski and Nicholas Szarzynski. The first historical work in Polish was by Martin Bielski, who was followed by Bartos Paprocki and Matthew Strykowski. Excelling in Polish prose was Jesuit Peter Skarga, head of the University at Wilno.[64] Among the domestic artistic masters were Gabriel Slouski, John Michalowitz, talented builder and sculptor, and John Bialy (1592). Besides these, Italian, German, French, and Flemish artists worked also for the Polish Court (the Magnates) and for the cities.

All important Polish cities, Krakow, Poznan, Plock, Wilno, and later also Lublin and Warsaw, have boasted monuments of Renaissance art. One may have an adequate picture of it from Professor Dvornik's estimate: "It must be confessed that although perhaps Czech literary activity during this period was more voluminous than Polish, the Polish literary production surpassed Czech in its quality and value."[65] Needless to say, under this influence, it was decided in 1696 that all official documents of administration and judicial procedure of the Grand Duchy should be composed in Polish.

This high cultural standard of the Poles appealed to the East, and some Kievan principalities were attached to Poland in 1569 by the Union of Lublin. Religious differences of Orthodox and Catholics were modified by the Union of Brest-Litovsk in 1596 and the Uniates came into existence in a peaceful coexistence. Subsequent failure must be attributed to the West in mishandling religious affairs of the Eastern rites, and this ineptness resulted in increased antagonism.

The Reformation in Poland

The Reformation[66] in Poland failed to achieve the lasting results it achieved in other countries, but there was a great influence on the cultural life of the Poles in the 16th and 17th centuries. The need to provide the faithful with Polish prayer books and to propagate the Reformation induced some of the Reformers to publish their books in the vernacular. Konigsberg, Duke Albert's residence, became the center where Polish religious books were printed. John Seklucyan was the main publisher and is credited with publishing the whole Bible in Polish in 1563, the so-called Bible of Brzesc.[67]

This was the best achievement of the Polish Reformation. The Protestants were unable to succeed in their propaganda to split the Polish Catholic mentality and scored but little in some chiefly intellectual corners. They never succeeded in establishing a Polish national Church. Nonetheless, their religious freedom was safeguarded by the *Confederation of Warsaw*, concluded at the Diet of 1573.

Partitions and Subjugated Status

The ties of friendship formed between the Jagiellonians and the Habsburgs at the Congress of Vienna (1515) proved of paramount importance for the history of Europe. For the Jagiellonians, however, it meant the surrender of their ambition to become a first-class power in Central Europe in favor of the Habsburgs. This, combined with the growing power of Russia under the Romanov expansionist policy, weakened Poland in the sense that it became a target, a land coveted by all its neighbors.

The anarchy in Poland, where confederates had deposed their King, speeded these developments. Through the first partition (1772), Poland lost a third of its territories to Russia, Prussia, and Austria. The second partition (1793) by Russia and Prussia followed, and the third (1795), made again by these three neighbors, Russia, Prussia, and Austria, brought an end to the Polish State.[68]

This blow was too much for freedom-loving Poles[69] who were nevertheless able with the help of Napoleon, who defeated the three powers responsible for the previous partitions of Poland, to reestablish at least the duchy of Warsaw. This was, however, annexed also to Russia after the Congress of Vienna (1814-15). In 1830, the Warsaw revolution broke out and in 1831 the Polish army was defeated and the Polish kingdom divided into provinces, which were treated as other Russian provinces; little relaxation in national spirit came after 1848 with the rise of nationalism and the appearance of the idea of Pan-Slavism.

Polish Republic — Aided by the Church

Poland's subjugated status lasted until the First World War (1914-18) when eventually Poland appeared as an independent republic, owing to President Wilson's famous declaration of January 18, 1918, with his *Fourteen Points*, which declaration was really a royal gift to the small nations. Poland also benefited from it. Perhaps a reflection on all these past sufferings of the nation can explain Polish nationalism, so strong that it was on occasion intolerant of other minorities, including Jews.[70]

When the Polish Republic was created in November 1918, the bishops had problems of organization. During the years of the restoration of the Polish State, the Catholic Church constituted the strongest effective, spiritual force in all that was regarded as characteristic of Polish life and culture.

In the rebuilding of Polish Catholicism, the leaders were the Archbishops Edmund Dalbot of Gniezno (1915-26) and Aleksander Kakowski of Warsaw (1913-38), who were made cardinals in 1919, and the nuncio Achille Ratti (1919-21), the later Pope Pius XI. The Concordat of February 10, 1925, and the bull *Vixdum Poloniae* of Pope Pius XI, issued October 28 of the same year, constituted the foundation for the new ecclesiastical order in Poland. Two new archbishoprics, Krakow and Wilno, were erected, and four dioceses were established: Czestochowa, Katowice, Lomza, and Pinsk. The new organization comprised five ecclesiastical provinces with a total of 15 suffragan sees.

Vitality of Polish Catholicism

The Polish census of 1930 indicated that Catholics comprised 75 per cent of the population. Under the leadership of the bishops, at whose regularly held conferences the Primate Augustin Hlond (1926-48) served as president, the Church, through an effective consolidation of its forces, exercised a strong influence on public life.[71]

The number of bishops in the period from 1918-38 rose from 23 to 51, and the number of diocesan and regular clergy increased by about 43 per cent, reaching a total of nearly 13,000. The religious orders enjoyed a marked growth in this same period. In 1939 there were more than 250 Catholic periodical publications, 38 of these being organs of the United Church. Every diocese had its own Sunday paper. The religious orders also exhibited marked zeal in the field of the Catholic press.

The scholarly life of the Church, which had a solid foundation in obligatory religious education, was promoted through the Theological Faculties of Warsaw, Krakow, Lvov (Lemberg), and Wilno, by the Catholic University of Lublin founded in 1918, and by the diocesan seminaries. This scholarly activity was reflected in a series of important theological journals.[72]

The Nazi Invasion

The independent Polish Republic (1918-39) was short-lived. The *German-Soviet Pact* and the German-Polish campaign of September of 1939 created a new political situation for the nation and the Church. The Nazi regime seized the territory of Gniezno-Poznan (Gnesen-Posen) and parts of the archbishoprics of Warsaw and Krakow, which it designated "the incorporated eastern territories." The Nazi invasion of Poland was the nightmare of all Poles. The cruelty of the Nazis is well reflected in their being—unjustly—accused of the massacre of Polish officers and prisoners of war in the Katyn forest,[73] for which the Russians were most likely responsible, and held accountable for it.

Following the outbreak of the German-Soviet War in 1941, the whole country was torn apart between Germany and Russia, when Russia invaded Poland and also fought against the Poles simultaneously with the Germans. Perhaps the greatest perfidy of the Russians was manifested when in the Warsaw uprising of 1944, the Russians deliberately halted their drive, to let the Polish patriots fight alone with the Germans.[74] The military basis for the decision of the Poles to fight in the capital was the belief that the Germans were decisively beaten on the Eastern Front and that the Red Army was about to enter Warsaw.

During World War II (1939-45), the Poles had their own government in exile, headed by General Sikorski and after his tragic death by Prime Minister Mikolajczyk in London, and a well-organized underground with the so-called Home Army led by General Bor-Komorowski. This constitutes the best testimonial to the steadfast resistance of the entire country against the German occupying army, as well as to its suspicion of the Russians, who never did shower much love on their Slavic brothers, the Poles. The Warsaw uprising was further evidence of the Poles' determination to handle their affairs independently of all their neighbors.

The Ordeal of the Polish Church

The archbishop of Krakow, Stefan Sapieha (1925-51, cardinal from 1946), served as spokesman for all the Polish bishops, making repeated representations to the administration of the General Government in order to obtain alleviations in the treatment of priests under arrest and sent into exile, to provide for the recruitment and theological training of seminarians, and to maintain the charitable activities of the Church in her age-old function of being a protective shield for all that was characteristic in Polish life and culture.

In all, 13 Polish bishops were exiled or arrested and put in concentration camps. There were 3,647 priests, 389 clerics, 341 Brothers, and 1,117 Sisters put in concentration camps in which 1,996 priests, 113 clerics, and 238 Sisters perished. On August 14, 1941, the Minorite Maximilian Kolbe met his death in the concentration camp at Auschwitz (Oswiecim).[75] He offered his life in substitution for that of a father of a family who had been condemned to die.

The diocesan clergy of the Polish Church, who at the beginning of World War II numbered 10,017, lost 25 per cent (2,647). The Nazi terror raged against leading Catholic laymen as well as against the clergy, and many laymen were put to death. The concentration camps of Auschwitz, Bojanowo, Dachau, Majdanek, Oranienburg, Ravensbrük, Stutthof, Treblinka, and others were sites of Polish martyrdoms.[76]

Liberation and New Restrictions on the Church

The collapse of the German East Front and the end of World War II introduced a new chapter in Polish history. The Polish Committee for National Liberation, the so-called Lublin Committee, in a manifesto of July 22, 1944, guaranteed, among other things, freedom of conscience and respect for the rights of the Catholic Church. Clergy and faithful devoted their efforts to healing the material and mental wounds caused by the occupation and the effects of the war. The Primate, Augustyn Cardinal Hlond—from 1946 also archbishop of Warsaw—undertook the rebuilding of ecclesiastical organization.

On September 12, 1945, the Polish government abrogated the Concordat of 1925. The nationalization of Catholic presses and the censorship of Catholic publications marked the beginning of restrictions on the freedom of the Church. They were followed (1948-50) by the censorship of all ecclesiastical publications of any kind, the elimination of Catholic youth associations and broadcasts, the dissolution of the Caritas Association, the nationalization of hospitals, and the expropriation of the largest portion of ecclesiastical property.

Under the Primate Stefan Wyszynski, who after the death of Cardinal Hlond (December 16, 1948) took over direction of the archdioceses of Gniezno and Warsaw (he was made a cardinal in 1953), an agreement was reached between the government and the episcopate on April 14, 1950. But the normalization of the relations between Church and State, which was expected, did not take place.

Open Conflict between Church and State

Out of the latent battle between Church and State, a more open conflict broke out (1952-55). The government decree of February 9, 1953, on the filling of ecclesiastical offices, subordinated episcopal jurisdiction to the supervision of the State. Some bishops were arrested and in 1953 Cardinal Wyszynski was likewise deprived of his freedom.

The absolute authority of the governmental office for ecclesiastical affairs; the dissolution of some major and minor seminaries, including seminaries of religious orders; the measures directed against the Catholic University of Lublin; the abolition of the Catholic Faculties at the beginning of the winter semester of 1954-55; the prohibition of January 1955 against the imparting of religious instruction in the elementary schools; the arrest and imprisonment of priests; and the expropriation of monasteries—all endangered most seriously the independence of the Church.

In addition to pressures from the outside, attempts were made to split the interior unity of Catholicism by means of the so-called patriotic priests, who were pushed into key positions in the Church by the office of ecclesiastical affairs, and of "progressive Catholics" who organized themselves as the Pax Movement and were supported by the government. These Catholics of leftist orientation developed the Pax Press and presented themselves as the true representatives of Polish Catholicism. The Church was pushed very much into the background in public life.

On December 8, 1955, concern for the unity of the Church in Poland moved Pope Pius XII to address a letter to the Polish episcopate. He not only dealt with the persecution of the Church, but he emphasized, among other points, the danger of the "progressive Catholics."

Improved Situation after the Thaw

In the fall of 1956 Wladyslaw Gomulka, after the thaw *(odwilz)* that freed Poland from Stalinism, took over the political leadership, and the situation of the Church improved. Cardinal Wyszynski was freed and returned to Warsaw, October 28, 1956. A commission made up of representatives of both Church and State was established to remove the existing tensions. The government decree of February 9, 1953, was withdrawn. All imprisoned bishops and clergy were given their freedom; the vicars capitular who had been appointed in the Polish West and North territories by the office for religious affairs in 1951 were now selected from loyal supporters of the cardinal.

Religious instruction was permitted as an elective subject in all elementary and higher schools before and after the hours set for obligatory studies. The Catholic laity obtained some influence in internal political affairs, the press, and journalism. In May 1957, Gomulka declared that he saw the necessity of a coexistence between believers and nonbelievers, between the Church and Socialism, and between the people's sovereignty and the hierarchy of the Church.

Polish Catholics were represented in the Sejm (Parliament) of 460 members, by a small number who represented three points of view in the parliamentary coexistence between Catholicism and the People's Democratic Government. In the last election of May 30, 1965, there were five belonging to the Znak group who were the strongest supporters of the rights of the Church, three to the "Progressive Movement," and five to the "Peace Movement."

Sufferings of Other Religions

It was owing alone to the vast Catholic majority that Catholics were able to defend their rights as they did. Despite this monolithic nature of the Polish nation, some non-Catholics suffered also for their rights. In retrospect, there was the total number of Protestants who were divided into 15 different religious groups, between 130,000 and 140,000.

The largest groups were the Evangelical Augsburg Church (Kosciól Ewangelicko-Augsburski) with 100,000 members, 279 parishes, and 112 ministers, and the United Evangelical Church (Zjednoczony Kosciól Ewangeliczny) with 7,500 members in 87 communities. The Adventists and the Methodists had 6,000 adherents each; Reformed, 5,000, and the Baptists, 2,500.

The Jews, whose number in Poland was reduced from 3 million in 1939 to 40,000 at the end of the World War II as a result of the mass murders of the National Socialists, belonged to the Religious Association of the Mosaic Confession (Zwiazek Religijny Wyznania Mojzeszowego). There was also a small Religious Association of Karaites (Karaimski Zwiazek Religijny).

The Mohammedan Religious Association (Muzulmanski Zwiazek) comprised a group of Polish Tatars.

In the Ecumenical Council created in 1956, the Evangelical communities, the Polish Orthodox Church, the Old Catholic Church of the Mariavites, the Polish Catholic Church separated from Rome, and the Christian Theological Academy at Chylice near Warsaw combined. Training was provided in three sections for students in Evangelical, Old Catholic, and Orthodox theology respectively.

Unique Communist Country from Religious Viewpoint

In this regard, Poland is a unique Communist country from the religious point of view. While the governments in other Communist countries either destroyed, mutilated, domesticated, or infiltrated various Churches and made them tools of their policies, the Communist government of Poland had to exercise some solicitude. More than 95 per cent of the population are Catholics and many Communists, including party functionaries, take active part in the life of the Catholic Church.

The Polish Communists were cautious in challenging the authority of the Catholic Church. The thousand-year-old history of the Catholic Church was closely interwoven with the history of Poland and her struggle for survival. Unlike Churches in other Communist countries, the Polish Catholic Church led by a strong and courageous leader Stefan Wyszynski enjoys now a considerable freedom of religious press and pulpit. Using this freedom fearlessly, intelligently, and responsibly, the Polish episcopate defends the Church against any harassment and encroachment of its religious freedom, and stands for human rights of all Polish citizens.

The Communist party in Poland apparently realizes that its government would be in serious trouble if the Catholic Church were openly harassed or persecuted. Consequently, they chose a policy of *modus vivendi* vis-à-vis the Catholic Church instead of a policy of open confrontation. Despite this unique position of the Catholic Church in Poland, however, there have been constant tensions between the two antagonists. These tensions, however, did not take such violent turns as in other satellite countries.

Meeting of Communist Head and Paul VI

The Communist government of Poland needed considerable time before its highest spokesman, Eduard Gierek, First Secretary of the Polish United Workers' Party, was ready to pay the first visit to the Vatican, to Pope Paul VI, on December 1, 1977. The uniqueness of the Catholic Church in Communist Poland and of the important role of the Vatican in the *Ostpolitik* and its relations with the Communist countries, as well as active participation in the Helsinki and Belgrade conferences, is nicely reflected in speeches of Gierek and Pope Paul VI, as significant documents of our time.

In his speech the Polish Communist leader Gierek emphasized "the absence of conflict between the State and the

Church; our will is to cooperate in the implementation of the great national goals. Concern for the prosperity of our Motherland, the Polish People's Republic, is the cause uniting all of us, as it was stressed by myself and the Primate of Poland, Stefan Cardinal Wyszynski, in a communiqué on our meeting."

On the other hand, Pope Paul VI underlined that "the Catholic Church does not ask for privileges for itself, but only for the right of keeping its identity and for the possibility of developing, without obstacles, its activities in keeping with its entity and mission."[77]

Natural Milieu for a Modern Pope

All these hopes which revived with the reestablishment of a new Polish republic after World War II were overdue for fulfillment. The upper hand of the Communists prevented their being always actualized. Communist pressure extended further the suffering of the Poles on the ideological front, in the sense that their human rights were drastically curtailed proportionate in lesser degree to their strongly religious antagonism to Communism.

No wonder that Warsaw remains an enigma to Moscow and vice versa. Poland, a country of 34 million people, 95 per cent of the Catholic persuasion, with a vast majority (80 per cent) faithful to the practice of their religion and determined nationals, is, to say the least, almost certainly a nuisance to Communists behind the Iron Curtain. Yet it would seem natural that the new Pope John Paul II should come from such a milieu as this strong Catholic nation surrounded by dangerous and hostile powers.

As a native son of Poland, the new Pope is a clear echo of national dynamism and religious zeal; as a son of his father, a military officer, he exemplifies patriotism by his participation in the Polish underground, and as an archbishop of Krakow he seems a visible perpetuator of all Polish religious, cultural, and national traditions. No wonder that the cardinals found him a fitting candidate for the highest office of the Church, which is the main pulse of a nation.

Chapter 5

EARLY LIFE OF KAROL WOJTYLA

Birthplace and Ancestry

THE birthplace of Pope John Paul II is Wadowice[78] a small town of 9,000 inhabitants (who now number 18,000). Located in Southern Poland approximately 40 miles southwest of Krakow, the region of Upper Silesia, it is not far from Oswiecim (Auschwitz), the ill-famed concentration camp where millions of Jews were massacred by the Nazis during the Second World War. Wadowice is in the foothills of the Beskidi Mountains which outline the boundary between Poland and Czechoslovakia. The people of that region are known as *górals* (from *góra,* mountain). Górals possess their own dialect, costume, literature, food, and dance.

The inhabitants are mostly small farmers but there is some industry too, though the economy is rather poor. Educational opportunities are, notwithstanding, very good, with a preparatory school, the ordinary high school (gymnasium), and vocational and professional schools. With its low houses and its 650-year-old parish church, rebuilt in the 18th century, Wadowice differs little from other towns of the Polish countryside. Its neo-classical castle, built in the beginning of the 18th century, adds a picturesque dimension to the region.

The parents of the future Pope, Karol Wojtyla and Emilia Kaczorowska, were natives of the village of Kety, likewise in Southern Poland, and belonged to the lower middle class, the agrarian background of the wife combining the traditional civil service of the husband. Their ancestors, of a mountain village close to the border of Czechoslovakia, were very much attached to the traditions of their native land.

Karol's father was a sergeant in active service with the Polish army, his mother a devoutly religious woman whose influence on her son was certainly salutary. The family lived in a three-room apartment on the second floor, which today is the home of Patyra, professor at the gymnasium and a classmate of Karol.

Religious Growth

In the parish church of the Presentation of the Blessed Virgin Mary, Karol was baptized,[79] received his First Communion, was confirmed, and celebrated his First Mass. The pastor of the parish was Canon Zacher, assisted by a chaplain. Father Franciszek Zak, who baptized Karol, was later replaced by Father Jakub Piotrowski, who remained for several years at this post. Besides the parish church, there were Carmelite and Pallottine Fathers with their monasteries and the Religious Sisters with their semipublic chapels, so that the faithful of the town were well served in their spiritual needs.

John Paul II was born in Wadowice in 1920; in the birth registry (p. 549, par. 71) there is the Latin entry: "Carolus Joseph born on May 18 and baptized on the 20th of the following June, confirmed on May 3, 1938, ordained priest on November 1, 1946, two days after receiving the Subdiaconate, made Bishop on September 28, 1958, Metropolitan Archbishop of Krakow on January 13, 1964, Cardinal on June 26, 1967, elected Pope on October 16, 1978."[80]

Early Loss of Parents

Karol's happy and serene childhood was disturbed at the age of nine by the untimely death of his beloved mother while giving birth to a still-born girl. Emilia's life had been very hard and laborious—when Karol was born, she was already close to forty. He was suddenly deprived of what is most indispensable in the life of a child—a mother's love—which in the life of Karol and his brother Edmund, 14 years his senior, was the more necessary because of their father's frequent and long absences in military service.

They had a cousin living in Krakow, Felicja Wiadrowska (a retired teacher and now 75 years old), who cared for Karol when his mother took sick and after her death. The two brothers had frequently, however, to cook for themselves and to care for the domestic chores concurrently with schoolwork. They managed with the help also of a good neighbor, mother of Karol's childhood friend, Boguslaw Banas.

Their father died in 1941 when Karol was 21 years old. A military man of high discipline, he demanded conscientiousness, diligence, and subordination of his sons. Often he deliberately left them in an unheated room to harden them, but he also cooked for them, washed and mended their clothes, says cousin Felicja. The toughening their father gave them paid off during World War II, especially for Karol who was able to endure the stone quarry where he slaved by day and studied covertly by night.[81] Both parents were buried in the Wadowice cemetery.

Dedicated to School, Church, and Sports

Karol attended grade school in his hometown from 1927 to 1931, and was better known by the diminutive Lolus or Lolek, according to 77-year-old Canon Zacher, who had also been his teacher in the gymnasium. Karol was a very good boy. He had many talents, and was first in his class. His piety made everyone believe he would become a priest. Most of all, Karol was devoted to the veneration of the Blessed Mother.

The Canon and his friend Boguslaw affirm that little Karol went to church every morning before school and every evening as well, after he finished his homework. We learn also from Boguslaw that Karol loved to pray. His mother had set up a small altar in the corner of his bedroom, before which the future Pope was wont to pray, often dressed in a white robe she had made for him.

Never did the two friends Banas and Wojtyla fight, for Karol did not like to quarrel. From boyhood he liked sports and began early with a kind of ping-pong.

From 1931 to 1938 Karol was a student at the gymnasium *(gimnazjum,* i.e., high school and college combined) located on Mickiewicz Street. One of the brightest students in the classical humanistic curriculum, he passed the baccalaureate *maxima cum laude* in June 1938, distinguishing himself especially in language and literature. The active temperament of the future Pope was noticeable already at this period. At the age of only 14 he was instrumental in erecting in Wadowice, with the help of Canon Zacher, a juvenile Marian Sodality. In his school years he also compiled a Catalogue of the region's historical monuments, thus showing his historic bent.

A transcript of Karol's baccalaureate study shows: A in conduct, religion, Polish language, Latin, Greek, German, mathematics, philosophy, and physical education; B in physics, chemistry, and history. His friend Zbigniew Silkowski says of him: "From the intellectual point of view, Karol was by far superior to all of us. He absorbed knowledge almost without having to study. On the other hand his interests were much more numerous than those of any of us."[82]

One must admire this against the background of the future Pope's difficult times. During his school years at the gymnasium Karol experienced hardship in making ends meet. Mrs. Zofie Warmus remembers him: "He had breakfast with us when his mother died. He was in charge of collecting the money that apprentices had to pay." When they asked why he should be in charge of the money, she always answered: "Karol is the most orderly of all of you!" This reveals not only his personal honesty and integrity, for which he earned the confidence others put in him, but also his understanding of the necessities of life.

Love for Native Place and Native Land

Karol evidently loved his native place very much, since he returned home frequently even after he had become cardinal. Since the house where he was born had been sold, he lived usually in the home of his childhood friend Zbigniew Silkowski. His behavior was the same, simple and always humble; he never showed off his ecclesiastical dignity, that his friends might feel at ease.[83] He made every effort to remain his old self, to be as his friends had known him.

One should recall also that Karol was affected during his school years by deep patriotic sentiments—he belonged to the Odrodzenie (Renaissance), a national movement organized by the then professor of sociology at Lublin Catholic University, Stefan Wyszynski, later the primate of Poland. The aim of Wyszynski's Odrodzenie was the revival of the old Polish Catholic national spirit: that national life must be infused with the religious faith of the people; that, indeed, without religious faith there can be no lasting national life.

This spirit became the firm ingredient of Karol Wojtyla's character with dynamic impact on all with whom he came in contact.[84] It is a paradox that World War II accounts for Polish Catholicism's stunning renaissance. The Nazi atrocities mobilized their full potential for compassion, charity, sacrifice, and determination to survive, along with the confirmation of the Polish Church's boldness and defiance.

Interruption of University Studies

Despite the enormous financial strain involved in maintaining two student sons—Edmund was in medical school—Wojtyla Senior had his son Karol enrolled at the University because of the boy's talents and interest. The family moved to Krakow in 1938, and Karol registered in the Faculty of Letters and Philosophy of the Jagiellonian University, the oldest university in Poland.

Founded in 1364, after the example of Charles IV University in Prague (1348), it was the same institution from which the famed Nicholas Copernicus had been graduated. Unfortunately, the young Karol could pursue his studies here for but a year and a half, since the Nazis, who had invaded Poland in 1939, for fear of possible student demonstrations, closed this university as they did all other institutions.

This was the usual Nazi procedure. Universities were closed for these reasons: (a) to handicap the intellectual life of the nation they occupied, (b) to use students for work in factories, and (c) to insure tranquillity. This followed a classic example, the similar closing of universities in Czechoslovakia[85] on November 17, 1939, when hundreds of students were deported to concentration camps or to forced labor in Germany. Some students were even executed. By this method, the Nazis succeeded in keeping the young people in an agony of suspense.

Chapter 6

WORKER, ACTOR, POET, AND SPORTSMAN

Firsthand Experience of Work and Suffering

TO AVOID deportation by the Germans, Karol had to find work in a hurry, first as a miner in the quarry of Zakozowek, then as a worker in the chemical plant of Solvey. There he founded a recreational club for the workers, motivated by his interest in their problems, not alone from a religious point of view but also from an educational, social, and cultural one. Thus the future Pope acquired direct experience in his own arduous work as well as in the hardships of those compelled to earn their bread by the sweat of their brows. It was the best way indeed for him to learn to understand the essence, the aspirations, and the anxieties of the working class.

He recalled this experience in a papal audience with some 2,500 workers from various countries, December 9, 1978: "For a short period of my life, during the last World War, I also experienced directly working in a factory. Hence I know what the daily exertion of working at the dependence of others means; I know the hardship and the monotony, I know the needs of the workers, their just exigencies, and their legitimate aspirations. And I know how important it is that work should never alienate nor frustrate, but correspond always to the superior, the spiritual dignity of man."[86]

This experience was valuable, for the young Wojtyla learned at firsthand some of the social problems of the people. At the same time, it not only developed in him a genuine social feeling with working people but also conditioned in him a special concern for universal distributive justice.

As if this interruption of study and the need to work with his hands were not enough, Karol was struck, in 1941, by a double sorrow. Both his father and his brother died—Edmund, already graduated from medical school in Krakow, and fulfilling his internship at the hospital in Bielsk-Bialej. Now Karol was alone. One feels how hard his life was. He was spared nothing; difficulty was part of his personal life. Deprived of the comfort of a family, he shared difficult times with a society terrorized by the Nazis. This was for him another experience, ascetical training in learning to take life realistically, as it is and as Providence provides.

Literary and Poetic Output

Already in high school Karol had revealed his literary talent; he took very hard the disruption the Nazi occupation caused in his studies. He turned his hand nonetheless to writing poetry and plays in which he gave vent to his artistic soul. He contributed to the contemporary existential poetry, writing under the pen name Andrzej Jawien. A series of his sophisticated poems appeared almost weekly in *Tygodnik Powszechny,* the weekly that served as a mirror for contemporary men and women suffering interior anguish from their faith and from their portion in the world.

Karol wished to deal with the problems of the main character in the famous novel *The Sky in Flames,* by Polish Catholic novelist, Jan Parandowski. The protagonist Andrzej Jawien, a young Catholic intellectual gradually losing his faith, was the source of his pseudonym. Another of his works is a social commentary on industrial life, wrestling with the frustration and the despair of a young factory worker alienated from himself and from society. Writer Julius Kydrynski recollects:

In his first year at the university, Karol wrote poetry, as he had done in the gymnasium. Our common interest in literature and the theater fueled our friendship. We came together for literary soirées. We advertised these events with posters in various towns. The turnouts were reminiscent of folk ballads, but in content they were reflective, philosophical lyrics.

The war broke out, interrupting our studies at the University. Our friends took odd jobs. My mother's friends secured for Karol and me a job in the quarry of the Solvey factory—later turned into the Krakow soda plant. We walked to work, across the Debuica Bridge, weather minus 30 degrees centigrade. Before leaving our house for work we smeared our faces with a thick layer of vaseline.[87]

When Wojtyla's father died of a stroke in 1941, Kydrynski's mother invited Karol to live with them. In the old house on Felicjanski Street his colleagues from the Polish philology department read the works of the romantics. Those reading rehearsals later turned into theater performances—often very risky. "In the flat where we are now having tea, we gave a performance for 30 people just half an hour after a gestapo search. Today it appears that half of Krakow was on first-name terms with Karol Wojtyla, and the other half had long expected that he become Pope."[88]

This vivid description by a good friend of Karol Wojtyla's certainly re-creates the atmosphere and circumstances that very much conditioned young Wojtyla emotionally, culturally, nationally, and spiritually so that he would soon mature into the integrated personality he is.

Influence of John of the Cross

Karol's growing up, other than through the great influences of his parents, his teachers, and his contacts with priests, came also through his rich experiences in life and from association with the good friends he kept always in his heart. Especially during the war years, one central influence on Wojtyla was that of a man named Jan Tyranowski, a simple tailor by trade, who was one of the rare people who not only knew and understood the great master of mystical prayer, the 16th-century Spaniard St. John of the Cross, but had himself the gift of mystical prayer.

Wojtyla, under Tyranowski's direction, read deeply and with understanding in the works of John of the Cross. Tyranowski reportedly observed to Wojtyla's intimates that Karol was one of the few young people he had met who had also the gift of mystical prayer. The influence of this friend had to be strong, as is indicated by the fact that Wojtyla later as a priest chose research on St. John of the Cross for his scholarly inquiry.

Here experimental knowledge mediated through human contact was being completed by philosophical and theological visions fused into an integrated spiritual synthesis, which ever after remained a distinct mark of the man's personality.

Participation in the Performing Arts

Another phase of his growing is illustrated by Wojtyla's association with another good friend who inspired him in the performing arts. This happened when he came into close contact with a prestigious actor, Miecyslav Kotlarczyk, to whom he offered the hospitality of his apartment at 10 Tyniecky Street, and with whom he founded the Rhapsody Theater. A clandestine activity, it went underground during the Nazi occupation; this foundation upheld his courage in time of danger and sustained the principles of the resistance movement. The Nazis strictly forbade any association in clubs not supportive of their regime and their ideology.

Karol's home became the center and meeting place of artists who programmed performances and poetry recitals. Karol himself wrote most of the plays and interpreted principal characters. Some offerings had a didactic or educational tone, but all afforded inspiration. Those who knew Karol Wojtyla at that time admired his outstanding gifts for acting; so much involved was he in this activity that he seriously considered becoming a professional actor.

Even later when he became bishop and archbishop, Karol continued to write critical articles on the theater and remained Kotlarczyk's friend. When a book was to be published, titled *The Art of the Spoken Word,* to honor Kotlarczyk, it was the Archbishop of Krakow, Karol Wojtyla, who offered to write the introduction. Another instance of his continuing interest in the performing arts is the circumstance that Andrzej Jawien's little known 20-year-old play, *The Goldsmith's Store,* was performed for the first time in 1979 on Italy's State Radio. Sudden interest in the obscure Polish actor and playwright—better known now as Pope John Paul II—was the reason.

The Goldsmith's Store recounts three separate love stories and was written under Karol Wojtyla's usual pen name. Written in Krakow while the Pope was a young prelate, it is his only published play.[89] Wojtyla's acting abilities were generally recognized for he had already proved himself a successful producer and leading actor in a school troupe that toured on occasion southeastern Poland, doing Shakespeare's *Hamlet* and modern Polish plays.

Singing Ability and Love of Music

With his acting Karol also developed his voice into a melodious baritone which frequently surprises his friends at occasional gatherings. Especially edifying is his voice in Church liturgy. It is said that Wojtyla is the first pope since Pius IX (d. 1876) to have a fine, well-trained singing voice, and according to some of the older hands at the Vatican, the "first in this century to sing the difficult *Ite missa est* ["The Mass is ended. Go in peace"] in tune.

His singing ability is immeasurably enriched by his love of music. He is especially fond of Frederic Chopin's music. Bach, Poland's Henry Wiemawski, the Czechs Smetana and

Dvorak, and folk and country songs are among his favorites. A New Hampshire lady remembers that when she broke her leg while skiing in Poland, she was serenaded in the nearby hospital by a group of fellow skiers—and only later was she to learn that the leading singer and guitarist was Bishop Wojtyla.[90]

Music is important also to his peace of mind, especially folk songs, which he sings in a mellifluous baritone while accompanying himself on the guitar. Unlike some prelates, he does not totally oppose rock music. In fact, when students performed a Polish version of *Jesus Christ Superstar* in a church basement, he made a point of being in the capacity audience and afterward congratulated the performers, pointing out that "love and joy" are very important in the Christian life of the young.[91]

Accomplished Speaker, Skilled Journalist, Poet

With frequent exercise of the performing arts, he developed well also as a public speaker with a skilled ability to convey messages easily and to communicate with the public. Perhaps in connection with this, Wojtyla was always, and still is, a tireless and voracious reader. He has in fact a disconcerting habit of reading and writing while carrying on a conversation, but is able all the while to display total recall of what he has read.

In expressing himself well in public, he became almost naturally a skilled journalist. He contributed frequently to the monthly *Znak* and several Catholic periodicals, later for the most part in line with his professional interests, moral and ethical problems. He wrote a cycle of articles in a column titled "Basic Ethics," which itself serves to indicate his journalistic acumen.

Uniquely perhaps did he distinguish himself as a poet. He wrote over the years a collection of poems, under his pen name, in *Znak* and in other journals. In fact Wojtyla's poems, all composed between 1950 and 1966, range over a wide field: work in a factory, artistic creativity, love, anger, evil, despair, the meaning of religious faith, and were translated by Professor Jerzy Peterkiewicz of the University of London under the title *Easter Vigil and Other Poems.*[92] It is a pleasure to read them.

One reflects that in the history of the popes the last pontiff who distinguished himself by writing poems of any number was none other than Leo XIII (1876-1903), who was polyhistor, scholar, and teacher.[93] It comes to mind too that Wojtyla in his new position as pope may have a special historic place also in this respect.

Love for Sports

With his passion for the arts, Wojtyla developed also a great interest in sports. He loved and practiced sports as a discipline equilibrating the spirit. He played soccer on the school team, usually on the defense. A member of his team, Dr. Wiodzimierz Piotowski, said of him: "Karol was not very strong in the beginning. But he exercised with perseverance that he might eventually develop muscles, which he really did. He seemed to radiate good cheer and had always lively conversation—a bit of gossip, a bit of humor, a Latin quotation."[94]

As an outdoor man who spends solitary vacations in the wild, Wojtyla enjoyed skiing best of all. Dressed in baggy work pants and old-fashioned lace-up boots, he made it a point to spend a week every year skiing in the Tatra Mountains of Poland. "He is a daredevil," says a ski instructor back home. "He loves the thrill and danger of it." When asked at his press conference whether he will continue to ski now that he is pope, he answered: "It will be difficult!"

There is a story he himself frequently tells from his skiing experience. One day while he was climbing the Tatra very close to the Czechoslovakia boundary, he was stopped by a policeman guarding the border. In his alpinist outfit there was no distinguishing him from any other alpinist, except by the small metal cross on his windjacket. "Identification," ordered the guard. The Archbishop of Krakow immediately showed him his passport, identifying him as "Karol Wojtyla, Cardinal of the Roman Church." "Where did you steal it?" the policeman asked rudely. "I did not steal it, it's mine," he answered.

After some effort, seeing that he could not convince the man of his identity and as it was getting colder, the Cardinal invited the officer to have a drink in the not-too-distant mountain hut. "We emptied some drinks and became friends," related the future Pope; "the policeman let me go at the end, but I think that he remained convinced that the document was indeed forged or stolen."

Not only is he a sportsman himself, but he enjoys also the excitement of the sports fan. During the summer of 1978 in Milan, while the World Soccer Championship was being contested in Argentina, the then-Archbishop Wojtyla was invited to a dinner after his conference on responsible parenthood, a favorite ethico-theological subject. He hurriedly left the table before the others and it was known later that he did so to watch the game between Brazil and Poland on television.

Religious Appeal through Sports

Wojtyla was very fond also of the canoe and paddled in the summer on the tributaries of the Visla River. But he is known mainly as an excellent skier. The inhabitants of Zakopane, the famous Polish winter sports resort in the Tatra Mountains, remember still his insuperable skiing. Certainly, he was not the lone Polish priest or bishop to love skiing. He explained once to the students in a Milan seminary how Polish and Italian bishops differ: by the fact that more than half the Polish bishops were skiers.

Another time, told that no Italian cardinals skied, he remarked innocently: "That's strange. In Poland 40% of our cardinals are skiers." Reminded that Poland had but two cardinals, he smiled: "That's correct, but Cardinal Wyszynski counts for 60 percent."

Hiking and mountain climbing he practiced regularly and everywhere. Appointed auxiliary bishop of Cracow in 1958, his nomination caught him on an excursion to Lake Mazuri, along with a group of young people. At that time he was parish priest of St. Florian in Krakow.

Wojtyla used the passion of young people for sports as an efficient means of apostolic activity. Did not Don Bosco do the same? And St. Augustine, did he not say, if you wish to attract children and young people, you must share their interests and love what they love in order to induce them to love what you love? In this Wojtyla had need of no lesson from anyone, for sports are second nature to him.

In order to have the closest contact with nature, he loved to sleep outdoors in a tent, camping with other young people. Is not nature the most eloquent witness of God? Karol Wojtyla seems to understand this perfectly, for he believed firmly in the harmony of the spirit with the body. Is not the slogan of the Scouts—"in healthy body, healthy spirit!"—in the same tune as Wojtyla's?

Chapter 7

CLANDESTINE SEMINARIAN AND UNDERGROUND WORKER

Blossoming Priestly Vocation

IN HIS spiritual life, Karol Wojtyla also seemed to follow the idea of a healthy body and a healthy spirit. His piety and religious zeal as a boy were generally known, for he was wont to serve regularly as an altar boy at Mass and devotions. Nevertheless, so long as he lived in Wadowice (until he was 18) he expressed no manifest vocation to the priesthood. The future Pope himself recalls that his vocation was strengthened and confirmed by frequent visits to the parish church of St. Stanislaus Kostka, administered by Salesians of Don Bosco, in Krakow, where he got much inspiration.[95]

Certainly the Christian education he had from his mother, the loss of his father and brother, the Nazi persecution, and the suffering of the Polish people in the war have all contributed to the evolution of his priestly vocation in accordance with the divine design. Yet, most instrumental in leading him to the final decision was again his fellow-worker, the tailor Jan Tyranowski, almost 20 years older than Karol. The long discussions of the two friends on the fundamental questions of life and their common prayers resulted in Karol's final irrevocable decision to be a priest.

Although this decision may have been maturing for years, to some friends it came as a surprise. Sofia Kotlarczyk, widow of the actor, remembers that unexpectedly one day Karol told the group he must renounce his lead in their next play, for he was about to enter the seminary.

Active in the Underground

When the Second World War broke out[96] Wojtyla was immediately active in the underground. At 19 he became a member of the Armia Krajowa (The Home Army), a military-type organization of national resistance.[97] He was a courier carrying messages, distributing resistance literature, participating in the underground canal that hid escapees and enabled them to reach the West. He was a member of the unit that obtained technical details and actual pieces of the German V-1 and V-2 missiles then being tested in Poland, and he forwarded the information to London.

The situation of the Poles became very tense, especially when the Germans launched their army against Russia from 1941 on. The Nazis used Krakow as an important transportation center during the War; their presence was very visible in the city. The main square around the cathedral was renamed Adolf Hitler Platz. Here was the residence of Hitler's general governor, Hans Frank, who ruled with an iron hand.

Cardinal Sapieha did not give in to him in any way, but bravely continued to discharge his duties as archbishop in spite of all chicanery and harassment. He was able even to organize a clandestine seminary counsel in his palace despite strict Nazi veto. Wojtyla failed in 1942 to return to his factory job and was not seen again until the end of the war in 1945. For his active part in the heroic anti-Nazi resistance movement he had to look for a hideout and found it eventually in the basement of the Archbishop's palace.

On the advice of a certain priest Karol Wojtyla requested of the Cardinal to be accepted into a seminary, once secretly organized. The Cardinal took him and some six or seven other young men into his residence where they pursued clerical studies clandestinely, the while quietly aiding the prelate in his opposition to the Nazi invaders; the Nazis had closed not only the universities but also the seminaries. Against this background the Cardinal acted with prudence and bravery. During the entire period of Nazi occupation, from 1942 to 1945, Karol was constrained to spend the day as worker while at night he attended classes in theology.[98]

Providential Survival

As a young seminarian in wartime Krakow, Karol distributed newspapers in the anti-Nazi underground and won himself a place on a list of wanted persons. He was furthermore an active member of the Polish underground movement Unia, which was the ideologically educational branch of the Social Christian Resistance Movement, whose legacy was to preserve Polish tradition and culture, which the Nazis were determined to annihilate.

During this period, young Wojtyla assisted hunted Jews in finding shelter and faking identification papers,[99] his situation further aggravated by his deep involvement in other underground activities for which his name had come to the attention of the gestapo. He would doubtless have been arrested and eventually executed by the Nazis had he not gone into hiding. There, for the last five months of the war (from August 1944 until the Nazis were replaced by the Soviet Army on January 18, 1945) he lived in fear, but meanwhile had plenty of opportunity to meditate and to mature in his philosophical and theological thought.

Karol's survival under such circumstances is in itself an example of providential divine care, especially if one considers the great number of Polish clergy who perished in the anti-Nazi struggle; the estimate is high: 3 bishops and 1,263 priests in concentration camps, with 584 other priests shot or executed—these outrages completed with the deaths of 6 million Poles during World War II. Then it is that we can fully understand a special divine intervention in Karol Wojtyla's case.

Help Extended to Polish Jews

One senses how great was Karol's courage in these underground activities. Without detailing much of these activities, we must mention one of special significance, for it concerns the Jews in the city of Krakow. Dr. Joseph L. Lichten, the Rome representative of the International Jewish Association, made the following declaration:

> During the German occupation of Poland, Karol Wojtyla, just a little over 20, was put on the Nazi blacklist, and he had to hide as he was in danger of being killed for helping the Jews in Krakow, as an active member of the secret Democratic Christian organization, UNIA. In fact, he had supplied many Jews with forged documents, prepared for them by the underground organization, thus saving them from deportation or even death. During the last months of the Nazi occupation, toward the end of the war, Wojtyla was hidden in Archbishop [Cardinal] Sapieha's basement to avoid arrest.
>
> After the War, there were only 500 Jews left in the whole city of Krakow, the only survivors from a substantial community. Monsignor Wojtyla helped to organize the restoration and provided for the permanent maintenance of the Jewish Cemetery of Krakow. In 1968, when he had been Archbishop of Krakow for four years, he opposed the expulsion of the remaining Jews from their city, which was as it seems in the period of tension that followed the Six Days' War in 1967.[100]

Lichten remembers also that *Tygodnik Powszechny*, Krakow's Catholic weekly, founded directly by Archbishop Wojtyla and distributed all over Poland, "played an important part in the defense of the Jews and the dialogue between Catholics and Jews."[101] This is a truly moving testimony of Wojtyla's generous human goodness.

As corollary to this, perhaps it can be mentioned that after his election, John Paul II received in private audience his childhood friend and schoolmate Jerzy Kluger, together with his children and grandchildren. Kluger is the son of the president of the Jewish Community of Wadowice, the Pope's birthplace. The young Wojtyla had visited his Jewish friend's home almost every day, and entered prep school with him. This friendship continued after the war.

The most precious memento of this friendship was certainly the photograph taken in the Vatican when the two friends met. This occurrence speaks itself for the voluminous documentary that could be drawn up on behalf of the personality Wojtyla developed in these crucial years.

Chapter 8

PRIEST, ACADEMICIAN, AND BISHOP

Ordination and Advanced Studies at Rome

AFTER the liberation of Krakow by the Soviet Army, the seminaries in Poland were reopened together with other universities. Karol was thus able to continue freely his theological studies at the major seminary in Krakow. He passed his last examinations in August 1946, *maxima cum laude,* and on November 1, 1946, at the age of 26 was ordained a priest by Cardinal Sapieha, for the Archdiocese of Krakow.

This same Cardinal, knowing the intellectual potential of the new priest, strongly advised him to pursue in Rome advanced studies in theology and philosophy. Father Wojtyla, chosen from hundreds of possible candidates arrived in Rome soon after ordination in the fall of 1946, with a colleague.

The economic hardship in Poland during and after the war resulted in his being undernourished. He was thin and his soutane almost threadbare. Some of his new colleagues were kind enough to give him a new one, that he might present himself at the university in a dignified manner. Wojtyla enrolled at the Pontifical University of St. Thomas Aquinas (the Angelicum), directed by the Dominicans, and he lived at the Belgian College, for the Polish College, closed during the war, had not reopened.

Several foreign countries have home institutions to lodge young student priests in Rome. The students distinguish themselves by their varied attire: the Germans from the Germanicum dress in red—that they may be singled out immediately should they be guilty of trespass, say the Germans. The Belgians wear black with a red and black belt; and the Polish, a black tunic with a green belt.

The two young Polish priests found themselves together with 14 Belgians under the direction of Monsignor Maximilian von Fürstenburg. By coincidence he would later be part of the same group of cardinals created in 1967 with Wojtyla and would participate at the conclave that would elect his former student to the pontificate.

Acquired More Than Book Knowledge

Wojtyla worked at his books very diligently, yet without neglecting to broaden his already wide background. He did thorough sightseeing until he knew every historical monument of the Eternal City, undertook hiking trips into the hills around Rome, and went often to the shrine of Mentorella, directed by Polish Resurrectionist Fathers. In the two years he spent in Italy, Father Wojtyla visited several other European countries as well, especially France, Belgium, and The Netherlands. At this period he was particularly interested in the workers' organization, Jeunesse Ouvrière Chrétienne (J.O.C. or I.O.C.).

Besides absorbing the texts taught in Latin in Rome and engaging in the normal academic arguments common among disputatious clerical students, the energetic priest from Krakow gave spiritual and pastoral assistance to the Polish refugees in Rome and to the innumerable former Polish soldiers and their families who as displaced persons were scattered through Germany, France, and Belgium in the post-war period. He thus achieved early acquaintance with much of war-torn Europe and perfected his knowledge of European languages and of English.

Karol's principal financial support came from the Pontificia Assistensa and from the Vatican through the generosity of the United States war relief services (NCWC) under Monsignor Andrew Landi and James Norris. During this period Wojtyla was providentially supervised by the substitute Secretary of State, Monsignor Giovanni Battista Montini, who exerted a great interest in pastoral missions of priests of various nationalities in refugee camps and elsewhere.[102]

His studies in philosophy completed, Father Wojtyla wrote his dissertation, "The Virtue of Faith in the Thought of St. John of the Cross," under the guidance of the famed French philosopher R. Garrigou-Lagrange and that of scholar Luigi Ciappi (later the Pope's official theologian, and cardinal), and was awarded a doctorate in philosophy (Ph.D.).

Continued Graduate Studies in Poland

Returning to Poland in the summer of 1948, Father Wojtyla went to his hometown of Wadowice where for the time being he served as coadjutor to a local pastor. Shortly after, he was appointed chaplain in Niegowic where he remained a year; and in 1949, he was transferred as chaplain to the parish of St. Florian in Krakow, working there until 1951.

Simultaneously, he continued his graduate studies at the Theological Faculty of his old alma mater, the Jagiellon University of Krakow, with its historic tradition as among the oldest and most respected European institutions. Founded in 1364, it was formally recognized by Pope Benedict IX in 1397 on the special request of Queen Hedwiga, wife of Ladislaw Jagiellon. Wojtyla shared a pride with this university, for when its Theological Faculty was suppressed in 1954 and eliminated from the university by the Communist regime, it was chiefly owing to Bishop Wojtyla's efforts that the Holy See reopened it by a decree in 1959; in 1961 it conferred on it also the dignity of pontifical institution.

Wojtyla was an ardent student and his excellence gained for him popularity. He majored in moral theology and after the defense of his doctoral dissertation, "The Problem of Faith in the Works of St. John of the Cross," under the direction of major professor Wladyslaw Wicher, he was awarded the degree doctor of sacred theology (S.T.D.), *maxima cum laude.*

His great talent as a linguist also helped. At this time he was already an accomplished polyglot: besides his mother tongue, the Pope speaks Russian, Czech, German, French, Italian, and English, and knows something of Spanish and Dutch, all these moreover without counting his Latin, Greek, and Hebrew. He soon began to be recognized by some professors as of exceptional talent, especially by Professors Rozycki and Wicher.

Chaplain to University Students

In the meantime, Wojtyla was entrusted as chaplain with the task of assisting and advising young students and graduates of the State University of Krakow. Given the difficulties and restrictions of the atheist government, it was not easy; but in guidance he could draw upon his valuable experience gathered during the war and from previous experience of parish work. His zealous, apostolic activity among the university students was greatly appreciated by Archbishop Stefan Sapieha and won respect for Wojtyla in academic circles. His good reputation began to grow.

> He was an excellent preacher. His diction was precise, clear, without inflection, and he used easy expressions, understandable to all. Definitely, he put his talents and experience as an actor to the best use. To teach his altar boys the basics of recitation, he invited his former actor colleagues to the church where they instructed the boys. Father Wojtyla could inspire universal enthusiasm. He was extremely communicative and while he was preaching required absolute silence and attention. As confessor, he inspired trust and ease without hurt to the penitent's feelings.[103]

The wholesome praise he evoked clearly indicates that Father Wojtyla's ability was well-rounded in that he was good in practically everything he attempted, directed always to the purpose of the project in hand, both to his superior's satisfaction and the people's benefit. He was simply a versatile man ready to perform the important task of the moment.

Ascending Academic Career

With his pastoral duties in the parishes and his apostolic activity with the university students Father Wojtyla did not let up in continuing his education. Gifted with an unusual intellectual capacity, he had a great yearning for an academic career. From 1951 on he kept himself busy with his scholarly works. He pursued this goal consistently; having already two doctorates, he had yet to achieve habilitation to become a docent as an opening to a university career. This is a standing requirement in all important European universities.

Father Karol wished to teach at the Jagiellon State University and, to earn the qualification appropriate for a post, presented in 1953 to the Theological Faculty of the university his habilitation thesis, "An Evaluation as to the Possibility of Establishing a Catholic Ethics on the Basis of the Ethical System of Max Scheler." This thesis was published as customarily required.

Although the young priest was well qualified for the post, his nomination was somehow delayed by the state authorities, and as a result he took advantage of other academic opportunities. His continuing philosophical research and his growing scholarly reputation opened for him, in 1953, the appointment to the rank of assistant professor of moral theology at the Major Theological Seminary in Krakow, lecturing on social ethics. In the following year (1954) he also accepted the post of assistant professor of ethics at the Catholic University in Lublin, the only one behind the Iron Curtain, where he soon became ordinarius professor and chairman of the department of philosophy.

For his scientific activity and for his growing scholarship in the skilled interpretation of adjacent ethical systems and values, he was elected a member of the Polish Academy of Sciences in 1959, a fitting recognition of his intellectual maturity. Professor Mieczyslaw Krapice, rector of the Catholic University at Lublin, expressed great praise and admiration of Karol Wojtyla as a well-esteemed professor of ethics. He is also hoping that the new Pope will visit the university when in Poland on the jubilee of St. Stanislaus and thus dignify that institution by his presence.

Upholder of Academic Freedom

Father Wojtyla was a good professor, one whose style of teaching was attractive to the students. One of his former colleagues at Lublin, the Dominican Father Adalbert Bednarski, at present professor at the University of St. Thomas Aquinas in Rome, states: "Wojtyla, with his warm heart, was loved by everybody who met him." He praises, as do many others, his intellectual vigor and doctrinal rigor.[104] He displayed great courage in expressing his views and did not let himself be intimidated by Communist threats.

One day a government inspector came to admonish the professors at the Catholic University at Lublin to be careful about every word they said, no longer to make any reference to Western thought. This did not hinder Professor Wojtyla from continuing to lecture on existentialism, on phenomenology, and on other Western ideologies. He insisted that academic freedom is a fundamental prerogative in scientific research. Very emphatic in his emphasis on free learning and teaching at all institutes of higher learning, he was open to every challenge of conflicting ideologies.

Such a cry for academic freedom was, to say the least, rather unusual, because it eschewed the monolithic method of indoctrination dear to Communist countries. Any interference of state authority to press this monolithic Communist ideology in state institutions he criticized as flagrant violation of academic freedom. He was thus the avant-garde fighter for human rights a decade before it became fashionable. One senses immediately that Father Wojtyla was a truly authentic academician, fully convinced of the biblical relevance that "the truth makes us free!"

Intellectual Opposition to Communist Ideology

The general public benefited also from Wojtyla's apostolate and zeal for learning. After the war, the public life of Catholics was restricted in many ways. Cardinal Sapieha founded a literary journal, *Tygodnik Powszechny* (Universal Weekly), "a gathering point for Catholics and liberal, anti-Marxist scholars and intellectuals." Threatened, the Communist party replied with attempts to corrupt, suppress, and isolate society hermetically by censorship and ruthless harassment by the administration.

During Gomulka's "thaw" when the Church and the Communist State sought a social truce, the Universal Weekly group was permitted a few delegates to "represent" Catholics in the "parliament." This group, both the organization and its publication, came to be known as Znak (The Sign) but was relegated to a shadowy position, for the general press ignored their speeches and their voting record.[105]

Professor Wojtyla became an architect of intellectualization strategy. As a Neo-Thomist with an outlook of existential and social philosophy, he was in a position to defend the Faith in a sophisticated, rationalist, and materialistic forum. Wojtyla belongs to that group of Catholic theorists who early descried the apt relevance of Thomas Aquinas' thought to the socio-political reality of our present century.

Spokesman for Christians in Atheistic Society

Wojtyla as a youth lived the horror of Adolf Hitler's moral "order." Soviet occupation of Poland subsequently confirmed him in the idea that nothing but defense and confrontation were possible for intellectual Christians in Eastern Europe. The only way to defend themselves, to survive, was to force the Communists to negotiate—this certainly an unlooked-for procedure to demand of people who bared the teeth to any who so much as suggested reasonable discussion.

Hence, even as the totalitarian State was priding itself on its ideas and concepts as being the most scientific, the mind of Aquinas appeared even more valuable than heretofore perceived. Thomism was becoming a signpost leading to "a theory of human liberty that is entitled to distinguish between the absolute and the dogmatic in matters of faith and firmly rejects determinant philosophies such as Marxism."[106]

This situation motivated Wojtyla to extend his talents to the general public as well, in such a way that he contributed numerous popular articles to a variety of above-named journals, in a determined attempt to make the life of the Christian intelligentsia and of the general faithful more livable in a Marxist society. He eventually became for them a forceful spokesman.

Youngest Member of Polish Episcopate

The stature of the priest was growing from the abundant merits he acquired in his apostolic and academic activities, conjoined with the strength of his faith, his ardent zeal, and his priestly spirit and piety. He was becoming, moreover, a prominent candidate for high position in the Church. Opportunity appeared sooner than one would expect.

With the death of Cardinal Sapieha (1951), the See of Krakow was vacant. Archbishop Eugeniusz Baziak was named apostolic administrator of the see and remained such because of government refusal to have a successor named. Pope Pius XII appointed (July 4, 1958) Karol Wojtyla titular bishop of Osubi and auxiliary bishop to the apostolic administrator of Krakow. At the age of 38, Wojtyla became the youngest member of the Polish episcopate when on September 28th he was consecrated bishop in Krakow, choosing a Marian motto *Totus tuus* (All yours).

Contributions to Conciliar Documents

As bishop in Krakow and with a scholarly reputation, Wojtyla participated in three sessions of Vatican Council II (1962-65), where participants greatly appreciated his intensive contributions. Given his familiarity with the problems of the contemporary world and his specific competence in the area of religious freedom, he was entrusted with the work on the drafting of the second and fourth chapters of the pastoral *Constitution on the Church in the Modern World.*[107]

On the theme of social communications, Wojtyla included very-much-appreciated specifications on the moral order and respect for the dignity of the person, and also on the importance of art as a means to transmit the message of the Gospel, exhibiting a distinct hierarchy of values.

He was a help in interpreting religious freedom, when he insisted that "the human being is the purpose and not the instrument of the social order; religion is the culmination and perfection of personal life and of the aspiration at truth." He faced, as well, the problem of contemporary atheism in these terms:

> Atheism should be considered not so much as the denial of God but rather as the interior state of the person and should be studied with sociological and psychological standards. An atheist is convinced of his "final solitude," since God does not exist. From this stems his wish to reach immortality, in a certain sense, in collective life. One must ask, therefore, whether collectivism favors atheism or vice versa. All these inherent ques-

tions make the dialogue with God very difficult, especially when atheism is joined by relativism and civic utilitarianism.[108]

If one conceives of atheism as the denial of God, he has then to begin the dialogue with human beings, respecting their interior freedom and evidencing that religious persons are not alienated at all from worldly reality. Such profound analyses of pertinent problems brought respect and esteem to Wojtyla from other Conciliar Fathers, who frequently used his services, his advice and guidance.

Skilled Negotiator in Church-State Problems

One clearly sees also that the young Bishop was intellectually and spiritually well prepared for the active part in the Council that he took so decisively. To his further credit it must be said that he kept himself in line to research the question whether Cardinal Wyszynski was the official spokesman for the Church of Poland. Out of loyalty to his older and esteemed colleague, Wojtyla took no part in the first session of the Council (1962) that he might show a solidarity with Wyszynski, whom the Polish government did not allow to go to Rome.

Bishop Wojtyla matured also into a skilled negotiator with the Communist regime on behalf of the Church's rights, which the government blatantly and consistently violated. He began his career as negotiator under such doughty veterans as Sapieha and Wyszynski, but soon developed as a more flexible apologist and contender, as well as diplomat both for the philosophical doctrine and the social postulates. As bishop for 20 years, then archbishop of Krakow, he warred with the Communists on everything: teaching of religion to children, the right to a Catholic press, the building of churches, even the nomination of priests, and so forth.

The situation of the Catholic Church in Krakow was then in a difficult position, since the Communist government was especially hostile to the apostolic administrator, Baziak, for his inflexible policies, in which government had pressed for some accommodation. As the way out of this impasse, perhaps, Wojtyla was frequently the preferred negotiating agent in Church-State problems.

Archbishop of the "Polish Rome"

When the apostolic administrator Archbishop Baziak died, Bishop Wojtyla was elected (June 16, 1962) capitular vicar of Krakow, and later (January 13, 1964) nominated by Pope Paul VI as archbishop and metropolitan of Krakow—becoming the first incumbent not of aristocratic origin. As archbishop of Krakow he automatically became a chancellor of the Catholic University of Lublin.

The prestigious historical city of Krakow has always been the heart and the center of Polish Catholics. Pope John XXIII called it the "most Catholic diocese of Poland." The Diocese of Krakow was founded in the year 1000, and it became metropolitan in 1925 with the suffragan Dioceses of Czestochowa, Katowice, Kielce, Tornow. For its great number of churches and the deep faith of its population, Krakow is called the "Polish Rome."

This was always a huge Archdiocese: it numbered before the war 1,230,000 faithful, had 305 parishes, 620 churches, 63 monasteries, and 227 convents for women religious. After the war (1945) the numbers increased to 2,000,000 faithful, 357 parishes with 1,700 secular priests, and 650 churches. As for its religious intensity, there were and are many priestly and religious vocations, as demonstrated by the presence of 1,500 students in its three major seminaries and several religious houses of study.[109] This statistical perspective indicates strongly that Wojtyla had to be constantly preoccupied with the church activities of his own Archdiocese.

Despite his many pastoral duties, the Krakow prelate was called often to Rome. He represented Poland's bishops at every Synod of Bishops. He frequently went to Rome for meetings of the Congregations for the Sacraments and Divine Worship, for the Clergy, and for Catholic Education, as well as for the Permanent Council of the Synod of Bishops.

Inherent Sense of Authentic Doctrine

Wojtyla always strictly defended in all these assemblies the fundamental principles of healthy Christian doctrine. A telling example is his book *Love and Responsibility*,[110] published before the pastoral *Constitution on the Church in the Modern World* (1965) and before Paul VI's encyclical *Humanae vitae* (1968).

Nevertheless, it is so consonant with the personalistic concept of love, which inspired both documents, and yet so markedly convergent on the same moral norms that it seems rather a subsequent writing. This is in itself a testimonial to Cardinal Wojtyla's inherent sense of authentic doctrine for which he consistently strove.

Origin of False Rumors

The sensitivity and realism of this book—a study of sexual morality—led to those foolish and false rumors that began immediately after the papal election: that he had been a married man before World War II. In this connection it should be mentioned that several versions circulated in Rome, originated accidentally by the unintentional remark of the secretary general of the Polish Episcopal Conference, Bronislaw Dabrowski, who once mentioned rumors of an unhappy love in Wojtyla's life.

One version ran that Karol Wojtyla married in 1944 and was a widower when his wife died after a lingering illness —hence his special attention to the sick. According to this version, Hedwig was always the name given the alleged wife. In another account, a more likely one, Karol Wojtyla was engaged for a few months to a Polish girl who perished in a way that is unclear, perhaps deported by the Nazis to Germany without there being further news of her.

The version of the Pope as a widower was categorically denied by the papal entourage though it did not exclude the possibility that in Wojtyla's heart there might have been a woman. It is a story or a legend that could account for the Pope's particular comprehension of the problems of couples, especially the young affianced whom he well portrayed in his book described above. One may be surprised how quickly the rumor took hold and spread so widely, despite its clear lack of substance from the start.

No Basis in Fact

Most judge it just a piece of gossip, for both versions are highly improbable. As regards the first, in 1944 Karol Wojtyla was already secretly studying theology while he hid from the Nazis. As for the second story, of his prewar engagement (1939), he was quite young (nineteen) then and immersed in his college studies, as well as beset by worry over his sick father and the tragic fate of his older brother.

"It is a thoroughly false tale," said Father Pastore, a Vatican press spokesman. "Nothing is true of what has been said in this connection. He was never engaged and he was never married. This is a very thorough denial."[111]

While it may be true that he had a woman friend and an active social life as a young man, these rumors have never been substantiated. With his decision to be a priest in 1942, Wojtyla gave up entirely his usual mode of life and dedicated it to God. Notwithstanding this, not surprisingly, many women are impressed by his rugged good looks. He has indeed an impressive physical appearance, much graced by his spiritual outlook. In the harmony of both lies his appeal.

Chapter 9

PRINCE OF THE CHURCH

New Power in Struggle with Communists

THE prestigious archiepiscopal seat of Krakow, occupied by such an illustrious incumbent, was yet open to another distinction. Pope Paul VI made Archbishop Karol Wojtyla a cardinal in the Secret Consistory of 1967, and in February 1968 invested him solemnly with the cardinal's insignia. This was certainly a great honor for Poland which, in addition to him and Primate Stefan Wyszynski, had a third cardinal, Boleslaw Filipiak, who was in the Roman Curia (d. October 12, 1978).

With this new dignity Wojtyla strengthened his position on the domestic front in frequent confrontations with the Communists and enhanced his prestige by frequent international contacts, with other princes of the Church and with dignitaries of other nations. He made numerous trips to the Vatican and visited various European countries, including those to the United States (1969 and 1976) and elsewhere.

Through his correspondence with the bishops of the Third World he kept in constant contact with the universal Church, through which he enlarged his vision, deepened his understanding of their problems, and developed a feeling for the needs of the people, meanwhile comprehending the orientations of the various ideological trends.

Together with Cardinal Wyszynski, Cardinal Wojtyla continued to be the outspoken critic of Poland's Communist government and of the restrictions placed on Church freedom.

Use of Religious Stratagems

Despite the fact that the Communist government had forbidden not only religious instruction in schools, but also any type of religious association, Archbishop Wojtyla organized catechism instruction in every parish, in every church, in monasteries and convents, and in individual families, to fight what he called "anti-catechesis." In Krakow alone there were dozens of centers for religious instruction and juvenile catechesis, with the participation of tens of thousands of students.

The Cardinal favored primarily the practice of religious and liturgical life and participation in cultural events. He developed into a religious activist, in the sense that he reacted to every anti-religious government move by various circumventions and by utilizing the psychological impact of Catholic crowds of people, not only to intimidate the Communists, who fear crowds, but to substantiate the issues he fought for by displaying the people's approval of them.

To increase the psychological effectiveness of crowds on the Communists, special attention was devoted to the veneration of the Blessed Mother and to the organization of popular pilgrimages to various shrines of Christ and His Mother: to the black Madonna of Czestochowa, to the shrine of the Holy Cross of Moglia-Nowa' Huta, Ludzimier, Myslenice, Staniaski, and Rychwald, especially to Kalwaria Zebrzydowka. He was impressed with this, for after being elected Pope, John Paul II himself recalled all these pilgrimages in a message to his former See of Krakow.

The Christian Patrimony of Poland

The Cardinal also stressed the historical merits of the Church for the preservation of the Polish nation and utilized as well national sentiments of people for the Church:

> When Poland was occupied and dismembered, it was the Christian patrimony of our culture and our history

> that allowed us to survive. Our first problem therefore is to remain faithful to this tradition. The history and culture of Poland come from Christianity. Thanks to these, we have our national character, our literature, and our tradition which distinguish us from all other nations of Europe and of the world. If we cherish this, we will preserve our national identity.[112]

Sensitive to national feelings in the populace, he employed theory in an interplay with government interference in the people's freedoms. For this reason the Cardinal took an active interest in national cultural affairs.

His interest in the Jagiellonian State University can serve as an example, for not only did he give on occasion conferences at the institution itself but he also defended the association of the Church with it.

In Krakow, Wojtyla organized the Pontifical Faculty of Theology, which was substitution and continuation of the Theological Faculty at Jagiellon University, closed by the Communist government in 1959. With the help of night classes held in the churches he intended to fill the gaps in official instruction and to correct distortions. He devoted a special effort to stressing Catholic contributions to Polish culture.

Celebration of the Millenium

The best way perhaps to indicate that the national life of Poland was connected with the Church, and that the Church kept this association alive, was manifested by the Millennium the Polish Catholics commemorated in 1966 with great celebrations, the thousandth anniversary of the baptism of their first king, Mieczylav I, called ordinarily Mieszko I. His conversion in 966 to Christianity, owing to the influence of his wife, Czech Princess Dubravka, introduced Poland into the culture of the community of Western Europe.

On May 3, 1966, in celebration of the Millennium[113] a huge procession took place at Jasna Gora. Paul VI was expected to be present, but was denied an entry visa. The procession began at the Basilica of Czestochowa and proceeded toward the wall where an altar had been erected. Beside the altar was a throne on which was placed a photograph of Paul VI, and an explanatory note distributed to the pilgrims read in part:

> We see a papal throne next to the altar. The Pope, Paul VI, was expected to be among us today. He would have celebrated the Eucharist and talked to us in Polish. Although the entire nation invited the Holy Father by cables and letters, unfortunately he was unable to come, for the Christ who lives in the Church in the Pope's person, was not welcomed by the authorities of our country. The way to Poland barred to him, our famed hospitality was as a nothing.[114]

During the nine years preceding the thousandth anniversary, a replica of the miraculous Blessed Virgin of Czestochowa was carried from church to church in the major Polish cities. On May 6, 1966, it was the turn of the royal cathedral of Wawel in Krakow. It had been raining for many hours. Thousands of believers waited on the hill in the open air much longer than expected since the state police obliged the bearers to take a route other than that previously agreed on by the government and the religious authorities.

Archbishop Wojtyla was to give the address on the occasion, but renounced it because of the delay. He gave only this short speech:

> Our Lady has instituted a new style. In the past she remained in her chapel and there awaited us. But for nine years now, she has gone out from her chapel and has begun her travels all over Poland, from diocese to diocese, from parish to parish. She visits all her children. This is a sign of renewal. It is necessary to go out to meet people as she has done.[115]

Our Lady of Czestochowa

A brief historical review may help explain the Poles' enormous spiritual and patriotic devotion to the Blessed Mother, Our Lady of Czestochowa.

The Diocese of Czestochowa, with her shrine located on the hill of Jasna Gora, is a suffragan to Krakow. The icon "Black Virgin,"[116] painted with the encaustic technique, is of Byzantine origin and was brought from Constantinople by Princess Anna when she married St. Vladimir the Great, Prince of Kiev, about 988, or perhaps sent later by one of the Comnenian emperors to a royal abbess at Polotsk. In Russian Galicia probably in the 12th century, the icon found itself in Polish territory again in 1382, some 600 years ago.[117]

During the attack of the Tatar and Lithuanian armies, an arrow of the enemy struck the right part of the icon. Subsequently a dense fog fell on this region causing the enemy to change its course. This eventually led to their annihilation by the Poles. The Madonna had thus secured the victory for her faithful people of Poland.

In 1432, after the conquest of Czestochowa by the Hussite Taborites [118] the wagon or carriage on which the stolen treasures from the monastery of Jasna Gora were carried away and among which was also the icon of the Virgin, could not be moved from the place until, with his saber, one of the Taborites struck the icon, which was thrown by the blow into the ditch, where it broke into three pieces. In 1434 the icon was restored and this most venerable image became the center of the religious history of Catholic Poland.

Manifestations of Love for This Madonna

As evidence of how much the Poles value this Madonna, one might point out that a replica was presented as a gift to President John Kennedy on his visit to Poland in 1962. (It is now located in the Texas Church of Our Lady of Jasna Gora to which the President donated it on his return home.[119]) In 1977 about three million Poles visited their beloved shrine at Czestochowa to show their affection for their Madonna.

In 1978, on August 15, the holy day of the Assumption of the Blessed Virgin Mary, over 30,000 people walked on foot from Warsaw, the entire 130 miles, to join in Czestochowa the other hundreds of thousands of pilgrims who came by train, bus, or car.

When Cardinal Wojtyla was asked about the significance of this incredible pilgrimage, he answered: "It is a pilgrimage which does not expect miracles and, as a matter of fact, no one speaks about miracles. Even if they occur, they are interior miracles. The significance goes beyond the faith and religion. Here, the people find, confirm, and celebrate their national unity, which gives them hope and strength."[120]

This strong religious and national loyalty of Catholic Poles can be explained in part by the circumstance that the great majority of the Polish people consists of a rural population, who maintain a traditional form of Catholicism, transmitted from father to son, from mother to daughter. They are satisfied with it. They still observe the laws of the Church and accept guidance from the priests and bishops also in spheres not exclusively related to religion.

Pro-Government Lay Catholics—Pax

More divergences occur in intellectual circles, divided into more or less strong groups of sophisticated intelligentsia with their liberal views on human affairs and an apparent apathy to religion. One such group is represented by the organization called Pax, formed immediately after the war in 1946, a pro-government group of Polish lay Catholics. This group was led by Boleslaw Piasecki, a World War II partisan fighter, as its president and is under the protection of the Communist regime. Perhaps the strange story behind its president will explain why Polish Communists tolerated this former Nazi renegade.

Boleslaw Piasecki (1915-79) had a rather unusual career; during World War II he was leader of a group of Fascists called Falanga and was known for his anti-Semitism. Arrested by the Russians in 1944, he was condemned to death, but somehow succeeded in persuading his jailers that he would be more useful to them alive than dead. Later with the consent of the authorities, he created in a Communist country an impressive commercial empire in private hands, owning business companies, factories, agricultural enterprises, and a publishing house.

With the blessing of the Communists, he was a member of the Council of State. He was director of the most important so-called Catholic publishing house in the country and became rather wealthy. Given his position in the government, his movement was controlled by it.

Pax performed the functions of an antenna that intercepts all movements of other groups and transmits them to the government. Piasecki was also a great promoter of "Marxist-Christian dialogue" with common responsibility for all cultural affairs. "Marxists and Christians" said Piasecki, "must struggle together against the general indifference, holding hands!"[121]

Tolerated by the Church

This group has five representatives in the Parliament. Thus it is the Communist party that gives it direction. Until 1956, it was clearly Stalinist, in the 60s it badgered intellectuals and writers, and then, in 1968, students and Jews. In the same year it approved the armed intervention in Czechoslovakia[122] by the powers of the Warsaw Pact.

The organization Pax has never been supported by the Catholic Church—on the contrary—for on several occasions priests were forbidden to be part of this group. Pax has, however, never been condemned by the Church officially—for pragmatic reasons. The religious authorities closed an eye, for reasons of strategy, in consideration of the fact that some Catholic authors publish their writings at the Pax publishing house, and some of the authors produce, indeed, valid literature worthy of printing.

Such an anomaly can exist only in a Communist country to keep bridges between hostile sides, while hiding in a Trojan horse to arrange the surprises for both and to maintain survival. It is interesting to note that Karol Wojtyla in spite of all his prolific writing never published any study or book at this publishing house. And yet Wojtyla was always a literary man, keeping up with the rest of the world and informed about the burning issues of the time.

Restrictions on Catholic Publishing and Broadcasting

Aware of the importance of means of social communication, Cardinal Wojtyla defended vigorously freedom of the press against incessant attempts of the government to obstruct the publication of Catholic newspapers and magazines. The Cardinal followed very closely the Catholic press trying to expand it despite the difficult conditions the restrictions created. A real apostle of the free press apostolate, he stressed it on every occasion he found opportune.

Presently, but three Catholic weekly papers with a combined total of only 200,000 issues must satisfy the thirst for instruction of 35 million ardent Catholics. The most important is *Tygodnik Powszechny* of Krakow. Wojtyla has supported and encouraged this paper with all his might. The number of issues cannot be increased, for paper is rationed. Only for the occasion of the election of John Paul II was it increased to 55,000 from its regular 40,000.[123]

One monthly magazine is published which discusses topics of Christian philosophy. Besides domestic journals, to keep himself up to date in the unfortunate isolation in which the Polish public lives, entirely deprived of Western publications, Wojtyla subscribed to the French daily *Le Monde*, which however arrived irregularly, and a journal in the Polish language printed in Paris, *Kultura*, the magazine most widely diffused among the 12 million Poles living abroad. This magazine and other journals, of course, were always obtained secretly.

One must note that religious broadcasts are authorized neither on television nor on the radio. The integral transmission of the papal Mass celebrated October 22, 1978, in St. Peter's Square was a special exception, given the importance of the event when a man of Poland became Pope. The situation had to be agonizing for such an avid reader, ready listener, and lover of books as is Wojtyla, who in his frequent travels could at least satisfy his thirst for information when official business called him abroad.

Early Maneuverings toward Dialogue

Together with Cardinal Wyszynski, Cardinal Wojtyla was an outspoken critic of Poland's Communist government and of the restrictions placed on Church freedom. State-Church relationship was that of a strong Church with a hostile State.[124]

The situation was further complicated in that some pressed for a compromise, to effect eventually a *modus vivendi* between Church and State. Especially after an interview by noted writer Ksavert Pruszynski with President Bierut in November of 1946, the group Pax submitted to Cardinal Hlond a memorandum containing a characteristic observation, that "the President's conciliatory position was not given enough attention by the Catholics."[125] This was the first pressure on the Church to negotiate an accord with the government.

When prolonged negotiations produced no results, in September of 1949, a Committee of Priest-Patriots was founded, connected with the Association of Fighters for Freedom and Democracy (Zbowid). Because there was danger that this organization was willing to make too many concessions to Marxists, within a year a Committee of Intellectuals and Catholic Activists under the Pax aegis came into being, offering a viable alternative to the Priest-Patriots.

The Pax group proved effective in lessening tensions within the joint Commission constituted for the purpose of negotiating the State-Church accord. Largely owing to Piasecki's role, the accord was finally signed on April 14, 1950. It was he who, together with Bishop Michael Klepacz, organized further meeting of the Commission at the critical moment when all seemed lost.[126]

Wojtyla's Type of Dialogue

The situation sharpened with the new Primate Wyszynski, who on taking intransigent positions was not disposed even to acknowledge a problem of confrontation. He is a shrewd manipulator and adamant defender of Church rights; he takes the Communists by surprise and they feel uneasy with his firm stand on the issues. While maintaining public solidarity with Cardinal Wyszynski of Warsaw, Wojtyla showed that he preferred dialogue with opponents to confrontation, that he trusted intellectuals and was keen to read the latest books, that he did not believe the religion of peasant folks could stave off indefinitely secularism in Poland. Hence, there was no substitute for an educated laity.[127]

Wojtyla, furthermore, felt a need for a challenge to Marxism, a strictly ideological challenge, which in his judgment presupposes a concrete proposal to humanity on the part of the Church, a proposal that searches anxiously social justice with an equitable distribution of wealth. He insists: "Even if a Church is not involved in politics, it does not renounce [its right] to intervene in history. Yet it intervenes with the means which are appropriate for the Church, i.e., spiritually, favoring the establishment and existence of civil culture which would offer an alternative to Marxism by proposing a model of free society, anchored on an advanced Christian vision of social reality."[128]

This intellectual approach did not prevent his being firm on fundamentals. In 1976 Wojtyla decried the drafting of seminarians. He also called for a system of education that does not impose ideologies on children: "We wish that every family in Poland might have the opportunity to educate their children according to their own religious and Christian beliefs."[129]

In the same year, in Wawel Square in Krakow, during the Mass celebrated for Corpus Christi, he declared: "We live in times when God is forgotten. He is not being confessed. He is being eradicated from publications, from books, from programs in public life. The world is deprived of God, is deprived of its beginning and its purpose. The world is torn away from its Creator: this is the ideology and the image which are being forced upon modern man under diverse forms, the world without God."[130]

Analysis of Situation in Poland

In March 1977, Cardinal Wojtyla was invited to speak in Milan to the students of the Catholic University of the Sacred Heart, on the occasion of the anniversary of its foundation. He spoke thus on the situation of the Church in Poland:

> We must have no illusion as to the ideological significance of Marxism: Marxism is atheism. Thus the situation of a Polish person, especially of a young person, is monolithic; either he is Christian and a believer, which means that he made the fundamental choice for the faith of Christianity, or he is on the opposite side. There are not those intermediate elements which may sometimes plunge the interior state of the conscience into somewhat of a fog. . . . All in Poland know, and the young ones know it very well too, that for the advancement of one's career not only in political life, faith and faithfulness to the Church does not help them. On the contrary, it is an obstacle.[131]

Outlined were the ways that such challenges with the Communists should be made, firmly but patiently, when he stressed to all the Polish bishops who flocked to Rome after his election to the papacy: "There won't be crusades, but a tenacious daily confrontation based upon the intangibility of Christian principles."[132] Such a "tenacious daily confrontation" was a constant in his drive toward the slow liberation of the people's rights from the yoke of Communism. This strategy is indicated in the case of the building of a new church in Nowa Huta.

The Church at Nowa Huta

In May 1977, Cardinal Wojtyla dedicated the contested church in the industrial suburb of Krakow. The name Nowa Huta was invented by Gomulka and means "new steelworks." As a socialist city, it could have no churches. But all its inhabitants, exclusively workers and their families, for years clamored to have a church, and attended Mass ostentatiously in public squares every morning and repeatedly on Sundays, when 12 Masses were celebrated each week. The people demanded their right to preserve their faith with very legal means, and even with violence when the people's Council office was burned down.

Finally in 1967 the authorities gave way and the laying of the first foundation stone, which Wojtyla brought from Italy, was blessed. But another 10 years elapsed before the church was consecrated. On that day, the Cardinal pronounced his important address, identifying religious rights and civil rights, mentioning truth but also freedom. The thundering applause with which his words were received convinced the governmental authorities that Wojtyla was one of their enemies who could no longer be overcome. Part of the Cardinal's vibrant and courageous address was:

> When this new city, this new magnificent industrial center was created, it was assumed that laws of economy, the laws of consumption and especially those of

production, would fully determine the history of man and would satisfy all his needs. When this thought was prevalent, and in the name of this assumption, Nowa Huta was built with the idea that it would be a city without God, without a church. And so Christ came into this city and with the help of its people worked here.

Through their very mouths he told the basic truth about men, namely, that the history of mankind cannot be valued simply on the basis of the economical criteria of production and consumption. Man is much greater. He exists to the image and likeness of the very God, and this truth was expressed by the people of Nowa Huta several years ago when they demanded to have a church. It is the Church that expresses this truth about man.

The people who demanded a church, who wanted a church, these people were inspired by Christ. This city is not a city of persons who do not belong to anybody, with whom you can do whatever you like, who can be manipulated according to the laws and the norms of production and consumption. This city is a city of children of God. . . . This event today is of historic significance. . . .

Man is not only entitled to work; he is also entitled to receive his just wage. But this is not sufficient to man. There are much deeper values and rights of the human spirit: freedom of conscience, freedom of opinion, freedom of religion, which cannot be violated or limited. Christ expresses these rights through the mouth of the Church.[133]

Clarity of Judgment and Love for Opponents

Carrying out his high and sensitive office, Wojtyla was characterized always by his clarity of judgment and confidence in his viewpoint or when he chose a side in a dispute. This resulted from his broad background and his interior and intellectual discipline. Very broadminded and constantly open to the contemporary problems of the world, he was not only strong and tenacious but proved himself a skillful diplomat when dealing with the authorities of Warsaw. His battles with the Communist government were concluded with success, even the small contests: the building of a church in Nowa Huta, or others as the harassment which slowed development in publishing activity designed to disseminate Catholic information.

There was another side for Wojtyla's patient dealings with the Communists. Cardinal Krol, a long-time friend of the Pope, said of him:

> He has an overwhelming love for man, for every man, not excluding sinners and the erring. He has had to deal with them in Poland, even Communists. He has never looked at them in any other way except as the image and likeness of God. While as of this moment they are in error, he never lets this color his obligations to teach them the truth. Even though they are card-carrying Communists, he regards them as ours, as His children. He doesn't believe in isolating Communists, but rather regards them "as people to evangelize." He has a real fatherly love for them. "We have to reach them, preach them the truth. Can you preach to someone you are not talking to?" Wojtyla would say.[134]

Noting the Pope's working-class background, Cardinal Krol remarked that he has "never lost that touch. It shows even in his rolling walk. Yet he is at home in the highest levels of academia."[135]

Contributions to Synods of Bishops

On another occasion all Polish bishops, including Cardinal Wojtyla, again did not take part in the first General Assembly of the World Synod of 1967 to express solidarity with Cardinal Wyszynski who had been again denied a passport by the Polish government. Nevertheless the Polish bishops sent to the Synod in Rome a noble message in which they confirmed their steadfast Catholic faith and their union with the Pope and all other bishops. As a response Pope Paul VI condemned the action of the Polish government in strong terms in his pronouncement at the Synod.

It should be said that Cardinal Wojtyla's name is tied very distinctly to the history of four general assemblies of the World Synod of Bishops as well as one extraordinary assembly held in 1969. In the years of 1967, 1969, and 1971 he was a member of the World Synod; in 1974 and 1977 he was in addition a member of the Council of the General Secretariat, to which he was elected in 1971 and foreseen for this office again in 1980. He served also as a member of several Congregations as mentioned before.

Especially significant was the contribution of Cardinal Wojtyla at the extraordinary assembly of the Synod of Bishops in 1969 of which he was a member by pontifical nomination. He intervened with several speeches replete with ecclesiological doctrine and was then charged to draft the final declaration on collegiality which was then approved by the Synod.

Synthesis of Thoughts on Collegiality

Its important doctrinal content can be asserted by this synthesis:

> Our scheme put appropriately at the center the concept of communion which indicates much more than the notion of community or common action. The idea of communion emphasizes the interpersonal relationships, from person to person, in the external exchange of goods and the interior participation of the very persons. Therefore, "communion" is a fundamental concept of episcopal collegiality: the communion of believers within the Church must find expression in the communion of the individual Churches. The fruits of the collegiate community were revealed in the last Council and are being revealed in the experience of the Conferences of Bishops.
>
> The idea of communion contains implicitly the idea of plurality and diversity inasmuch as it draws on the dynamical aspect of unity which can be obtained among many and diverse persons by means of communication. Plurality and diversity, on the other hand, always imply a certain tendency toward unity. Collegiality is sup-

portive also of supreme authority, for it means responsibility and coresponsibility. Whoever must "pasture" Christ's flock is called to promote communion.

The idea and practice of collegiality can and must be developed proficiently and in perfect harmony with the Second Vatican Council. This requires the search of the spirit for communion with all brother bishops; mutual communication of ideas, of work, of initiatives, all in the spirit of dialogue and service, and in cooperation with the Pope with whom the episcopate often actively collaborates and gives direction, precepts, and advice to the universal Church and from whom it frequently receives them.

It is very important to develop both the collegial exercise and doctrine without being frighted off by difficulties and false interpretations that occur at times. Men of today in the agitation of the diverse systems of public life desire collegiality in the Church as a sign of brotherly communion.[136]

Views on Doctrinal Aspects of Priesthood

Cardinal Wojtyla distinguished himself on another occasion, namely, the second regular general assembly of the Synod in 1971, which revolved around two topics of basic importance: *priesthood* and *justice.* On the priesthood, he presented two written contributions, one on the doctrinal and the other on the practical aspects. From the former we choose excerpts:

> It is very useful not only to priestly spirituality but to the very doctrine on the priesthood to reflect on the personal vocation, which is the answer to Christ's invitation to leave everything and to follow Him. In this sincere offering of himself, the priest may find his personal identity and his place in contemporary society.
>
> The call to a more perfect following of the Savior borders on the connection between the sacred Order and celibacy which must, as in the past, remain intact. By taking part in Christ, every priest, through his vocation, participates also in His virginity no less than in

> His obedience and poverty. The personal and spontaneous pledge of the priest must be accompanied by the law of the Church; the two neither contradict nor exclude the other.
>
> Such deep insertion (infusion) of the priestly vocation into the very vocation of mankind as manifested by Christ is of utter importance, for the Church considered as *ad intra* and *ad extra* [in itself and in its relations outside itself]. The Church is a sign in Christ; it is necessary that this sign be especially visible and readable in His ministers.[137]

The Cardinal concluded by citing the example of priestly devotion of the Franciscan Father Maximilian Kolbe, who saved Frank Gajowniczek, condemned to death by the Nazis. Father Kolbe has been beatified (October 17, 1971). Referring perhaps to the numerous recent priestly apostasies, Wojtyla quickly transferred an appropriate thought about their search of conscience.

> In a time when so many priests of the world are searching for their own identity, Father Kolbe rises among us, not with theological speeches but with his life and his death as a teacher who gives testimony to the greatest love. Heroism is certainly not within reach of everybody, but renouncing any appreciation for it, is this not in itself a defeat?[138]

Ideas on Practical Aspects of Priesthood

Cardinal Wojtyla's ideas on the practical aspects of priesthood can be summed up as follows. The mission of the Church, the apostolate, the diverse vocations in the communion of God's people, these and more must be considered in the certain and mandatory light of the Vatican Council, and also must be considered in the relationship between, on the one hand, the ministry and the life-style of priests and, on the other, the tasks and actions of lay people.

The two elements equilibrate and complete one another; this must be borne in mind to make a good determination of the specific mission of the priest, necessary indeed for his very formation. This report defines in an excellent way the necessary limits to the profane activity of the priest and describes his relationship with the laity. Excessive engagement in tasks reserved to lay people must however be avoided.

The cooperation of lay people, in those fields where it is indispensable for the Church's mission, is strictly tied to the priest's ministry and also to his formation—which fact does not mean any laicization of the priestly existence. In Poland, an organized apostolate of lay people is very necessary and is provided as best can be done by linking the family tightly to the work of the parish, this in the spirit of true love for the Church and in full solidarity of lay people and the hierarchy of the Church.

The Cardinal also emphasized one element which seemed to be missing in the preparatory document on the priesthood, the importance of the sacrament of penance in the life of the spirit and the priest's ministry. This entails the spirit of penitence, personal frequentation of this sacrament, and assiduity in administering it to others, after the example of the Curé of Ars, St. John Vianney, and many other priests who became freely slaves of the confessional. He cited the recent beatification of Father Kolbe as providing an opportunity for recall to a special devotion to the Blessed Mother as very beneficent in the priest's life.[139]

Wojtyla's reaffirmation of the priestly dignity is really a follow-up of traditional theology with the concept of *sacerdos* [priest] in the sense of sacrificial undertone and with co-identification of a priest with Christ as representing another Christ not only in the liturgy but also in the imitation of Christlike perfection, so much needed in this modern decadent era with its hedonistic exploitation and sexual permissiveness. A need for the good, celibate priest is for Wojtyla still a valid postulate should the Church succeed in the renewal decreed by Vatican Council II.

Approach to Social Justice

More progressive is Wojtyla's approach to social and distributive justice, which he also outlined in the Synod of 1971. Here he exhibits not only a scholarly erudition in moral theology and ethics, but also his personal social concern for the people in whose problems he is deeply interested, for justice is for everyone.

The following is part of Cardinal Wojtyla's contribution to the topic of justice:

> The Synod cannot devote less attention to the aspect of justice, which touches upon freedom of conscience and of religion, than on that devoted to poverty and economic misery.
>
> The importance of culture must be exalted in such a way that it appears as an asset fundamentally attached to human dignity, to the life and development of every nation and to the justice due the emigrants.
>
> Let us find a better way to connect the doctrine of justice to that of communion within the Church. This doctrine demands that no individual Church can be concerned with itself without consideration of the other Churches. The individual Church must communicate with the others in the unity of the universal Church, whose foundation, established by God, is Peter; at the same time they draw from this unity a value which belongs to them in the highest sense.
>
> Without the true and sincere realization of unity, the problems of justice within the Church *(ad intra)* cannot be resolved. Without going too closely into the sphere of temporal competencies, doctrine to be exposed should demonstrate the faith of the Synod in the justice which is a gift from God and was manifested to us in Christ and through Christ.[140]

The Cardinal dealt with this topic of justice frequently and dedicated much of his writing to it. It is for him a natural thing to do, for he lived always in close contact with the people, taking active part in their pains and sorrows, their hope and struggles. His house was always open to anyone and on any occasion. All turned to him for consolation and advice. The poor were his preferred; nobody was sent away without receiving help and kind words. Defender of the weak and helpless, he was always close to those who suffered, raising his voice now softly, now aloud and strongly to defend the rights of the people, of the workers.

This personal concern for the working people was also a great asset to him in his dealings with the government, for he was given lessons in many aspects of social action by having in some cases outdistanced the government. Social justice was for him always a moral question of the highest priority, a belief exemplified by a high social consciousness without his being in the political sense socialistic.

Sense of National Corporate Justice

In this connection one should mention the new Pope's strong sense of national corporate justice. Wojtyla felt an urgency and a need to make reconciliation with the Germans, in spite of all the experiences he had during the Nazi occupation of Poland. He associated himself with and maintained contacts with the German bishops.

In September of 1974 Wojtyla celebrated *Versohnungs gottestdienst* (liturgical conciliation services) together with the late Julius Cardinal Döpner, archbishop of Munich, at the spot of the infamous concentration camp in Dachau. Then in September of 1978 he accompanied the Polish Primate Wyszynski and Bishops Jerzy Stroba and Wladyslaw Rubin on an official visit to the Federal Republic of Germany to make this conciliation public and effective.[141]

Anyone who knows European history must be acquainted with the tense relationship between Poland and Germany[142] in the past, especially in the recent past, and must appreciate the significance of this event. It was Wojtyla who really initiated and promoted this idea, which represents certainly a great act, humanly, nationally, and diplomatically—especially when viewed against Wojtyla's active part in underground activities in World War II as well as the patriotic involvement of Cardinal Wyszynski against the Germans. It also is a reflection of Cardinal Wojtyla's deep spiritual concern for a peaceful solution of controversial issues among the nations, and it is an indication of pastoral care for the people by a zealous pastor.

Chapter 10

PASTOR, SCHOLAR, ECUMENIST, AND DIPLOMAT

A Veritable "Good Shepherd"

IN SPITE of all his busy involvement in the Council, the Roman Synods, and other activities abroad, Cardinal Wojtyla did not neglect his primary responsibilities in his archdiocese and was the affectionate and zealous pastor of his people. During the 20 years of his episcopal activity, he several times made pastoral visits to the parishes of his archdiocese, bringing to all encouragement and light.

Though he took particular care of the sick and of the suffering, his preference went to the priests. To them he was father, friend, brother, and confidant. With his open and sensitive character he understood their problems and he encouraged them, supported them, and assisted them with paternal affection. One could really say of him that he was the "good shepherd" ready to give his life for his sheep.

With the spoken and the written word he had defended the right of Catholics to free expression of their faith. His famous homilies were followed with affectionate interest by all believers, especially on special occasions such as Corpus Christi, Marian pilgrimages, or national holidays, when he employed his oratorical ability for the great crowds of faithful he always attracted.

Faithful Administrator and Effective Negotiator

In the administration of his archdiocese Wojtyla was constantly faithful to the conciliar decrees of Vatican II and made their practical application. A Catholic weekly of Posen conducted an inquiry in 1971 on the rights and obligations of Catholics and asked his opinion. He answered that this question had to be understood as an inquiry as how to actualize the Church, and he specified this objective according to three major orientations: (a) the testimony of a Christian who participates in the redemptive mission of Christ, takes pains to give the proper value to all that is good in nature, and has reliance on the workings of grace; (b) the responsibility of Christians to safeguard everything authentically human; and (c) the ecumenical attitude not alone in the religious sense, but as the social expression of Christians.

Coherent with these principles he favored lay participation in the life of the Church.[143] These were also guiding principles for his pastoral care of his archdiocese. He had a well-developed sense of loyalty to the Church, with a strong *sentire cum Ecclesia* ("union with the mind of the Church"), as the famous Father Reginald Garrigou-Lagrange, his former professor at the Angelicum, was wont to instill in his students. Soon he would be tested in his undivided loyalty to the Church. He has also a well-developed theological balance, for his theology is deeply Thomistic.

Immediately after his appointment as archbishop, the Polish Communist government attempted to profit by the difference between his opposition to its oppressive tactics and that of the hard-hitting and intransigent Cardinal Wyszynski in Warsaw. But the effort proved futile. In dealing with the government, Wojtyla proved to be smoother, more diplomatic, but just as effective as the man of strong will and iron fist, Cardinal Wyszynski.

The two high prelates, as well as their courageous bishops and their faithful priests, gradually forced the government to let them build the churches and institutions necessary for the growing population of the faithful. They pressed also for relaxation in censorship and abolishment of the various restrictions laid on the Catholic press. In this they scored at times, but never fully to their satisfaction. The Polish Communists, however, know well that the Church is not an easy target for their oppressive methods.

Cardinal Wojtyla was much admired by Pope Paul VI, who frequently called him to Rome for consultation on theological issues and on Vatican relations with Eastern Europe.

Retreat Master to the Holy Father

In 1976 Wojtyla was also invited to preach Pope Paul VI's Lenten retreat in the Vatican, which in itself is a great distinction as well as a testimonial to the Polish Cardinal's own spirituality.

Not without apprehension, yet with docility and confidence in the grace of the Holy Spirit, the Archbishop of Krakow accepted this honorable task. In order to cope with it he added to his faith his intense prayer and the wealth of his pastoral experience. Enriched with these gifts he tried to fulfill the task with the optimism of a strong Christian and with the simplicity of a son of that nation which is accustomed to saying "yes only to God, to the Church of Christ, and the Blessed Mother." This yes—free of any hesitation—is also the characteristic of all the conferences in the Vatican.

The meditations he gave during the papal retreat held at Mathilda Chapel in the presence of the Holy Father were later collected in a book and published as *Sign of Contradiction.*[144] Characteristically enough, a topic of the conferences was that biblical "Sign" perceived by Simeon as "the blessed fruit of the womb" of the Mother of God, who also revealed herself to the world as a "great Sign in the Heavens" (Rv 12:1), "A woman clad with the Sun." It is this Sign against which the world fights. Yet she does not cease to remain present in the mystery of Christ and His Church.

Recalling this hope during the spiritual exercises in the Vatican, the Archbishop of Krakow offered to the Holy Father and his household a faithful and precious service of the Word in its full Christological and Mariological context —in view of a "new advent of the Church and mankind, which means a time of a great test, but also of great hope,"[145] and all rendered in a truly scholarly fashion to the satisfaction of members of a demanding papal court.

In the Line of Modern Popes

It is expected from the Pope, the leader of a worldwide spiritual community, that he be well versed in religious and spiritual problems. Thinking of him as a leader, one generally accepts that he be an administrator and a practical man. Looking to all the popes of the 20th century one finds several types represented.

Leo XIII (1876-1903) was a scholar par excellence, skilled diplomat, teacher, and also administrator; St. Pius X (1903-14) was a pastoral man with great dedication to spiritual needs and reforms; Benedict XV (1914-23) was a diplomat and peace-maker; Pius XI (1923-39) was a great scholar interested in historical research and a teacher; Pius XII (1939-58) is known as an erudite theologian of theologians; John XXIII (1958-63) was a diplomat and Church historian, pastor and ecumenist; Paul VI (1963-78) was diplomat and Church reformer in a time of great change; John Paul I (1978) was the pastor with a literary interest.

John Paul II (1978-) represents a combination of scholar, philosopher, literary man, poet, writer, moral theologian, pastor, and upcoming reformer; hence there is much to be expected from him. He has a fine sense as an ideological analyst, Church reformist, social activist, and student of modern thought, well able to bring his Church on with the modern age.

Serious Thinker and Productive Writer

In scholarship Wojtyla shows himself a serious thinker and productive writer. If the American proverb in academia "publish or perish" is a valid reminder for professors in the United States, their Professor Wojtyla gives example in his scholarly endeavors for many to follow. If one, moreover, takes into consideration his impressive activism, one must be surprised by the quantity as well as the quality of Wojtyla's work, which may also be evaluated and singled out for its complex variety as *multum et multa.*

The evidence for it stems from the fact that in a comparatively short time he has already produced six substantial books, and has over 300 philosophical and theological published articles to his credit—certainly not a bad achievement for a man so active. Frequent translation of his works into various languages serves moreover as an indication that his thought must be sufficiently relevant to be translated and to reach a wide public.

His books to date are: (1) *Love and Responsibility*, published first in Polish (Lublin, 1960) with its second edition (Krakow: Znak, 1962) and translated already into Italian, French, Spanish, and English; (2) *The Philosophical System of Max Scheler, Used as a Basis for a Foundation of Christian Ethics* (published in Polish, Lublin, 1959); (3) *Person and Act* (published in Polish, 1969); (4) *The Basis of Renewal: The Study and Realization of Vatican II* (published in Polish in 1972, and translated into Italian, 1976); (5) *Sign of Contradiction* (published in Polish, Poznan-Warszawa, 1976, and translated into Italian in 1977 and into English in 1979); (6) *Fruitful and Responsible Love* (New York: The Seabury Press, 1979); (7) *Il Buon pastore, scritti, discorsi e lettere pastorali* [*The Good Shepherd: Writings, Discourses, and Pastoral Letters*] (Rome: Edizioni Logos, 1978, translated by Elzbieta Cywiak and Renzo Panzone). As the titles indicate, philosophical, existentialist, personalist, and theological, moral, ethical, and pastoral thought dominate his writings.[146]

Participant in Various International Congresses

In regard to Karol's 300 learned articles, about half are of a philosophical nature and the other half theological, which is proportionate to his professional training in philosophy and theology. That Wojtyla was concerned about modern thought is indicated among other things by his frequent scholarly participation in various international congresses. To mention at least some of recent times, he took active part in 1974 at the International Thomistic Congress in Rome on the 700th anniversary of the death of St. Thomas where he read a paper, and in 1976 at the International Congress in Genoa. In July of 1976 he lectured at Harvard University[147] on "Participation or Alienation" as a sharp critique of Marxism.

Moreover, Wojtyla had frequently a part in theological conventions where he usually was an official representative. Perhaps the most important was his part at the International Congress on "Fruitful and Responsible Love: Ten Years after *Humanae vitae,*" held at Milan June 21-22, 1978. He gave the opening address, "Fruitful and Responsible Love," [148] which served as a theological and pastoral foundation for an ecumenical dialogue of this international gathering.

Accomplished Author and Poet

Karol Wojtyla may be the most prolific and accomplished author to succeed St. Peter as Bishop of Rome in modern times. Even more impressive than the number of his published works is the range of his interest—philosophy, theology, spirituality, sociology, political science, history, ethics, poetry—and the high quality of his writings. Not surprising then is one consequence of his startling election to the papacy, a rush to publish translations, articles, and even his poetry.[149]

If an additional uniqueness should be mentioned it is that Wojtyla is also a poet, an actor, and a dramatist. His scholarship then has come full circle. It seldom happens that a pope is a poet, an occasion associated rather with the Renaissance or humanistic times.

It is interesting also in this respect to note that Wojtyla is a member of the Polish Odrodzenie and indeed to stress that he is fully behind the spiritual renaissance in modern Poland. This is the concerted effort to resurrect Poland politically from post-World War II ruins and to revive it culturally and spiritually from the Communist persecution and oppression, which is a heavy burden on the freedom-loving Poles and on the rest of the people under the Russian yoke in every country behind the Iron Curtain.

Most appropriate, perhaps, was what Bishop Thomas Kelly, general secretary of the National Conference of Catholic Bishops, said of him: "He's witty, funny, yet right away you know you are in the presence of a scholar."[150]

Dedicated Ecumenist

With his broad education and scholarly mind it logically follows that Wojtyla should be—as he really is— a dedicated ecumenist. The circumstance that Poland itself is basically monolithic in a religious sense insofar as the majority of its population is Catholic did not help him much in this ecumenical orientation. His frequent trips and study abroad, as well as his repeated contacts with other Christians, Jews, and neutral religious systems, were instrumental in this orientation.

The greatest impulse, however, toward his understanding of ecumenism came from his participation in Vatican Council II, where Cardinal Wyszynski as one of a board of twelve presidents and Wojtyla as a well-trained theologian were involved in the commissions dealing with doctrinal and pastoral problems. Here, unlike most other prelates from

Communist countries, Wojtyla took a comparatively open, progressive stand on the issues dealing with marriage, sex, and family life.

The Archbishop of Krakow likewise showed himself sensitive and open-minded on the issues involved in religious freedom, coming out strongly for the right of the faithful as well as the theologian to discuss the Church's teachings freely and to hold differing opinions within the circle of the orthodoxy of the faith.[151] His experience with other progressive prelates and his interactions with other progressive theologians and the *periti* of the Council swayed him completely toward ecumenism. So decisive was the influence exerted on him by Vatican documents, namely, *Decree on Ecumenism,*[152] *Declaration on Religious Freedom,*[153] *Constitution on the Church in the Modern World,*[154] that ecumenical theology became also the fabric of his theological thought.

Undoubtedly, the hardship which the Catholic Church has had to bear under the Communists and the circumstance that other Churches shared the same fate helped also—in the sense that an additional support was welcomed in their struggle for survival.

Not least in influence was Wojtyla's confrontation with the new and secularized world outside that emerged after World War II, a world replete with progressive and liberal views.

Wary of Marxist-Christian Dialogue

Perhaps the appropriate characterization of Wojtyla's thought came, just after his election to the pontificate, from the Polish Communist government official in charge of religious affairs, Kazimierz Kakol, who confided to several Western diplomats: "We put much trust in the flexibility of John Paul II, who is intransigent in matters of principle as many Polish bishops are, but more disposed to a dialogue."[155]

There must be made here some distinction between ecumenical dialogue with other Churches, in which Wojtyla was quite open, and between Marxist-Christian dialogue, which he really distrusts. His frequent contacts with the prelates of other Communistic countries, especially of hard-line Communist Czechoslovakia, namely, the archbishop of Prague, Francis Tomásek, and the late Stephen Cardinal Trochta[156] of Litomerice, increased his doubts about the play of Communists.

The experience of not being allowed even to concelebrate at the funeral Mass for Cardinal Trochta on April 16, 1974, in Litomerice, together with Cardinals Franz Koenig of Vienna and Alfred Bengsch of Berlin,[157] left a great mark on him, causing him to remark sarcastically: "I am just beginning to experience a new kind of socialism in this truly Communist country. Over 25 years I have lived in my socialistic country, but not till now can I see what is real Communism!"[158]

Goal of Christian Unity

Cardinal Wojtyla was nevertheless unreservedly at home with ecumenism as he reaffirmed in his message *urbi et orbi*, after his election:

> We cannot forget our Brothers of other Churches and Christian confessions. The ecumenical cause is actually so great and delicate that we cannot now let it go unmentioned. How many times have we meditated together on the last will of Christ, that asks the Father for His disciples the gift of unity (John 17:21-23)? And who does not recall the insistence of St. Paul on the "communion of the spirit" which leads one to be united in love with a common purpose and the common mind in the imitation of Christ the Lord (Philippians 2:2,5,8)?
>
> It does not seem possible that there would still remain the drama of the division among Christians—a cause of confusion and perhaps even of scandal. We intend, therefore, to proceed along the way already begun,

> by favoring those steps which serve to remove obstacles. Hopefully, then, thanks to a common effort, we might arrive finally at full communion! [159]

This explicit statement should leave no doubt about the fact that Koral Wojtyla is a truly ecumenical soul. One might add that he has also the ecumenical personality to go with it. Just four days before Wojtyla's election Protestant Evangelist Billy Graham preached to the people at St. Anne's Roman Catholic Church in Krakow, at the personal invitation of Cardinal Wojtyla.

Personally Diplomatic by Nature

Karol Wojtyla is by nature a diplomat, understood as one having the ability to get along in every circumstance without losing one's identity or betraying one's principles, without acting for the sake of expediency. A retrospect of Wojtyla's life indeed reveals how remarkably well he lived, managing his conversation, his actions, his endeavors, and the whole of his personality to fit the framework of the various conditions that he faced, so that he seemed always to be the "right man at the right time, with the right people."

As a child Wojtyla was an obedient lad, pleasing his parents, and in school he was always the studious and industrious pupil, appreciated by his professors. In underground activities he was reliable, courageous, prudent; he took care to avoid unnecessary danger and made a determined effort to survive. When abroad he was eager to learn the languages and customs of the place he visited.

In time of pressure or tragedy he was patient, when he held lower positions, was ever respectful to the authorities, and when he assumed a higher role, knew how to treat those under him in a kindly manner, respectful and yet firm. Deeply integrated in his personal makeup is the virtue of prudence, a viable factor responsible for the success he achieved in life. This discretion is perhaps the source of his tremendous appeal to people and his attraction for them.

Professionally Diplomatic through Experience

It should be noted, however, that while Wojtyla possesses such natural abilities, and a personal fitness for diplomatic lore, he had in fact no experience in professional diplomacy. He neither attended the Vatican's distinguished Collegium Capranicum for the training of diplomats nor served in any papal nunciature. Notwithstanding, he had in Poland firsthand experience in one of the most delicate diplomatic activities in which the Holy See is engaged.

Several instances will serve to show Wojtyla's diplomatic sense. First we note his handling a close relationship with his older colleague and superior, Primate of Poland, Cardinal Wyszynski. According to Richard T. Davies, former U.S. ambassador to Poland[160] the Polish government had tried to set up a rivalry between the two cardinals, with intent to exploit them.

When prominent Europeans or Americans visited Poland, government officials would take them first to Cardinal Wojtyla. Well aware that he was being used, he would manage either to be out at the time or he would act as escort to Wyszynski's headquarters. Yet he had no fear, nor did he shrink from confrontation, this even to the point when he judged necessary of baiting the regime. He insisted on being recognized by the government.

When he became archbishop in 1964, he refused to do business with low-ranking Communist officials. Once, when a local official managed to get through to him by phone, Wojtyla rang off: "Until you officially recognize us, I don't see how we can talk to each other. Good day!"[161]

Status of Church-State Relations in Poland

Another example of Karol's diplomatic acumen is his skill in dealing with his nation's Marxist regime. It is well known how Catholicism and Communism have been on a collision course ever since Karl Marx damned religion as "the opium of the people,"[162] and how under dictator Joseph Stalin (who dismissed the Pope with the cynical quip: "How many divisions has he got?") thousands of Eastern Europeans suffered imprisonment and death for the one crime of having faith in God.

The contemporary delicate coexistence of Church and State in Eastern Europe is primarily owing to the Communists' grudging acknowledgment that international Catholicism cannot after all be destroyed by government decree. A British expert on religion behind the Iron Curtain, Michael Bourdeaux, states: "By the mid-50's it was perfectly clear to the Communists that their hard-line policy was failing."[163]

Furthermore, Catholicism and nationalism have been closely interlinked in Eastern Europe. Accordingly, outright suppression of the faith runs always the risk of provoking national rebellion; as Earl Pope, an American analyst puts it: "In an atheist society, the rebel goes to church."[164]

As a result, Church and State relationship throughout much of Eastern Europe has entered a period of mutually wary accommodation, and nowhere is such detente more visible than in Poland. The Church in Poland was always strong and in persecution her strength has yet the more increased. "Church is the alternative State. What's more, unlike the State, it works!" insists one professor. Catholicism is both symbol and substance of fierce Polish nationalism.

Example of Wojtyla's Shrewd Diplomacy

This was, of course, of great help to the Church in her demand for recognition by the Communist State, and to obtain some concessions. Cardinals Wyszynski and Wojtyla were in a position to make demands on behalf of the Church because the Communists could not aggravate the faithful too much without alienating them. Wojtyla was able to recruit also support of some liberal Catholic intellectuals who became an influential group in Krakow. By this, Catholic strength increased. With Wojtyla's consensus, furthermore, the vote of the Catholic group of deputies (Znak) rejected approval of a new Polish Constitution, since it did not agree that in it the Polish Communist party be named "a leading power of a nation."

In general, a direct confrontation was as much as possible to be avoided. Rather, the people learned to get around governmental pressures, bans, laws, restrictions, guidelines. One example may be given regarding the regime's ban on the teaching of religion in state schools. To circumvent such a ban, Catholic parents decided to support more than 20,000 religious instruction programs on parish properties, where government could not interfere.

Perhaps the most visible example of Wojtyla's shrewd diplomacy is reflected in the building of a massive church in Nowa Huta, a town built on Stalin's orders to represent a model socialist community—with everything except a church. Cardinal Wojtyla simply channeled the outrage through an avalanche of petitions and protests, so effective that the authorities feared open revolt of the people.

He had merely applied the Communist methods to incite people for a cause, but was careful enough to avoid incitement to any violence, although ultimately the Catholic protesters did burn the townspeople's office. After this demonstration, the Communists let them have their church, because the "people" want it. Thus the whole design of the city was changed.

Greater Freedom to Negotiate

Owing to the circumstance that the Polish bishops must live in a constant State-Church collision and are from this experience well acquainted with the problems at home, the Vatican gave them certain broad freedoms to make their own decisions and to plan their own strategy against a hostile government. This happened when bishops became increasingly skeptical of the Vatican minister for extraordinary affairs, Archbishop Agostino Casaroli, who directed the dealings with the Communists, although they felt some need for the so-called Ostpolitik of Pope Paul VI.

As a result the Pope tightened the reins on Vatican diplomats. Thus, chief Vatican negotiator in Poland, Archbishop Luigi Poggi, began to spend more of his time in consultation with Polish bishops than in dealing with the nation's Communist authorities.

This uneasiness between the Holy See and the Polish bishops was responsible subsequently for the agreement that was effected: that the Vatican and the bishops would work together when negotiating with the Communists. The decision was influenced mainly by Cardinals Wyszynski and Wojtyla. The Vatican, in fact, yielded little under their pressure and let the Poles act in many cases on their own. As mentioned above, in 1977 Wyszynski began a series of unprecedented private talks with the Communist party leader, Eduard Gierek. The talks broke down, however, and the Church continues its struggle to have Poland's government recognize it as a legal institution.

Perhaps the best sign of the awareness of the Church of Poland in her struggle with the Communists is apparent in the fact that Polish major seminaries have additional courses titled Church-State Relations, designed to prepare newly ordained priests with some diplomatic skills to handle the inevitable problems. It is needless to say that emphasis was being placed on Catholic ecclesiology as against the so-called Communist ecclesiology,[165] which Communists forced not only on Poland but on all Iron Curtain countries. Wojtyla had indeed much influence and merit in challenging this unwanted "Communist ecclesiology."

Use of Diplomatic Ability at Vatican II

Wojtyla's diplomatic abilities were perhaps best displayed in his activities at Vatican Council II. His heavy involvement in the formulation of conciliar documents was conditioned and motivated by his own struggles with problems in Poland, by his expectation of having the documents as effective tools in further struggles with hostile agitators.

Thus, during the Council, he urged in numerous interventions that the fathers insist clearly and without equivocation that every person has a right to follow his own conscience. Intervening with reference to the *Decree on Religious Freedom* and the *Constitution on the Church in the Modern World,* he stressed the state duty to protect the right of religious freedom. He repeatedly challenged any state system that denies a person his religious rights, beyond what is necessary for the common good.

Speaking on "The Church in the World," he stressed also the duty of lay Christians to be active witnesses and apostles of their faith. He declared that the State must recognize this duty as their right. With Wojtyla's backing and that of others, the accent on the right of personal conscience (which had been pioneered and promoted by the American Jesuit John Courtney Murray) won the day at the Council. This reversed the centuries of tradition in which the Church had stressed, as its role in religion, the State's obligation to protect the truths of Catholicism rather than to defend the right of conscience for its citizens.

These all were certainly useful tools conveniently ready for quick supply of a rationale to substantiate the Church's demands and to serve as armament against an adamant enemy, as are the Communists. Needless to say, a good diplomat must know not only all his points of strength and of weakness, but also how to apply every weapon accessible to him in a situation of challenge. In this respect, Poland has truly produced an able challenger in Church-State crises, Wojtyla the diplomat.

Influential and Prestigious in Office

Owing to Wojtyla's demonstrated diplomatic skills, Pope Paul VI frequently called on him for consultations in several congregations on theological issues and on Vatican relationships with the countries of Eastern Europe. The Pope placed in him a great measure of confidence because of his ever-competent performance and reputation for fair play, and gave him precedence despite his comparative youth.

It is little wonder, then, that Paul VI made him a cardinal when he was but 47 years of age. This was certainly a distinction in recognition of his abilities and a reward for the services he rendered, always with generosity and selflessness.

Recognition was given also because of the historical importance of the archiepiscopal seat of Krakow, where already from 1484 the archbishop bore too the title of prince and this with the right to crown the Polish kings, for until 1596 Krakow was also a capital of Poland. Krakow was distinguished by several previous archbishop-cardinals beginning with Bishop Zbigniew Olesnick (1389-1455) as the first Polish cardinal.

Simple and Unaffected in Life

Coming from a background of a humble family and disciplined by various hardships in his young life, Wojtyla kept a wholesome simplicity in his life always, even in later days of success and in a high position. His friends described his surroundings:

> From the splendor of the palace halls we come to a cramped corridor, a staircase much in need of fresh paint. The door painted with dark oil. A small hall, a large study, a tiny sleeping room: a simple desk with peeling varnish, a simple bed with a worn spread and a colorful pillow with a gay folk decoration. On the wall a Renaissance madonna, a Polish winter landscape. On the desk papers, on the night table a rosary, a thermos flask and a glass. On the floor a pair of used black shoes.
>
> The cardinal usually got up at 5 or 6 A.M. He went to Mass at 6:30 and then had his breakfast in the kitchen. His favorite foods were white cheese, scrambled

eggs, buckwheat gruel and sour milk, homemade egg noodles and milk.

His housekeeper, Maria Mordzianka recalls: "If he did not go out he read books in many languages in a special small room from 9 to 11. If he held a meeting, I brought in weak tea at 11, so that he could ease his dry throat; he took sugar but was not extremely fond of sweets. He had neither a radio nor television, because he felt them a waste of time. He only read, wrote, met people."[166]

His was truly a Spartan life, with a thoroughgoing simplicity, as orderly as the life of a soldier. It is the consequence of his spiritual makeup.

Chapter 11

WORLD TRAVELER AND FAITHFUL CHURCHMAN

Worldwide Travels

WOJTYLA'S travels were conditioned by interest, need, and office. Since the period of his studies in Rome (1946-48) he has been practically on the go all the time. While still a student he traveled to France, Belgium, Holland, and to other countries to assist in the spiritual needs of Polish refugees widespread over Europe. After his return home he was not restricted to his homeland.

With the opening of Vatican Council II (1962), Wojtyla was frequently in Rome, mostly in an official role. In 1973 he undertook a trip to Melbourne, Australia to the 40th International Eucharistic Congress, then to the Philippines and other Asian countries. He was concerned with the diffusion of devotion to the Blessed Virgin of Czestochowa and as a result made frequent pilgrimages to Marian shrines. He was several times in Lourdes, at Fatima, and at almost all Mary's shrines in Italy.

He came to the United States in 1969 and 1976 to visit many Polish centers here. In 1969 he was a representative of the Polish Primate, Cardinal Wyszynski, come to thank the American people for their generosity to the Polish Church. In 1976 he was at the Eucharistic Congress in Philadelphia.

People evaluated him from contacts with him. Cardinal Wojtyla "is a deeply spiritual man. He has a good smile, a good sense of humor, but he's not anywhere visibly flamboyant in his actions," according to the priest who gave him a tour of Washington after the Eucharistic Congress. Father Philip Majka, who often arranges tours for visiting Polish hierarchy, handled the arrangements when 17 Polish bishops and Cardinal Wojtyla went to Washington in that summer of 1976. He had also been with the Cardinal on his United States visit in 1969.

Two Visits to the United States

Cardinal Wojtyla's 12-day itinerary in 1969 included Buffalo; Hartford and New Britain, Connecticut; Cleveland, Ohio; Detroit and Orchard Lake, Michigan; Boston; Washington, D.C.; Baltimore; St. Louis; Chicago; the National Shrine of Our Lady of Czestochowa in Pennsylvania; and Brooklyn, New York. His second visit during the 1976 Eucharistic Congress in Philadelphia lasted almost six weeks. Before the Congress Cardinal Wojtyla went to Washington and lectured at The Catholic University of America.

Wojtyla's travels abroad were usually connected with official assignments or missions, very seldom of personal interest only. His growing reputation led to his being frequently invited as a speaker for causes for learned societies or Church affairs. The success of one insured a call to another so that Wojtyla had more invitations than he could well handle.

A most memorable, and perhaps the most profitable was his appearance at the 41st International Eucharistic Congress in Philadelphia where he gave at Veterans' Stadium, in English, a very important homily, "The Eucharist and Man's Hunger for Freedom." It was on August 3, 1976, the day of Peace and Justice. This talk singles out basic principles and rationale for man's hunger for freedom and in it Wojtyla became its forceful spokesman who explored it on every level and in a variety of circumstances. It would seem of general benefit to reproduce it *in toto.* Moreover, it helps one decisively to plumb the feelings and grasp the thought of him who was soon to become Pope.

Homily at Eucharistic Conference

" 'The Spirit of the Lord is upon me; because he has anointed me; he has sent me to announce good news to the poor, to proclaim release for prisoners, and recovery of sight for the blind; to let the broken victims go free, to proclaim the year of the Lord's favor' (Lk 4:18-19).

"Such were the words of Jesus on the day when, according to St. Luke, at the age of thirty He arose in the synagogue of Nazareth, facing His fellow countrymen officially for the first time. By these words He reveals His messianic mission. 'Messiah' means 'the Anointed One.' And thus Israel, the people of the Old Covenant, is faced by the Messiah, by Him whom the Father had 'anointed with the Holy Spirit' (Acts 10:38) and 'sent into the world' (Jn 3:17).

"This same Jesus Christ today faces us all, the people of the New Covenant, here on American soil, in Philadelphia, the City of Brotherly Love, where the Eucharistic Congress is taking place. And again Jesus defines Himself and His mission in the same way, for He had said to His disciples: 'I am with you always, to the end of time' (Mt 28:20). He has instituted the sacrament of His Body and Blood precisely in order to *be,* to be really and sacramentally (Trid. sess. XIII, I) with us. When we are gathered here in such numbers from all parts of the world, it is therefore right to be with Him (cf. Mk 3:14, Greek text), with the eucharistic Jesus, in a special way. It is right to return to the words with which He described Himself and His mission at the beginning of His work in Galilee: 'The Spirit of the Lord is upon me, because he has anointed me; he has sent me to announce good news to the poor, to proclaim release for all who are deprived of freedom' (cf. Lk 4:18-19).

Man's Hunger for Freedom

"The Eucharist is the food which satisfies man's deepest hunger. Created in the image and likeness of God Himself (Gn 1:26), man can find the final appeasement of his hunger and fulfillment of his desires in God alone. 'Our heart is not quiet until it rests in You' (St. Augustine, *Confessions* 1, 1). At the same time created from 'the dust of the earth' (Gn 3:7) and placed among the creatures of the visible world, subjected to the laws of creation and even to some degree to the laws of nature (cf. Gn 8:20), man hungers in many ways. He hungers according to the demands of this earth whose master he was made (cf. Gn 1:26).

"We have a true vision of the man of our times and we speak truthfully of him when, while remembering the physical hunger of millions of brothers, men of all continents, we intend to speak now of the hunger of the human soul, which is no less than that of the hunger for real freedom.

"What this freedom is each of us knows to some extent according to his own experience. It is the principal trait of humanity and the source of human dignity. We read in the Pastoral Constitution of the Second Vatican Council: 'Our contemporaries make much of this freedom and pursue it eagerly, and rightly so. . . . For its part, authentic freedom is an exceptional sign of the divine image within man. For God has willed that man be left "in the hand of his own council" (Sir 15:14), so that he can seek his Creator spontaneously. . . . Hence man's dignity demands that he act according to a conscious and free choice. Such a choice is personally motivated and promoted from within. It does not result from blind internal impulse nor from mere external pressure' *(Constitution on the Church in the Modern World,* 17).

A Gift and a Task

"Freedom is at the same time offered to man and imposed upon him as a task. It is in the first place an attribute of the human person and in this sense it is a gift of the Creator and an endowment of human nature. For this reason it is also the lawful right of man; man has a right to freedom, to self-determination, to the choice of his life career, to acting according to his own convictions. Freedom has been given to man by his Creator in order to be used and to be used well (cf. Gn 4:7). But man may not abuse his freedom (cf. Gal 4:31—5:1), for, as we know perfectly well from sad experience, he can abuse his liberty. He can do wrong because he is free (cf. 1 Pt 2:16).

"But freedom has been given to him by his Creator not in order to commit what is evil (cf. Gal 5:12), but to do good. God also bestowed upon man understanding and conscience to show him what is good and what ought to be done, what is wrong and what ought to be avoided. God's commandments help our understanding and our conscience on their way. The greatest commandment—that of love—leads the way to the fullest use of liberty (cf. 1 Cor 9:19-22; 13:1-13). Freedom has been given to man in order to love, to love true good; to love God above all, to love man as his neighbor and brother (cf Dt 6:5; Lv 19:18; Mk 12:30-33 par). Those who obey this truth, this Gospel, the real disciples of eternal Wisdom, achieve thus, as the Council puts it, a state of 'royal freedom,' for they follow 'that King whom to serve is to reign' *(Constitution on the Church,* 36).

"Freedom is therefore offered to man and given to him as a task. He must not only possess it, but also conquer it. He must recognize the work of his life in a good use, in an increasingly good use of his liberty. This is the truly essential, the fundamental work on which the value and the sense of his whole life depend.

Jesus Teaches Us How to Use Freedom

"Jesus Christ who stands before us, as He did in the synagogue of Nazareth, to proclaim freedom to those who do not possess it, fulfills now what He has declared. In reality He teaches us and helps us to make good use, the best possible use of our freedom (cf. Jn 8:31, 36). He warns men while they are free and protects them from becoming slaves of their sins (cf. Rom 6:16), weaknesses and passions (cf. 2 Pt 2:19). He protects them from becoming slaves of the flesh, of self-indulgence, of money; He entreats them to be internally free, to remain themselves; and to allow neither their career nor riches and the applause of the world to enslave them (cf. Rom 6:12-14; also Mk 13:22 par).

"Jesus Christ reveals in the deepest way that there exists in man's soul a real hunger for freedom and teaches him what the freedom consists in and how this hunger may be truly satisfied. Christ has been teaching this by His whole life; that was the continual lesson given by His person. He does not cease to give us this lesson, not only for the obvious reason that His deeds and words have been recorded in the Gospel, but above all because He remains with us in the Eucharist. 'The Son of Man did not come to be served, but to serve' (Mk 10:45 par).

"These words of Christ came true on Holy Thursday, while he was washing the feet of His disciples, and most of all on Calvary and in the Eucharist (cf. Lk 22:19; Gal 1:4; Eph 5:25). In this act He gave Himself and continues giving Himself utterly to God His Father and to men.

Best Use of Freedom Is Love

"We all, who participate in the Eucharist, if we are to do it with the right interior attitude, must at the same time accept the messianic program of liberation, according to which the best use of freedom is love (cf. 1 Cor 9:19-22). And love itself is expressed in the service of God and man, in laying down one's life for one's brothers (cf Jn 15:13).

"The hunger of freedom passes through the heart of every man, and the richer the heart, the greater that hunger.

"The Eucharist is the chief source of the wealth contained in the human heart. For God, who in this sacrament, 'gives Himself wholly to us,' through this spiritual Communion, enriches man most magnificently and brings out from the secret of man's heart all the treasures which its Creator has enclosed in it.

"In this way the Eucharist is the wealth of the poor, even of those who are poorest, and food for the hungry.

Jesus—the Inspiration and Hope for Freedom

"The hunger for freedom passes also through the history of the human race, through the history of nations and peoples. It reveals their spiritual maturity and at the same time tests it.

"This year is the bicentennial of the day when the hunger for freedom ripened in the American society and revealed itself in liberation and the Declaration of Independence of the United States. Tadeusz Kosciuszko and Kazimierz Pulaski, my compatriots, participated in this fight for independence. The heroes of the Polish nation became heroes of American independence. And all this took place at the time when the Polish Kingdom, a big State consisting of three nations, the Poles, the Lithuanians and the Ruthenians, was beginning to lose its independence, and by degrees became the prey of its rapacious neighbors, Russia, Germany and Austria.

"At the same time while the United States of America was gaining independence, we were losing it for a period of more than a hundred years. And many heroic efforts and sacrifices, similar to those of Kosciuszko and Pulaski had been necessary to ripen anew the freedom of the nation, to test it before all the world, and to express it in time by the independence of our country.

"I wish to confess here, before the Eucharistic Jesus, that during those old struggles, for liberty in the past twenty centuries and in the later ones of this century, He was our inspiration and our only hope. The faith in His Resurrection from the dead after His Passion and death has never left us, and in spite of all kinds of distress and persecutions, it has created continually the will to live and the desire for freedom.

Jesus Fulfills His Promise

"And thus Jesus Christ fulfilled His messianic promise, once given in Nazareth: 'The Spirit of the Lord is upon me, because he has anointed me; he has sent me to announce good news to the poor, to proclaim release for all who are deprived of freedom' (cf. Lk 4:18).

"We believe that in the Gospel there is the full and fundamental program of liberation of man (cf. Gal 4:31). Jesus Christ is the true prophet of men's freedom, and also of the liberty of nations and peoples, of all the oppressed who suffer from hunger for true freedom. Are we not witnesses in our times of the many-sided limitations and even of the deprivation of freedom of whole societies, nations and states? And all this is happening while colonial nations, up to now subjugated by others, have ripened to freedom and have achieved their independence, a fact which gladdens all those who really love liberty.

"But it is already being said that old forms of colonialism are being superseded by new ones. The Synod of Bishops spoke of it in the following terms in 1971: 'Our action should be directed in the first place toward those men and nations, who owing to different forms of oppression and to the present character of our society are silent victims of injustice and are deprived of the possibility of making themselves heard' ("Injustice without Voice," in *Justice in the World).*

Hunger for Freedom Still Unsatisfied

"And so the hunger for freedom continues to be unsatisfied. Individuals and societies, groups and social classes, and above all the peoples and nations of our twentieth century have acquired a more acute consciousness of the fact.

The laws of human freedom have been more fully formulated, as has been the case of the law of nations; they have entered the constitutions and codes, the international declarations and the conventions. But have they actually entered real life to the same extent?

"In our times, on the background of the maturing social and human consciousness, the principle of the freedom of the human spirit, of the freedom of conscience, of the freedom of religion has become much more evident. The Second Vatican Council has expressed it in many places and especially in the separate *Declaration on Religious Freedom.* But is this principle really respected *everywhere?* Do we never meet with the case of those who are underprivileged because of their religious convictions? May we not even speak today of actual persecutions of those who confess their religion, especially Christians, persecuted as they were in the first centuries after Christ?

"This is what the *Declaration on Religious Freedom* (15) says on the subject: 'Forms of government still exist under which, even though freedom of religious worship receives constitutional recognition, the powers of the government are engaged in the effort to deter citizens from professing religion and to make life difficult and dangerous for religious communities.'

Demand for True Freedom for All

"And so today we bring to this great community of confessors of the Eucharistic Christ, gathered at the Eucharistic Congress in Philadelphia, the whole hunger for freedom which permeates contemporary man and all humanity. In the name of Jesus Christ we have the right and the duty to demand true freedom for men and for peoples. We therefore bring this hunger for real freedom and deposit it on this altar. Not only a man, a priest, a bishop, but Christ Himself is at this altar, He who through our ministration offers His unique and eternal sacrifice.

"It is the sacrifice of all times. It is also the sacrifice of our twentieth century and of its last quarter. It contains everything of which the earthly existence of each man and of all people consists: 'the joys and the hopes, the griefs and anxieties of the men of this age' *(Constitution on the Church in the Modern World,* 1). Christ, the Son of God, comes to them all and to all of us, as He had once come to the synagogue of Nazareth, and says:

—" 'If you dwell within the revelation I have brought, you shall know the truth, and the truth will set you free' (Jn 8:31).

—" 'Where the Spirit of the Lord is, there is liberty' (2 Cor 3:17).

—" 'You were called to be free men. It was for liberty that Christ freed us all' (Gal 4:31).

—" 'Live as free men; not however as though your freedom were there to provide a screen for wrongdoing, but as servants in God's service' (1 Pt 2: 16)."[167]

Travels in America

This "hunger for freedom" is the reason that Wojtyla was so compassionate to all deprived of liberty and why in his words there was a strong spiritual undertone pointing out the real roots of freedom. It was, coincidentally, under the spell of Wojtyla's influence that the subsequent Conference of Czech hierarchy, clergy, and laity who had been participants at the Congress (held August 3, 1976, in the Gruber Theater of Chestnut Hill College) formulated the *Catholic Manifesto for Religious Freedom and Its Restoration in Czechoslovakia*[168] and sent it to the chief public authorities to make them aware of the blatant violations of religious freedom in their native lands.

After the Congress in Philadelphia the Polish delegation returned to the Baltimore-Washington area. Cardinal Wojtyla celebrated Mass at the Polish chapel at the National Shrine of the Immaculate Conception, and the delegation toured the nation's capital.

"His interest was very thorough," said Father Majka. "I pointed out the space museum and he was very much interested in technology, in the educational aspect." Father recalled the Cardinal's 1976 itinerary after the Washington tour. Wojtyla again visited Detroit and Orchard Lake, where there is a Polish national seminary. He went again to Boston, Buffalo, and Niagara Falls, and then on to Ontario. From Canada, he visited Chicago, which contains the largest community of Poles outside Warsaw, Poland. He went also to Stevens Point, Wisconsin, and then returned to Chicago. Thence he returned to Boston to lecture at Harvard University, went west to Los Angeles, and then to Great Falls and Billings, Montana; back again to Chicago and then on to Cincinnati. His final stop was New York.

Broadened by Travel

From his contact with the Cardinal, Father Majka said he feels that he "has a keen awareness—he's aware of what you're saying. He thinks on his feet, he has that ability. He 'tells it like it is,' you don't play politics with him. I wouldn't dare, that's not his style. His style is very Christ-like."

Father Chester Zielinski and his parishioners at St. Peter's Church in Stevens Point recalled the Cardinal's 1976 visit: after a brief appearance at the parish the Cardinal went to a farm nearby for some Polish cuisine and conversation with the Polish well-wishers.[169]

Among the last trips before his election was his pilgrimage to the Sacred Shroud in Turin, September 1, 1978. This interest in the Sacred Shroud was intensified by recent scientific findings in regard to its authenticity. After he became Pope, he went several times into the city of Rome, visited Assisi (1978), and flew to Mexico to attend the National Conference of Bishops of Latin America at Puebla (January 1979).

If it is said that traveling is learning and education, then Wojtyla is really a good learner, whose travels are always with purpose and an interest. They helped him to acquire not only a cosmopolitan outlook but to get a feel for problems internationally and needs of the universal Church, all of which was beneficial in forming him as a true cosmopolitan, a shepherd.

Humble Steward and Faithful Churchman

A sign of deep spirituality is one's realization that all talents and qualities are given in one's stewardship[170] only, that there is nothing not given by God. One's consciousness that every gift is from God really keeps one humble. Wojtyla was indeed conscious of his great talents, which he used always prudently and for the benefit of society, as we see throughout his life.

Mindful always of that biblical warning: "Give an account of your stewardship," Wojtyla strove to be a faithful servant. As a real steward he was well aware that if his service was to be acceptable to God, this must be proportionate in accord with Jesus' own measure: "To whom much is given, much will be demanded" (Lk 12:48). Aware of this he was always very generous with his time and talents in His service, and as he prayed "that our sacrifice may be acceptable to God, the Almighty Father" he also realized that God can never be outdone in generosity, for God's reward is always greater than one's service: "Consider the lilies of the field, how they grow, they neither toil nor spin; yet I tell you, even Solomon in all his glory was not arrayed as one of these" (Mt 6:28ff). He would frequently say: "*Inutiles servi sumus*" (We are useless servants indeed; Mt 25:30, Lk 19: 22).

So involved did he become in work that some would call him, in the colloquial term, a workaholic. He actually toiled like an ox, it was said. If the concept of total stewardship reflects the full use of "time, talent, and treasure," then Wojtyla was that sort. Diligent as he always was, he busied himself in God's vineyard so that nothing was left for his leisure. He really emptied himself in the service of God.

Wojtyla's sense of fidelity and of loyalty was well developed in all of his life. Since childhood he was very appreciative of his parents, from his youngest years he appreciated the friendship of his associates, in schools he valued highly his teachers, during his public life he shared a beautiful association with his coworkers, and as a churchman he truly treasured his brother bishops and cherished a filial devotion to the Holy Father. Nothing was difficult when he was asked to do any task for Rome.

Regard for Paul VI

One feels Cardinal Wojtyla's sentiments for the Holy Father as demonstrated on one occasion. On May 30, 1970, Pope Paul VI received in audience in the Hall of the Consistory 260 Polish priests, some on the 25th anniversary of their liberation from various concentration camps, to convey their respects to the Pope. Wojtyla, as their spokesman, addressed the Holy Father:

> Most Holy Father,
>
> At this time the whole Church of Christ celebrates with Your Holiness the fiftieth anniversary, the Golden Jubilee of your priestly ordination, and with you returns thanks to almighty God, Father, Son, and Holy Spirit. In this thanksgiving it seems that today a specially privileged place has been given to us, the bishops and priests from distant Poland. By our presence here "*regale sacerdotium*" [as a royal priesthood], we also render present the whole People of God in our country. In a spiritual sense they are always close to you, Holy Father, and are, so to speak, always linked with you, the Shepherd of the universal Church, in a union of prayer and sacrifice. It is a union not just of mind, but of heart. Today we want to lay bare the heart of our people to you.

It is a faithful heart, following the example of fidelity of the Blessed Virgin, who, beneath the cross of the Redeemer, became for ever the mother of our priesthood. It is a heart "tried by fire," as the bishops and priests here present wish to show. There are those here —saved from the fire—who are living witnesses of the many, the very many, who not only suffered much for Christ, for the Church and for the fatherland, but also gave their own lives as a witness to faith, hope and charity. This happened during the last World War when, of all the peoples of Europe and of the whole world, our nation experienced unequalled and almost unheard-of disasters.

But we are not here to recall such things; we are here rather as a gift providentially foreseen and prepared, most Holy Father, for the time of your Jubilee. The gift is spiritually offered to you by our whole people, by laity, religious, priests and bishops; it is offered from the very womb of Mother Church and of Mother Poland who brings forth her children in sorrow, not for this life only, but in the hope of life eternal. A symbolic offering is attached to this gift which we shall leave with you, most Holy Father, begging you to accept it and place it in the Treasury of the Church. (It is a "chalice" and "missal" used for the secret celebration of the divine sacrifice in the Oswiecim prison camp.)

In the name of the bishops of Poland, in the name of the Cardinal Primate, I now present to you this body of priests who left behind a part of their priestly life in the concentration camp of Dachau and elsewhere, and humbly request your apostolic blessing.

We have left our good wishes at the altar of blessed Peter the apostle and elsewhere in Rome during these last few days that they may remain there for you, Holy Father, ever gracious, ever faithful, ever true.[171]

Appreciation for John Paul I

In the light of this truly beautiful relationship of Wojtyla to the Holy Father, it is interesting also to know that the Cardinal had always many friends, from all walks of life, at home in Poland and abroad. This was certainly because he kept contact with them and knew the value of friendship and of loyalty. He seems to follow the maxim of Socrates: "Be slow to fall into friendship, but when thou art in, continue firm and constant!"

Ominous as it may appear, among the last official performances as archbishop was Wojtyla's homily delivered on October 1, 1978, in St. Mary's Basilica in Krakow during the Mass for the repose of the soul of Pope John Paul I, in which he gave high tribute to this well-loved Pope. The whole Polish text appeared in *Tygodnik Powszechny*, and in translation was carried in many journals. He spoke of him in part thus:

> We expected so much from him. He gave us so much promise with his human, priestly, episcopal, and papal personality. So quickly he became that which he was destined to become by reason of his calling. It was with amazement that I witnessed this that evening in the Sistine Chapel. The accuracy and speed of the election seemed to confirm it all.[172]

And it would seem that an account of a responsible steward, a good servant, and an ever-faithful churchman, which was brought by Wojtyla into the new conclave after the papal throne was left vacant by the untimely death of John Paul I,[173] was promptly caught up by the cardinal-electors, who then brought to fruition the biblical promise: "Come you, faithful servant, because you were faithful in less, I will put you in charge of more!" (Mt 25:23), by making him the good Shepherd[174] of the universal Church, a mission for which he was prepared in Krakow of Poland.

Chapter 12

A SURPRISE ELECTION

The Year of Three Popes

THE year 1978 was really the year of three popes[175] who were in turn duly elected to the office. On August 10, 1978, Pope Paul VI died; on August 23 John Paul I was elected and died on September 26 after 33 days;[176] on October 16th of this same year, again a new pope was elected who took the name of John Paul II. In this chaotic time when the transition of popes was so quick and unexpected, the greatest of all surprises came when a non-Italian pope[177] was chosen, thus bypassing the old tradition for an Italian. This caught unaware not only the whole world but the candidate himself, who was stunned by this unexpected turn of events.

Did Cardinal Wojtyla himself ever think it might happen? No one can be sure, but the Italian photographer Franco de Leo recalls an interesting exchange with the Cardinal as he arrived at the Rome airport for the funeral of Pope John Paul I. De Leo relates that as he shot picture after picture of Wojtyla, the Cardinal asked good-naturedly: "Why are you taking so many pictures of me? You don't think that I'll be pope, do you?" The future Pontiff then put his hand on the photographer's shoulders and laughed heartily.[178]

The well-structured conclave, so well described by some writers,[179] insuring the voting process as "secret and free from all outside influences," developed into its present form after frequent historical experiences, when the papal election was subject to every sort of outside pressure from concerned parties and even nations. The last example of a blatant outside interference was when Emperor Francis Joseph exercised the Habsburg's ancient privilege of veto against the favored Cardinal Rampolla, Leo XIII's secretary of state, on August 2, 1903. The conclave refused to accept this veto, but in succeeding ballots instead elected Giuseppe Melchiore Sarto (Pius X).[180]

The conclave as such is then conditioned by such historical experiences and as a relic of the medieval times remains a rarity, a unique feature which cries out to be updated with the 20th century while still serving well its purpose, i.e., the election of the pope free and independent of human politics but with full reliance on the assistance of the Holy Spirit.

Inconveniences of Present Way of Election

Considering these facts, it would seem that this may perhaps have been the last election in the traditional way, with the segregation of the cardinals and the smoke signal. Many reasons support this, among them the greyish puff of smoke at John Paul I's election—neither black nor white. Then there are the medieval inconveniences: the cells not only lack air-conditioning, but are red-hot in the summer sun; the beds are uncomfortable; the rest rooms are very few with a minimum of baths.

Already the American Cardinal, Francis Spellman, New York's archbishop, had offered John XXIII to erect a modern building for the conclaves, with convenient facilities, inside Vatican City. Funds would be provided by donations and collections from Catholic Americans. The edifice would hold at least 150 mini-apartments, a large meeting room or hall, one big church and several small chapels, a dining room, and lounge rooms for smaller group meetings.

Cardinal Spellman was said to have been moved by his own bad experience during the conclave that elected John XXIII. It so happens that he himself was assigned a cell without a bath (the cells being assigned by lot), and he had to wait at times an hour and a half for a shower. Despite the good will of the Cardinal, the project was not realized for lack of space in Vatican City, but mainly perhaps because of the short duration of John XXIII's pontificate (1958-63).

Origins of Strict Seclusion

The cardinals were also exasperated by the rigorous, strict seclusion to which they were subjected pursuant to the regulations of the conclave, "a seclusion deriving from three episodes which happened 700 years ago which could be finally forgotten," once commented Dutch Cardinal Alfrink.[181]

The first incident had occured in 1216, when the cardinals were called to elect the successor of Innocent III. Since the sessions continued for a long time, the inhabitants of Perugia, where the election took place, locked the cardinals in, thus forcing them to speed up their voting. The second incident was in Rome, after the death of Gregory IX in 1241, when the electors were locked in what remained of the palace of Septimus Severus on the slopes of the Palatine. But the most clamorous of the incidents was in 1270. At the death of Clement IV, the 18 cardinals gathered in the papal palace in Viterbo, but they were unable to agree.

After several unsuccessful interventions of King Philip III of France, and when more than 18 months had elapsed from the Pope's death, the Franciscan St. Bonaventure convinced the Viterbians to lock the cardinals in. When even this brought no result, Alberto di Montebuono, mayor of the city, and Raniero Gatti, commander of the papal militia, had the roof removed from the palace and ordered that the cardinals be fed only bread and water. The exhausted cardinals finally elected Teobald Visconti of Piacenze, apostolic legate in Syria who took the name of Gregory X.[182]

The new Pontiff promulgated immediately a series of laws to avoid future interminable conclaves. The cardinals were to be locked in a common room and if within three days there was no result, they were to receive but one dish for lunch and one for dinner for five days. If after these five days they did not come up with a solution, the electors would be left with bread and water.

The reform had served to some purpose, for the successor of Gregory, Innocent V, was elected in a single day in 1276. In that year the conclave had twice more to be repeated. Both Hadrian V and John XXI, successors to Innocent, had discarded (abrogated) the strict rule of Gregory X. The result was that for the election of Nicholas III in 1277, seven months and eight days were necessary; for that of Martin IV in 1281, ten months and nineteen days; and for that of Nicholas IV in 1888, ten months and twelve days. At the death of this Pope, his see remained vacant for two years and three months.

It was Celestine V who, in 1294, restored the validity of the Gregorian laws or regulations which have been in use with some modifications and adaptations to the present time.

The Procedure of the Conclave

The present procedure of the conclave is conducted by the rules issued by Pope Paul VI, October 1, 1975, with the Apostolic Constitution *Romano pontificii eligendo.*[183] This imposes a great deal of secrecy about what is going on in the conclave, making it even more independent and perhaps even more mysterious. As a result the human maneuvering of the cardinals' voting is rather a matter of speculation—based on hearsay or hinted at by the cardinals obliged to keep silent.

Moreover, from the voting procedure itself several details may be detected. It is known, for instance, that the cardinals vote both at the morning and the afternoon sessions; two ballots are expected at each session unless the first is successful. If no name received the two-thirds plus one required for election, the second voting process begins immediately. According to the number of days of the conclave, one can figure out easily how many voting ballots a certain pope needed for his election.[184]

First Appearance of the New Pope

The signal that the new Pope has been finally elected is revealed when the white smoke issues from the chimney of the Sistine Chapel, and when the senior cardinal deacon traditionally accompanied by two other cardinals and preceded by the crossbearer comes out on the balcony to announce to the world that a new Pope has been chosen.

More suspenseful minutes and, finally, onto the balcony came the new Pope, flanked by the papal masters of ceremonies and by Cardinal Wyszynski. When his name was announced by Cardinal Pericle Felici, the crowd reacted with excitement yet with great surprise, for the choice was a non-Italian. The reaction, "Oh, a foreigner," was short-lived when Cardinal Wojtyla gave his brief address in flawless Italian to the cheering crowd:

> May Jesus Christ be praised. Dearest brothers and sisters, we are all still grieved after the death of our most beloved Pope John Paul I. And now the most eminent Cardinals have called a new Bishop of Rome. They have called him from a distant country, distant but always so close through the communion in the Christian faith and tradition. I was afraid to accept this nomination but I did it in the spirit of obedience to Our Lord Jesus Christ and of total confidence in His Mother, the most holy Madonna.
>
> I do not know whether I can explain myself well in your . . . our Italian language. If I make a mistake you

> will correct me. And so I present myself to you all to confess our common faith, our hope, our confidence in the Mother of Christ and of the Church, and also to start anew on this road of history and of the Church, with the help of God and with the help of men.[185]

The new Pope then imparted his first apostolic blessing, *urbi et orbi* (a blessing for the city and the world).

Ramifications of New Pope's Choice

Perhaps more of a surprise than that he was not an Italian was the circumstance that the new Pope comes from a country behind the Iron Curtain, a Communist land. Wojtyla's election as pope not only was the first severe blow to the logic of agreements made at Yalta in 1945[186] dividing Europe into Russian and Western zones, but it was also something of a moral lesson for Western Christianity for lack of appreciation of Christian values. They now see the Christians of the West in contrast with Christians of Eastern Europe who are not permitted to practice their religion as much and as freely as they wish. That the new Pope comes from Poland, a country of living Christian faith, would serve furthermore as indication that this surprise choice of a son of Poland was in a manner a reward for that nation's steadfast witness to Christ.[187]

There is perhaps another rationale behind this surprise choice, namely, the fact that Italy, a country of popes and Christian traditions, is at the present in great danger of a Communist takeover. This circumstance is of no little significance. Certainly it indicates that the Church in Italy was too little aware of the numerous impending problems to be solved lest the Communists overwhelm it. In contrast with previous Italian popes, John Paul II is likely to be more confrontation-free and more detached in his view of Italian politics.

One example of this can be seen in the struggle of Christian Democrats and Communists. Cardinal Wojtyla was once present at a discussion initiated by a letter of General Secretary Berlinguer of the Italian Communist party to Bishop Betazzi as to whether a Catholic can be a party member. He cautioned: "Beware! This is their classical trick. We know it well; they attempt to divide the episcopate by every means! As soon as a little split appears, they intrude into it and widen it. The Polish episcopate built against this tactic a unity of iron. This was and is our strength!"[188]

The increasing polarization of the Christian and the Communist worlds and their forthcoming confrontation perhaps conditioned the cardinals to look for someone skilled and ready to take up the sword and fight for a survival of Christian ideas, values, and principles, to defend every freedom that the Christian life may live. Interesting and certainly not accidental was it that the first task of major importance in the present pontificate was on the occasion of John Paul II's attendance at the Latin American Bishops Conference in Mexico at Puebla.[189]

There the new Pope examined the problems of liberation theology and how close the Church should come toward Marxism in order to oppose successfully the military and the wealthy that they may have more understanding of the social problems of the vast majority, the poor, in all the Latin countries. Certainly it is no small task to be resolved by the man from Krakow, who can speak the same language, literally and figuratively, when he sits down with Latin American bishops who point to exploitation by the left, the right, and the center: guerrilla terrorism, military dictatorships, and the rape of the poor and of the land by the wealthy—all of them Christians.

Shock to Russians

Perhaps the election of the Pole Wojtyla to the papacy was the greatest shock to the Russians themselves if one may infer from the meeting of the Pope with Foreign Minister Andrei Gromyko of the Soviet Union on January 24,

1979. The meeting was, on the Soviet initiative, "to take up the measure of the new Polish Pontiff."[190]

The Pope's personal stature and background are such that he can bring about changes, if he so wishes, in attitudes of the people toward the Communist regimes not alone in Poland but also in the other East European countries with large Roman Catholic populations: Czechoslovakia, Hungary, East Germany, and even in Soviet Lithuania, the only Soviet Republic with a large Catholic population. Furthermore, Pope John Paul II's forthrightness—he already several times stressed that "the days of the silent Church are over" —had to cause concern in Moscow, for the Pope is known to feel strongly that improved relations between the Vatican and the Soviet Union should be associated with similar relaxation in ties between individual national Churches and East European governments.

Soviet leaders are worried also about the Pope's forthcoming visit to Poland, [191] for they fear it may incite not only religious feeling but also a wave of nationalistic fervor in the Poles, Czechoslovaks,[192] and other Slavic peoples of satellite countries which never had much love for their Big Brother, despite all talk about Communist solidarity.

Sign of Hope for Future

Other elements of the surprise choice of Wojtyla are his comparative youth, his academic ability and scholarly maturity sufficient to be able to cope with various ideological world views, his physical strength to withstand the heavy burden of the office, and his intellectual capability alert to know how to give orientation to a confused world.

To one thinking over the surprise of his choice, it appears clearly a suitable vehicle of the divine design to deal adequately and successfully with contemporary problems. In accord with the popular saying: "God's ways are mysterious ways," one is all but compelled to see a special divine favor and grace in this surprise choice of Karol Wojtyla as John Paul II, Pope.

As an anthropological feeling of surprise is open to being changed into awe,[193] so in a very short time the world will stop to wonder over its surprise and will be eager to learn more about John Paul II and what may be expected of him, for he was so early explicit in his message to the world,[194] to the cardinals,[195] to the diplomatic corps,[196] and to the press.[197] Enthusiasm for him began to build, for he was seen as a Pope who would be a positive force in the Church, a strong leader in the modern world.

Especially reassuring appears his choice of the name John Paul II, clearly indicating his intent to continue the pastoral interest and concern of the beloved John Paul I. In addition to the same concern the new Pope's great knowledge of diplomacy, his scholarship, his versatility in theology and in world matters give him strengths and advantages whereas John Paul I was perhaps somewhat uninformed.[198] As a result this surprise choice gained not only a quick acceptance but brought a great promise of hope, expectation, and assurance for better times so much desired and so long overdue.

Symbolized by Coat of Arms

That this promise is taken in full seriousness by the Polish Pontiff is well symbolized by his coat of arms, intended as an act of homage to the central mystery of Christianity, the Redemption:

> . . . its main representation is a cross, whose form, however, does not correspond to the customary heraldic model. The reason for the unusual placement of the vertical section of the cross is readily apparent if one considers the second object inserted in the coat of arms—the large and majestic capital M. This recalls the presence of Mary beneath the cross and her exceptional participation in the redemption.

> The great devotion of the Holy Father to the Virgin Mary is manifested in this manner, as it was also expressed in his motto as Cardinal Wojtyla: *Totus tuus* (All yours). Nor can one forget that within the confines of the ecclesiastical province of Krakow there is situated the celebrated Marian shrine of Czestochowa, where the Polish people for centuries fostered their filial devotion to the Mother of God.[199]

Thus, to the Pope's spiritual strength described above one must add the determination of a holder of this coat of arms. This serves to reassure all the faithful that he will discharge the entire trust put on his shoulders by them with the service of a good shepherd that they expect from him.

To achieve this, in his humility he is beginning his pastoral ministry in prayerful confidence in God's help and with a request to everyone: "Help me to be able to serve you!"[200]

Chapter 13

THE INAUGURATION OF A NEW PONTIFF

Worldwide Interest and Participation

JOHN Paul II chose to have outdoors the simple installation services in the manner initiated by his predecessor, John Paul I. He moved the ceremonies, moreover, from the afternoon to 10 o'clock in the morning the better to accommodate the European television public, while relays to other continents followed.

The solemnity of the event itself was accented by the multitude of the faithful, some 300,000 or more from every corner of the world, and the presence of numerous state and national delegations (103), the diplomatic corps. Most impressive was the crowd of faithful come from Poland and other countries behind the Iron Curtain.

The ancient Church ritual was observed. Again were seen the clerical garb, the brightly striped costumes, and plumed helmets of the Swiss guard, the folk costumes of Italian, Slavic, and Polish villagers. All contributed to the drama of the Vatican scene enacted in St. Peter's Square on the occasion of this Pope's inauguration.[201]

Promptly at 10 the solemn ceremony began. It is estimated that more than 700,000,000 people from all over the world watched or listened to the papal inauguration. The solemn Mass concelebrated by the cardinals, as described so well elsewhere,[202] was meant as a public celebration for the beginning of the papal ministry and was held in accordance with liturgical rules for such an occasion with the sole exception of the ritual of conferring of the pallium on the shoulders of the Pope, which replaced the former rite of coronation. The other parts of the Mass followed prescribed ritual for a period of two and a half hours. All was in Latin save only for the second reading in Polish, and the prayers of the faithful chanted by four ministers in Polish, French, Spanish, English, and German.

The Pope's Homily

The center of attention for all the faithful present and for the television audience was the homily in which John Paul II outlined the main thoughts of his pontificate:

"'You are the Christ, the Son of the living God' (Mt 16:16).

"These words were spoken by Simon, son of Jonah, in the district of Caesarea Philippi. Yes, he spoke them with his own tongue, with a deeply lived and experienced conviction—but not in him do they find their source, their origin, '. . . because it was not flesh and blood that revealed this to you but my Father in heaven' (Mt 16:17). They were the words of Faith.

"These words mark the beginning of Peter's mission in the history of salvation, in the history of God's People. From that moment, from that confession of Faith, the sacred history of salvation and of the People of God was bound to take on a new dimension; to express itself in the historical dimension of the Church. This ecclesial dimension of the history of the People of God has its origin, is, in fact, born from these words of Faith; and is linked to the man who uttered them: 'You are Peter—the rock—and on you, as on a rock, I will build my Church.'

"On this day and in this place these same words must again be uttered and we must listen:

"'You are the Christ, the Son of the living God.'

Christ Reveals the Father

"Yes, brothers and sons and daughters, these words first of all. Their content reveals to our eyes the mystery of the living God, the mystery to which the Son has brought us close. No one has in fact brought the living God close to men and revealed Him as He alone has done. In our knowledge of God, in our journey toward God, we are totally linked to the power of these words: 'He who sees Me sees the Father.' He who is infinite, inscrutable, ineffable, has come close to us in Jesus Christ, the only-begotten Son of God, born of the Virgin Mary in the stable of Bethlehem.

"All of you who are still seeking God, all you have the inestimable good fortune to believe, and also you who are tormented by doubt:

"Please listen once again, today in this sacred place, to the words uttered by Simon Peter. In those words is the Faith of the Church. In those same words is the new truth, indeed, the ultimate and definitive truth about man: the Son of the living God—'You are the Christ, the Son of the living God.'

The See of Peter

"Today the new Bishop of Rome solemnly begins his ministry and the mission of Peter. In this City, in fact, Peter completed and fulfilled the mission entrusted to him by the Lord.

"The Lord addressed him with these words:

"' . . . when you were young you girded yourself and walked where you would; but when you are old you will stretch out your hands and another will gird you and carry you where you do not wish to go' (Jn 21:18).

"Peter came to Rome!

"What else but obedience to the mandate received from the Lord guided him and brought him to this City, the heart of the Empire? Perhaps the fisherman of Galilee did not wish to come here. He would perhaps have preferred to stay there, on the shores of Lake Gennasaret, with his boat and his nets. But guided by the Lord, obedient to his mandate, he came here!

"According to an ancient tradition (given magnificent literary expression in a novel by Henryk Sienkiewicz) during Nero's persecution Peter wanted to leave Rome. But the Lord intervened: He went to meet him. Peter spoke to Him and asked: 'Quo vadis, Domine?'—'Where are you going, Lord?' And the Lord answered him at once: 'I go to Rome to be crucified again.' Peter came back to Rome and here he stayed until his crucifixion.

A Roman by Choice

"Yes, brothers and sons and daughters, Rome is the See of Peter. Down the centuries new bishops continually succeeded him in this See. Today a new Bishop comes to the Chair of Peter in Rome, a Bishop filled with trepidation, conscious of his unworthiness. How could one not tremble before the greatness of this call and before the universal mission of this See of Rome.

"To the See of Peter in Rome there succeeds today a Bishop who is not a Roman—*a Bishop who is a son of Poland*—but from this moment he too becomes a Roman. Yes—a Roman. He is a Roman also because he is the son of a nation whose history, from its first dawning, and whose thousand-year-old traditions are marked by a living, strong, unbroken, and deeply felt link with the See of Peter, a nation which has ever remained faithful to this See of Rome. Inscrutable is the design of Divine Providence!

"In past centuries, when the Successor of Peter took possession of his See, the *triregnum* or tiara was placed on his head. The last Pope to be crowned was Paul VI in 1963, but after the solemn coronation ceremony he never again used the tiara and left his Successors free to decide in this regard.

"Pope John Paul I, whose memory is so vivid in our hearts, did not wish the tiara; nor does his Successor wish it today. This is not the time to return to a ceremony and an object wrongly considered a symbol of the temporal power of the Popes.

A Call to Service

"Our time calls us, urges us, obliges us to gaze on the Lord and immerse ourselves in humble and devout meditation on the mystery of the supreme power of Christ Himself.

"He who was born of the Virgin Mary, the carpenter's son (as he was thought to be), the Son of the living God (confessed by Peter), came to make us all 'a kingdom of priests.'

"The Second Vatican Council has reminded us of the mystery of this power and of the fact that Christ's mission as Priest, Prophet, Teacher, and King continues in the Church. Everyone, the whole People of God, shares in this threefold mission.

"In the past perhaps the tiara, the triple crown, was placed on the Pope's head in order to express by that symbol the Lord's plan for His Church, namely, that all the hierarchical order of Christ's Church, all 'sacred power' exercised in the Church is none other than service, service with a single purpose: to ensure that all the people of God share in this threefold mission of Christ and remain always under the power of the Lord, a power that has its source not in the powers of this world but in the mystery of the Cross and Resurrection.

"The absolute and yet sweet and gentle power of the Lord responds to the whole depths of the human person, to his loftiest aspirations of intellect, will, and heart. It speaks not the language of force but expresses itself in charity and truth.

"The new Successor of Peter in the See of Rome makes today a fervent, humble and trusting prayer: Christ, make me become and remain the servant of your power that knows no eventide. Make me a servant, indeed, the servant of your servants.

Open Wide the Doors of Christ

"Brothers and sisters, be not afraid to welcome Christ and accept His power. Help the Pope and all those who wish to serve Christ and with Christ's power to serve the human person and the whole of mankind. Do not be afraid. Open wide the doors for Christ. To His saving power open the boundaries of States, economic and political systems, the vast fields of culture, civilization, and development. Do not be afraid. Christ knows 'what is in man.' He alone knows it.

"So often today man does not know what is within him, in the depths of his mind and heart. So often he is uncertain about the meaning of his life on this earth. He is assailed by doubt, doubt which turns to despair.

"We ask you therefore, we beg you with humility and trust, let Christ speak to man. He alone has the words of life, yes, of eternal life.

"Precisely today the whole Church is celebrating World Mission Day; that is, she is praying, meditating, and acting that Christ's words of life may reach all people and by them be received as a message of hope, salvation and of total liberation.

Gratitude to All

"I thank all of you here present who have chosen to participate in this solemn inauguration of the ministry of the new Successor of Peter.

"I heartily thank the Heads of State, the Representatives of the Authorities, and the Government of Delegations for so honoring me with their presence.

"Thank you, Eminent Cardinals of the Holy Roman Church.

"I thank you, my beloved brothers in the episcopate.

"Thank you, priests.

"To you, sisters, and brothers, religious of the orders and congregations, I give my thanks.

"Thank you, people of Rome.

"Thank you, pilgrims who have come here from all over the world.

"Thank all of you linked with this sacred ceremony by radio and television.

Words to Polish Pilgrims

"I speak to you, my dear fellow-countrymen, pilgrims from Poland, brother bishops with your magnificent Primate at your head, priests, sisters and brothers of the Polish religious congregations—to you representatives of Poland from all over the world.

"What shall I say to you who have come from my own Krakow, from the See of Saint Stanislaus of whom I was the unworthy successor for 14 years? What shall I say? Everything that I could speak would fade into insignificance compared with what my heart feels, and your hearts feel at this moment.

"Let us then leave aside words. Let there remain just a great silence before God, the silence that becomes prayer. I ask you: Be with me! At Jasna Gora and everywhere. Do not cease to be with the Pope who today prays in the words of the poet: 'Mother of God, you who defend Bright Czestochowa and shine at Ostrobrama.' These same words I address to you at this moment in particular.

Appeal for Prayers

"That was an appeal and a call to prayer for the new Pope, an appeal expressed in the Polish language. I make the same appeal to all the sons and daughters of the Catholic Church. Remember me today and always in your prayers!

"I open my heart to all my brothers of the Christian Churches and communities, and I greet in particular you who are here present, in anticipation of our coming personal meeting, but for the moment I express to you my sincere appreciation for your having wished to attend this solemn ceremony. . . .

"I appeal also to all men—to every man (with what veneration the apostle of Christ must utter this word man)

—pray for me!

—help me to be able to serve you!

"Amen."[203]

Reflective of Pope's Personality

This compassionate homily reflects truly the new Pope's personality, humility, gratitude, concern, love, openness, sincerity, and pastoral care for all entrusted to him. The faithful instinctively shared their feelings with the Pope by placing in him all their hopes and expectations. Most people seemed to find the appearance of the new Pope pleasing and were satisfied with the many things reported to him and what he had to say about some reforms so that they felt that with him "a new era"[204] was coming.

As a stunned and amazed world gathered either in St. Peter's Square or before the television, they found the newly elected Polish Pope ready to go far to acquaint himself with the people, both curious and proud, and to bring himself to the world with his visions of making a better Church in a better world. In this John Paul II appeared to be determined[205] to assert his leadership.

Chapter **14**

NEW STYLE OF JOHN PAUL'S PONTIFICATE

Changed Traditional Procedures

THE new Pope revolutionized the traditional procedures of caution and prudence in his first public appearances and declarations. He also displayed a seemingly unconcerned attitude in what he did.

He began in his own bedroom, next to the study at whose window the popes were wont to show themselves each Sunday. As soon as he was alone, he threw open the shutters and left them wide all the next day, to the great anxiety of the prelates in charge, who feared the Pope could be spied on through a strong electronic telescope, from the Pincian hill. John Paul had brought with him to bed the special issue of *Osservatore Romano,* whose title framed in yellow announced to the world that he had become Pope. But he did not enjoy a good rest.

"Not because of emotion," he hastened to explain; "because of the mattress." A regular woolen mattress on which Paul VI and John Paul I used to sleep was for Karol Wojtyla definitely too soft. The next morning, as soon as he got up, he asked Father Magee (an Irishman already engaged in the secretariat of Wojtyla's two predecessors) to have a board put under the mattress to make the bed harder.

Polish Cooks Added

The day after the election, on Tuesday, October 17, the nuns of the Child Mary (in Italian *Maria Bambina*), who care for the papal apartment, served him a meal without *pastasciutta.* The Pope, who had learned to appreciate it during his Roman studies, asked right away: "How come, Reverend Mothers, there is no pasta?" The abashed nuns prepared it then for dinner, but it was spaghetti, and the Pope needed several minutes to cut them small with knife and fork.

Msgr. Caprio, to whom the sisters talked about this, asked the Pope discreetly whether he would prefer a Polish cook. He answered neither yes or no, but later, having thought it over, he returned to the question and told Caprio that perhaps for a time Mother Germana, the Sacred Heart sister who had been taking care of Msgr. Deskur, could help the Italian sisters.

Thus three days after his election, Thursday, October 19th, John Paul II could have at last a Polish dinner. For him and for his guests (Secretary General of the Synod of Bishops, Bishop Wladyslaw Rubin, rector of the Major Seminary of Krakow, Msgr. Franczziszek Maharski, and Msgr. Caprio), Sister Germana prepared boiled potatoes with sour cream, with meat which had first been fried and then boiled in the fashion of the countryside near Krakow.

Msgr. Caprio was the only one to drink the red wine served with the meal, the others contenting themselves with mineral water and several small glasses of vodka. A favorite dish of the Pope is *bigos,* a national specialty of Polish cuisine made of pork cut into small pieces and cabbage boiled for hours with onions.

Precedent-Setting Visit

Another happening not only showed the new Pope's sensitivity to his friends but also acted as the immediate expression of his style of action, with little regard for the customary, tradition-bound papal restraint. It may well illustrate that the new Pope has a style of his own.[206]

His countryman and friend Bishop Andrea Marie Deskur, president of the Pontifical Commission for Communications, was hospitalized after a heart attack three days before the Conclave, and his condition was quite serious. He had expressed his hope to live long enough to see the next pope. When the new Pope John Paul learned of this, he said to the deputy secretary of state, Archbishop Giuseppe Caprio: "Let's go."

The Secretariat of State immediately contacted the Ministry of the Interior through the nunciature in Italy. Very soon carabinieri and local police mushroomed in the streets that led to the Gemelli hospital, which seemed to be transformed into a barracks. Never in this century has it happened that a pope left the Vatican in the 24 hours after his election. In the streets and in the hospital, crowds greeted the new Pope enthusiastically.

Speaking in New Languages

John Paul introduced new ways also in his public addresses. In contrast with his predecessors, who customarily spoke the traditional languages: first Italian, then Latin for official occasions, and French chiefly for diplomatic groups, the new Pope introduced other languages to accommodate the audiences he addressed. Since he is a linguist, this did not pose any difficulty for him. In addition to Italian he makes every effort to learn any new tongue that he sees of benefit to his mission.

Thus weeks before Pope John Paul II set out for his trip to Santo Domingo and Mexico, he began to study Spanish, getting up an hour early at 5 A.M., to find the necessary time. The new Pope has shown himself fluent in English, French, German, Italian, and Latin. He has already achieved some proficiency in Spanish. He has a command of Russian, which he used in conversation with Soviet Foreign Minister Andrei Gromyko, January 25, 1979, in Rome.

The Pope took all the trouble to learn to speak to Latin Americans in their own tongue. It is typical of the enthusiastic and dogged determination the Pope brings to everything he tackles.

Other Departures from Traditional Ways

The Apostolic Palace was likewise transformed in appearance. While the Pope is essentially the man he always was, the manner of Vatican life is being revolutionized as his own style comes to the fore.

Even the pleasant, time-honored custom of the siesta, when all from prelates to workers would take time off for sleep in the early afternoon, is obsolescent.

The new Pontiff avoids the impersonal "we" that has marked even private papal conversation. Already, in John Paul II's first speech to the diplomatic corps, he referred to himself as "I."

Though the Pope addresses the visitors to the Vatican and other audiences with the hallowed greeting, "Praise be to Jesus Christ," yet after casual talk with them he startles with his crisp and loud signal that it is time for a blessing.

Unpretentious and Accessible

There is nothing at all stuffy in the Pope's manner. He acts freely during audiences. He walks instead of being carried on the throne, and expresses his feelings freely with the people, especially the children, to the great displeasure of his aides who prefer that the Pope restrain himself a little.

To the surprise of some, in his recent trip to Latin America (1979) as he stepped from the plane, he knelt and kissed the ground, which was certain to please the people of the respective countries. This friendly gesture Paul VI had made occasionally during visits in his Archdiocese of Milan and on his trips abroad. In the Dominican Republic the thousands allowed into the airport erupted in cheers, and in Mexico[207] bands burst out with marches and popular Mexican songs. Handed a shoulder-wide Mexican sombrero, he clapped it on his head over the traditional skull cap[208] or zucchetto.

His appearances are delightful in the sense that he acts openly, sincerely, and freely. A good illustration of this is his open relationship with members of the press. Not only did the new Pope give them a blessing and an address, but he held an impromptu press conference, answering the questions of each journalist in the appropriate language. (And he does this with complete self-confidence and without restraint on his emotions.) He gains thereby the lasting affection of international journalists, photographers, cameramen, and broadcasters, whose jobs are always difficult at best.

There were about 1,000 news personnel covering the Vatican events. He met them in the Hall of Benedictions in St. Peter's, walked through the Hall talking with them one by one, shaking hands with them, and often speaking directly into the microphones proffered him from the crowd.

Genuine Regard for People

The new Pope's directness was moreover shown in his relationship with the cardinals: in a break with normal ceremonial precedence, the second one to pledge obedience at the inauguration Mass was Stefan Cardinal Wyszynski of Warsaw, Primate of Poland. The Pope rose as the 77-year-old prelate approached and when Cardinal Wyszynski knelt at his feet, the Pope knelt also and held the Cardinal in a strong embrace.

At the same time his warm relationship with the others was also evidenced, for instead of receiving the cardinals' acts of homage while he was seated on the papal chair, John Paul II approached each cardinal individually.

During this short time, one can already see definitely that this Pope seems bent on restoring some of the informality and joyfulness the papacy had 20 years ago under John XXIII. In that process the present Pontiff has become the most visible pope in modern times.[209] Not only has he doubled the number of papal audiences but he has gone out from the Vatican to greet the Roman crowds—often with an eye for babies to kiss and bounce in the air.

Moreover, in the words of one long-time Vatican observer: "It's no act. He thrives on people. If he has his way, we are in for a return to old-fashioned religion with the accent on the family, the old values, and moral force as the key to relations between people and nations."[210] He appears to be truly a people's Pope.

Direct in Church Controversies

In regard to policies the Pope is direct also in Church controversies: he spoke out his strong and traditional views on celibacy for priests, on abortion, on the unbreakable bond of marriage, and on the necessity for priests to wear clerical attire and for religious women to wear habits. His stands are causing concern among some liberal Catholics in Europe as well as in the United States and a storm of angry press commentaries and cartoons from those who would uphold Italy's liberal abortion law.

Yet there are among those who oppose John Paul II's ideas some who think his stress on religious discipline is aimed at the conservatives, so that they may support his ideas on social issues. But friend or foe to his ideas, all agree that he brings a new vigor to the Church.

Evidently he wants for the Church, so to speak, a clean house. He believes that self-reform must precede a reform of any kind; it is in this perspective that one should view his strong statements about the principles involved. He has expressed these views clearly, directly, and without any "diplomatic cover-up."

Understanding toward Those Outside the Church

In contrast to his strict and firm stand on affairs within the Church, the Pope is generous, conciliatory, benevolent, and understanding to those outside, i.e., without the Church. As one critic expressed it: "He is general to his priests (staff) but friend to the faithful."

Thus, hours after his inauguration Mass the Pope met with the representatives of other Christian Churches. He affirmed: "The commitment to the ecumenical movement as it has been solemnly expressed in the Second Vatican Council is irreversible."[211] Continuing in this reassurance, he added:

> Your presence in fact bears witness to our common willingness to establish closer and closer relationships among ourselves and to overcome the divisions inherited from the past. The divisions are, as we have already said, an intolerable scandal putting an obstacle in the way of the proclamation of the good news of salvation given in Jesus Christ.[212]

Collegiality and Popular Devotions

John Paul is open with the people. At his first general audience, held October 25, 1978, he lamented the fact that "one pope is not enough to embrace everyone." He made this comment after greeting, with an individual embrace, many of those who attended the audience. He then added: "Thanks be to God that there was, not only one, but 12 Apostles; thus, with collegiality, we can touch everyone."[213]

This is not only a typical example of the Pope's quick and skilled pragmatic use of an occasion for a purpose, but that very point, collegiality, seemed one that might become a landmark of Pope John II's papacy. And although in his first weeks as Pontiff, he provided no blueprint for the future, nor showed indication of intent to produce one, a few points nevertheless, like this one, were clear.

The new Pope showed quickly that he had no mind to be confined within the Vatican only. Ten days after his inauguration, he went to the papal summer villa at Castel Gandolfo. A little later he flew by helicopter to the Polish-run shrine of the Presentation of Our Lady of Mantorella, about 50 miles from Rome. Since in the past he had visited practically all the Marian shrines in Europe and elsewhere, this could signal what may well become another hallmark of his papacy: a new burgeoning of popular devotions, especially Marian ones,[214] a point of practical devotion so much overshadowed by post-Vatican II's theology.[215] In this regard he does not miss the opportunity to stress the rosary as his favorite prayer and the Stations of the Cross as an effective devotion.

Resemblances to Predecessors

In speeches, public appearances, and meetings or conferences with various groups, the Pope's personality has emerged as somewhat like one or the other of his immediate predecessors. Clearly though, he is more at ease with the crowds, more outgoing and ebullient than was Paul VI, and his spontaneity is somewhat more muted than that of John Paul I.

Unlike John Paul I, who left many with the impression of "an ordinary man to whom something extraordinary happened,"[216] the present Pope, from the moment of his first appearance, has given the impression of a man fully in control of the situation, aware of his own abilities, and confident that he can handle the job.

Again, unlike John Paul I, who almost immediately after his election sweepingly reappointed all Curia officials, the present Pope cautiously in his first weeks made but one major appointment: he renamed Cardinal Villot secretary of state "until it is provided otherwise."[217]

Relations with the Roman Curia

His action was received as a clear sign that great changes would be made in all departments of the Roman Curia and that the new Pope takes his time to get acquainted with the problems as well as with the people. This careful procedure perhaps reveals to us that John Paul II is definitely his own man, decisive and somewhat authoritative, but a forceful leader in his own right, for he has all the qualities of one as expected of him by Catholic and Christian people.

This Pope was expected to have little trouble in learning to govern the Roman Curia or directing the Holy See's network of diplomatic activity, for unlike his predecessor, who inferred openly that he knew little about the Curia, this Pope John Paul II was well acquainted with the functioning of the central offices of the Church.

As Cardinal, he had served on several Vatican Congregations and World Synods of Bishops and was a member of various curial bodies. While in Rome on Church business, he lived with the Polish Curia officials and heard from them about their work. All this indicates that he came well prepared to his pontificate and that he has no need to learn the issues while in the office.

Issues Facing the Church

Furthermore, all Wojtyla's major speeches opening his pontificate highlight some very important issues that now face the Church, and these help considerably for every good Christian to perceive that a new type of papacy is coming. At the Mass inaugurating his pontificate he stressed the spiritual and pastoral role of the papacy and the Church's primary mission to announce the good news of salvation of mankind in Christ. Addressing the diplomats, he pointed out that the Church's primary role in the international sphere is the formation of consciences.

Nor did he rule out direct intervention by the Church in political issues when human rights or values were at stake.

He promised that the Church would continue to engage in dialogue with nations and international organizations to promote peace, justice, and progress.

An issue most talked about following the election of a Polish Pope was its possible effect on Pope John Paul's policy of detente with Eastern European nations. The new Pope mentioned free exercise of religion several times shortly after his election, but did not discuss it or relate matters in detail.

Versatility in Handling Communists

On at least two occasions, however, the Pope publicly expressed the hope that Poland would ease travel restrictions so that Polish Catholics could visit him more freely. He also indicated a strong interest in his own travel back to Poland, possibly for a major religious festival in 1979.

The Pope's versatility in handling the Communists is, according to Polish Professor Kolakowski, "very important, since he has spent his pastoral life in a politically adverse, but in a socially friendly, environment. He knows very well the essence of confrontation between the Church and the Communist system, and this is greatly comforting in our time of crisis."[218]

Likewise, Professor George H. Williams of the Harvard Divinity School insists also that the fact that the new Pope has mastered Marxist dialectic and can therefore deal effectively with Marxists of the Euro-Communist kind and also of the type dominated by the Soviet Union, probably may help also in dealing with the "Italian social and political problems, which now frequently involve the Italian Communist party," This is without a doubt a great asset to a new papacy,[219] serving to increase the confidence of the people in a new Pope and their respect for the papacy.

Advocate of Social Change

Another ingredient of a new papacy is the circumstance that the present Pope is a champion of social change, for he considers himself a friend of the downtrodden, the handicapped, and the poor. His experience in Poland prompts his warning: The Church should not interfere actively in politics nor entangle itself in any way in the Marxist ideology.

Many Church observers believe, accordingly, that he will strive for a balance of the political goals of progressives and the evangelical emphasis of conservatives. Attempt at such a balance was made in Latin America with some success[220] despite some fears that the Puebla Conference could erupt in a bitter squabble among the bishops and among the proponents and foes of liberation theology.[221]

In the direction of peace, John Paul II appears to have taken a line of conciliation, with dramatic success in averting a shooting war between Chile and Argentina. A papal envoy shuttling across the Andes persuaded both nations to withdraw their troops and warships from disputed islands near Cape Horn in favor of papal-mediated negotiations.[222] In this the present Pope is a faithful follower of his zealous predecessors, the peacemakers Leo XIII, Benedict XV, Pius XI, and Pius XII, but especially of Paul VI with his dramatic personal appearance before the United Nations in New York in 1967 with his plea for "no more wars."

Champion of Human Rights

Very distinctly, however, John Paul II appears in the role of a champion for human rights, a topic which may well be a highlight of his pontificate. Since the day of his election, his fellow Poles have clamored for the Pope to come to their national event, that marking the 900th anniversary of the death of St. Stanislaus, Poland's patron saint who became a symbol of Polish resistance to every form of government tyranny and oppression.

The anniversary of the martyrdom of the patron saint of Poland is the date that John Paul II had selected for his first return to his homeland, yet mention of the saint in the

Pope's Christmas message was deleted as potentially explosive. He said in part: "We see in St. Stanislaus a spokesman of the most essential human rights and the rights of the nation. True freedom of the nation depends upon those rights."[223]

Even the Communists are aware of the parallels to the present-day situation in the minds of many Polish Catholics. The reason is obvious to experts on Eastern Europe: Poland's rulers fear that the return of the Pope for the country's greatest sacred event in a century might result in an uncontrollable flood of religious and nationalistic sentiment. While unlikely to topple the regime, it would emphasize the relative unpopularity of Soviet-style Communism and anger the Kremlin.

To understand the reason for all the maneuverings of the Polish government to postpone the Pope's visit till June 2-10, 1979, thus avoiding the traditional May festivities in honor of St. Stanislaus, one must know the background. The Pope generously accepted this compromise,[224] and postponed also the main festivities until a time when he can be present.

Fearless Social Activist

The Pope's insistence on using this historical event in its fullest manifestation shows that he himself is an advocate of every human right, including religious freedom. The new Pope is fearless whenever he defends truth, especially in these last years after the Helsinki Conference (1975) when human rights were at stake. He upholds the right to freedom, not only political freedom and liberty of conscience, but also freedom of movement and the right to information without any government censorship.

His concern for human rights should also be seen as the motivation behind his visit to Latin America and the projected one to Lebanon that might help to end civil warfare in that country. In this respect, special care should be taken to include in the Pope's concern for human rights his adamant defense of the social rights[225] of human beings—particularly in terms of distributive and social justice—of which he proved to be so forceful a proponent all his life. His was, moreover, a delicate concern for all involved.

Even more important, however, is that his is an experimental knowledge of the social problems gained in his homeland; and this has to be taken seriously especially by all his Communist or Socialist challengers worldwide. Although several previous popes distinguished themselves as social theorists by well-known social encyclicals,[226] including those of Pope John XXIII and Paul VI, this new Pope goes even further; he is not only a social teacher or doctrinaire, but a social activist par excellence. This makes his service very different and marks certainly a milestone in the new papacy.

Promising Reformer

Not the least sign of John Paul's new style is the fact that he appears to be a promising reformer. In major addresses to the College of Cardinals the new Pope emphasized continuing reform and spiritual renewal of the Church in the spirit of the Second Vatican Council. "For us," he said, "it is a formal obligation that [the Council decrees] be studiously put into effect." He emphasized in particular the development of a deeper understanding of the nature of the Church and the way in which it acts out the mystery of salvation in history.

His stress on collegiality in this context and a suggestion that collegial structures,[227] especially the Synod of Bishops, might be developed more fully led to widespread speculation that his intent is to go much further than Pope Paul had gone in making the bishops share more fully in development of Church policy.

The future is hidden, but it is apparent that the See of Peter is in the care of a capable and confident man. An extraordinary period of papal transition is now past. The

Church now turns its eyes expectantly toward a new profile of the Pope.

New Style as Outgrowth of Pope's Personality

This new style of papacy is a natural outgrowth of a new personality of the upcoming Pope. The most valuable testimony of this is that of Bishop Wladyslaw Rubin, the secretary general of the World Synod of Bishops, an intimate friend of John Paul II since 1962, who characterizes the Pope in this way:

Ability to Think on His Feet

The Holy Father is not a man who will be buried by functionaries. He is a man who demands to know what is going on at all times and you must show him. He is a man of many exceptional qualities which include great intelligence, good disposition, deep religious feelings, and deep compassion. Probably his greatest work talent is being able to get right to the heart of the most complex of problems.

Now Pope Paul VI wasn't like that. Pope Paul VI was very intellectual and he would speak at length about a problem before he could begin to go into the problem. This Pope goes right to the core. It is a talent few men have. He is a man about whom you don't list a lot of qualities, and then say "but this or that." With him there are no buts. He is very outgoing man and he likes to be with people.

He is extremely interesting to speak with. He can easily present very clearly what he wants to say. He has the mind of a philosopher and theologian but can express those thoughts so they can easily be understood. He writes all his own speeches, except for those dealing with a particular group or issue. He has a faculty for speech writing and writing of any kind and he has done a great deal of it. He writes fast and he writes well.

Man of No Pretense

The Holy Father is a very natural man. When he was named a cardinal he did not change one bit. When he became pope, he did not change. He is the same today to his friends as he was when he was just a bishop.

Because of his physical ruggedness and athletic stance and movements there are times Pope John Paul II doesn't look like what the world has come to expect of a pope. Sometimes the way he moves around and waves his arms and laughs and hugs old friends and picks up children to kiss, you think he does not act like a pope. But you must understand that this man is so very genuine. No pretenses.

Good Sense of Humor

I think he is enjoying being Pope just as he enjoyed being all the other things he has been over the years. He lives life as it comes and he always enjoys it. If God wants him to do something, he does it with joy, liberty and conviction. That is him. The moment he was elected, he became Pope as completely as he ever will be.

He does everything in that manner. He has a very good sense of humor and is able to laugh at himself when it is called for. I do not mean that he sits around telling jokes, I mean that the Holy Father can see amusement in certain situations. And most valuable of all, he can laugh at himself.

I was not surprised that Cardinal Wojtyla was selected by the cardinals once they decided on choosing a non-Italian.

I think the cardinals started out trying to find another Pope John Paul I and when they couldn't find one and they started looking outside Italy for a pope, I honestly think Cardinal Wojtyla was an obvious choice because of his qualities.[228]

A Pope with Charisma

Bishop Rubin's characterization of John Paul II is indeed a festive profile of a dynamic, religious man with a vision of the modern Church for modern times; with its truly spiritual mission[229] in the spirit of the Pope's prayer: "O Mother, help us to be faithful stewards of the great mysteries of God. Help us to teach the truth proclaimed by your Son and to spread love, which is the chief commandment and the first fruit of the Holy Spirit."[230]

All the people, conservatives as well as progressives in the Church, have much to look forward to from John Paul II, a man who has suffered a lot and who all his life has survived by outmaneuvering the wily governors of his native Poland and elsewhere. He is certainly a Pope who is not easy to label as going in any specific direction, since he intends to be in Christ's following "all to all" and is very much determined to be one "with a style all his own,"[231] attempting to effect a balance of all extremes and converging them—to use Pierre Teilhard de Chardin's[232] term—into a Divine Milieu of brothers and sisters and all people of good will.

Polish-born Zbigniew Brzezinski, national security affairs adviser to President Carter, said: "I am delighted by this choice. The Pope is a theologian who understands the reality of the modern world; he is a former worker-priest who has a feeling for suffering and hardship; he is a dedicated leader of the faith and of his people. He will make a great Pope."[233]

Rabbi Balfour Brickner characterized the Pope thus: "The man has charisma. I liked his looks and found myself initially drawn to him. But there is more. In his face, one finds a kindness, a gentleness. It seemed to me that his academic background, the scholarly side of his personality, is his obvious strength. The combination is compelling. I felt myself in the presence of a man who takes his personal spirituality very, very seriously."[234]

He will surely know how to satisfy both the Catholics who want a strictly law-and-order life in the Church and their fellow Christians seeking "the freedom . . . of the sons of God" (cf. Gal 3:26; Rom 8:21), preached by Christ in the Gospel, so that all of good will shall find benefit from the ever-ready and generous service of the "servant of servants" (title given for centuries to the pope; cf. Is 42:1-4; 49:1-7; 50:4-11; 52:13—53:12) that he has declared himself to be.

Chapter 15

THE SPIRITUALITY OF JOHN PAUL II

Testimony of Cardinal Wyszynski

ALTHOUGH high-caliber spirituality is an expected prerequisite for any pope as vicar of Christ, certainly that of John Paul II is a natural outgrowth of a personality maturing through many a hardship, suffering, sacrifice, persecution, and struggle, a journey really as St. Ignatius worded it, *per aspera ad astra* ("through adversities to the stars").

Before giving a detailed analysis or delving into important testimony of the eyewitness, it should be most helpful to sketch the spiritual profile of the present Pope, adequately and properly.

Certainly the most interesting are the remarks of the man who knew him best. Of the new Pope, Cardinal Wyszynski[235] said:

A Man with a Good Heart

The election of Cardinal Wojtyla as Pope is an extraordinary event for the Church Universal, and especially for the Church of Poland. This election is beyond the normal course of events in that the death of one pope is necessary before the election of another.

The cardinals, who dedicate their lives to the Church, sought a man with a living faith, one who conscientiously carries out his episcopal office, one whose education is appropriate. Above all else, they sought one with a good heart, a man who is good, open, sensitive to the problems of others, who is able to show forth in its fullness God's love, and who gives it out to the world.

So universal and so strong was the desire to make such a choice that it overcame the 400-year-old barrier of Church tradition, the barriers of language and of nationality. It has elected a non-Italian Pope. How will the other cardinals, how will the Roman people accept this?

The Romans did indeed receive their new Bishop and Pope so sincerely and enthusiastically that all saw in it the spirit of a living faith and a hope that the Church may easily, in this time of constantly growing nationalism, overcome this barrier also, one which till then had seemed insurmountable. By this election the evangelical spirit of universal brotherhood, the unity of all languages and of all nations was made manifest, as well as the vitality of an eternally young Church, concerning which not a few had already indicated considerable doubt.

Sincere Faith and Prayerful Spirit

For the time being I cannot speak adequately of the life of this man who is so close to me in many ways, who has been for so many years my closest collaborator. In this cooperation our friendship grew steadily, and our love for the Church and for our Polish fatherland.

What can be, however, of interest to the world in this new Pope, who comes to Rome from Poland? It is his sincere faith and his prayerful spirit.

I came to know Wojtyla about 20 years ago, when I announced to him the will of the Holy Father, who had named him an auxiliary bishop of the Krakow Archdiocese. Then already I recognized in his face a spiritual readiness and a deep spirituality. I told myself: "Here is the man for whom prayers are his personal power, to be got only on one's knees, with folded hands, as is the faith of children."

From his fully developed personality as philosopher and moral theologian, prayer shines out in the opportunity of daily life and of the moment, for fervor was already there, when he made his daily Stations of the Cross, when he celebrated Holy Mass, or when he talked, sang, or conversed with his faithful people.

Character of Goodly Fellowship

His education is a good one, fitting the university professor. Nonetheless, even with his many books, manuscripts, articles, and dissertations he has never lost his character of goodly fellowship, of the affable man who laughs with those who enjoy themselves, who is ready to enter into sports events: to play volleyball or soccer, to hike in the mountains, to walk the forests and fields.

So much did he enjoy walking in the meadows and in the woods, or strolling the streets of Royal Krakow, that tears come to my eyes when I but think that he must leave these beautiful places. The question comes to my mind: "Mountain-man, are you not sad that you must leave this, your native land?"

Our Mountain-man from Wadowice, when from the Vatican windows his spirit will look toward his forests, and when he will have dried the tears from his eyes, will surely answer: "It must be so for God's sake, for Christ, His Church, her mission and her great goals which are before those of all mankind."

Yes, it is a great sacrifice and denial of self for him to leave his beloved fatherland, whose gem is Bishop St. Stanislaus of Wawel, to leave after him the royal tombs, to go from dear Queen St. Hedwig, to leave childhood behind and the smiling eyes of all the students, those to whom he gave his heart, his thoughts, his very life, his own unforgettable smile which attracted them to Christ and to His Blessed Mother.

Poland's Gift to the Church

Let each heart learn from such a great person his sacrifice, and let each consecrate himself to God and the Church so dear and so close to us. Now must he let go his own customary Stations of the Cross and must begin those which, for centuries, many of the faithful have made who follow the Cross of Christ into their eternal homeland.

The native and the lost paradise will be now for you the way of the nations to Christ, Whose Vicar you now are. Let the Blessed Virgin of Czestochowa, the Queen of Poland, give you happiness and peace!

Rejoice, Poland, for you gave the Church and Christ's Mother the most beautiful flower which has sprung from the struggles and sufferings of our Nation![236]

Based on Christian Personalism

Such a tribute given by this spiritual prelate accentuates the circumstance that the spirituality of a new pope is a real one, earned through the experiences of life, one learned not only from books or extracted from theology, but got on his knees. His spirituality is no cliché.[237] It is his own, it is deep, reaching the living waters of mysticism of St. John of the Cross, about whom he wrote his doctoral dissertation (1948), and it is personalist, which quality he acquired when he prepared his habilitation thesis, "The Possibilities of Catholic Ethics on the Basis of Max Scheler" (1953).

This work reveals that his spiritual maturity went hand in hand with his intellectual formation, together with the experience of living faith with no vacuum left between theory and practice, for it was dynamic not only in its motivation but in its strength, simply the wellsprings of his own spiritual life. His spirituality is solidly based on the theology of Christian personalism.

Personalism, as a philosophical movement, has taken divergent directions. Owing to a logical postulate that religion is (a) objectively conditioned but (b) subjectively made, it makes of it a personalized affair. Its essential, unifying perspective, however, is that all thought should be referred to personhood. Persons and personal relations are more basic than things, more basic than abstract ideas like being, nature, substance, or essence. Personalism insists on the supreme dignity of the human person and the centrality of personhood for understanding all reality.[238]

Leading Exponents of Personalism

The best expression of this fact is what is called the history of personalism as represented by (a) Emmanuel

Mounier, (b) Gabriel Marcel, (c) Martin Buber, (d) Jacques Maritain, and others. Thus Mounier's *Philosophy of Personalism*[239] is an attempt to re-create a sense of spirituality to challenge modern mass dehumanization. One has to free himself from self-interest and have a dialogue with others. There is no true inwardness that is not nourished by its interaction with an outer reality.

Marcel's *Ontological Personalisms*[240] insists that one is inseparable from a situation and must relate directly to the circumstances. To enter into a loving relationship requires a person to exercise all feelings of one's personality to become aware of other persons so that mutual enrichment may be felt.

Buber's theory of *I-Thou*[241] says that the *Thou* must be encountered in the full freedom of his otherness that is addressed and responds. In meeting another person, one meets oneself and, using the same *I-Thou* relationship, one may meet God as well. He sums up the whole idea that "all real living is meeting." God is also this "eternal Thou we meet in all our relations with other persons, or even in the deepest part of our being." In the depersonalizing world of today, it seems appropriate that someone should be able to contrive a means for one to reach God and to believe in Him again.

Maritain's personalism[242] involves one also in a complete relationship with great emphasis on a value, worth, and need of such personalization to make one's religion effective. Personalism insists on the supreme dignity of the human person and the centrality of personhood for understanding all reality.

Examples of the Pope's Personalism

The spirit of personalism breathes throughout the entire pastoral *Constitution on the Church in the Modern World,*[243] on whose preparatory stages Cardinal Wojtyla labored and on whose final stages he had more than a little influence.

Especially important is the chapter, "The Dignity of the Human Person." Here the Council canonized the basic principle of personalism when it stated: "All things on earth should be related to man as their center and crown" (chapter 1, no. 12-22).[244]

The challenge of atheistic humanism had obviously been for Wojtyla an important issue. He has wrestled with the thought of such critics of Christianity as Ludwig Feuerbach and Friedrich Nietzsche, with the existentialism of Martin Heidegger, and the humanism of Polish philosopher Leszek Kolakowski[245] and others.

The experience of Vatican II must rank along with Wojtyla's experience of the war, the Nazi occupation of Poland, and atheistic Communism as having left an indelible imprint on his personality and spirituality. Even when he speaks about God, he does so from a personalist standpoint. "We cannot think about our lives other than by looking at the personal character of our existence," he said, "by looking at the intelligence and freedom which distinguish us from the rest of visible creation."

As persons, we are pilgrims of the absolute: "We tend to God as to our ultimate end. We are on a pilgrimage to the Holy City (Ps 122:1-4), to the sanctuary accessible only to us. The dimension of the Holy, of the sacred, is the highest and definitive sphere of human existence. It is the sphere of the fullest self-realization of the human person." Referring to St. Augustine, he affirms of the human heart: "The deepest desires of the spirit cannot be satisfied except by God alone."

This basic transcendence of the human spirit unites the Church with all peoples. Creation and covenant reveal a God who, from the very beginning, desired to be a Gift for people and source of all gifts: "To be created means to be gifted, to be constantly gifted with existence." This is essential for Wojtyla, who firmly believes that "from this consciousness there must be created another culture, another civilization, another system of economics, of production and distribution of the world's goods, another understanding of values."

Humanistic and Phenomenological Approach

As St. Augustine prayed, "May I know you, may I know myself," Wojtyla also reflects: "The human heart reveals that human existence[246] means existing 'for,' existing in relationship, in self-giving" and this is a true personalism; whatever the topic, Christ, or conscience, sin or salvation, he takes always a personalist approach.

Perhaps this aspect is best clarified by Professor George Williams of Harvard when he asked: "What is man?" That question will be central to John Paul II's papacy. "He is very much interested in the human person and in personal relationships. He is so much concerned with the doctrine of man that he might be moved to call a Council. I think he would like to clarify new kinds of alienation, new kinds of exploitation. He has the philosophical and theological training to preside over such a Council and for the first time, I think the experts will not necessarily be Catholic. John Paul is a blend of finely honed intellect and deep spirituality."[247]

Another Boston-area intellectual, Anna Teresa Tymieniecka, head of the Institute for Advanced Phenomenological Research, praises Wojtyla as an expert in phenomenology, a theory of knowledge that bases scientific objectivity upon the unique nature of subjective human perception. He has written a major work, *Person and Act* (1969), which she is translating into English. Summarizing the Pope's complex thought, she says: "He stresses the irreducible value of the human person. He finds a spiritual dimension in human interaction, and that leads him to a profound humanistic conception of society."[248]

A Spirituality of Contestation

There is another characteristic of Wojtyla's spirituality, namely, that it is marked by the feeling of opposing to or being opposed from, and the opposition he consistently encountered from the Communist regime never permitted his personalism to become optimistic or naive, but always rather realistic. His spiritual life has known too well the uses of adversity. Jesus Christ for him is not only the Prophet of Christian personalism, but also a sign of contradiction, "a sign that is spoken against" (Lk 2:34).

We are witnessing, he said, a programmed attack on religion and faith in God. But it is only a contemporary expression of a process that goes back to the beginning of human history. The sin of Adam is not some Promethean "I will not serve," but a turning to the world as a field for autonomous human endeavor.[249] The anthropocentrism[250] that sees humanity as ultimately alone, as beyond God, beyond good and evil, he describes as the antithesis of the Christian method, an anti-gospel.[251] The depth dimension of human existence, where we encounter the Holy, is precisely that sphere where we achieve fullest self-realization as persons.

Yet Marxists and other secular humanists see God and the idea of the Holy[252] as alienating us from ourselves, as the source of dehumanizing self-alienation.[253] Not only the Christian individual but the Church as institution finds itself caught up in a struggle against the program that is bent upon desacralizing the world, a program that cannot help but dehumanize humanity.

The Dignity of Human Beings

The Pope has touched already several times on the dignity of human beings. One instance was his *urbi et orbi* speech for Christmas:

> *Uniqueness of Every Human Being*
>
> I am addressing this message to every human being, to man in his humanity. Christmas is the feast of man.

A human being is born. He is one of millions and millions of people who have been born, are being born, and will be born on earth. . . . It was not without reason that Jesus came into the world when a census was being held, when a Roman emperor wanted to know the number of subjects in his territory. A human being is an object to be counted, something considered under the aspect of quantity, one of many millions. Yet, at the same time, he is a single being unique and unrepeatable.

If we celebrate with such solemnity the birth of Jesus, it is to bear witness that every human being is somebody unique and unrepeatable.

If our human statistics, human categories, human political, economic, and social systems and mere human possibilities fail to ensure that man can be born, live, and act as one who is unique and unrepeatable, then all this is ensured by God. For God and before God, the human being is always unique and unrepeatable, somebody thought of and chosen from eternity, someone called and identified by his own name. . . .

A New Human Dimension

A human being lives, works, creates, suffers, fights, loves, hates, doubts, falls and recovers, in fellowship with others.

I address, therefore, all the various communities—the peoples, the nations, the regimes, the political, economic, social, and cultural systems—and I say: Accept the great truth concerning man, accept the full truth concerning man that was uttered on Christmas night, accept this dimension of man that was opened for all human beings on this holy night, accept the mystery in which every human being lives since Christ was born; respect this mystery; allow this mystery to act in every human being; allow him to develop in the outward conditions of his earthly existence.

Humanity's power resides in this mystery. The power that permeates everything that is human. Do not make it hard for that power to exercise its influence. Do not destroy its influence. Everything that is human grows from this power. Without this power it perishes. Without this power it falls to ruin.[254]

A Spirituality of Liberation

As Christ is a sign of contradiction, so a good Christian human being has to share the same lot, for the same reason and for the sake of Christ. This is part of one's coidentification with Christ in the Christlike manner.

Although the spirituality of the present Pope is definitely personalist, it is by no means individualist or without practical, social, and economic consequences. Christian discipleship, continuing the ministry of Jesus, meets opposition because of its implications. The Pope asks:

> Who is Jesus Christ for whole continents, traditions, cultures, political situations? He is a sign of liberation from unjust economic and social structures in Latin America and elsewhere, and a sign of liberation for people from whom freedom of conscience and religion has been taken away or limited. He is—and certainly should be—a reproach to affluent consumer societies. He is also the basis for the self-identity of those nations beginning their independent existence. He is the Word of God's wisdom for the ancient tradition of spirit and culture to be found among the peoples of Asia.[255]

In the same connection—according to the Pope—"the theology of liberation" is often associated (sometimes too exclusively) with Latin America; but it must be admitted that one of the great contemporary theologians, Hans Urs von Balthasar,[256] is right when he demands a theology of liberation on a universal scale. Only the contexts are different, but the reality itself of the freedom for which Christ set us free (Gal 5:1) is universal. The task of theology is to find its real significance in the different concrete and contemporary contexts.[257]

Joyful Union with the Church

Another aspect of the Pope's spirituality is, as manifested in all his public appearances, its joyful tone. One can feel it from the spontaneity of his zeal, his charisma, and his complete devotion in everything he does. He shares St. Philip Neri's hilarious mind with the readiness of St. Don Bosco for "my Father's business." For some he is a "workaholic," so to speak, to others a true zealot for the Church.

His identification with the Church, the institution, through his willing, generous, and dynamic apostolic involvement reveals that his *sentire cum Ecclesia* ("union with the mind of the Church") is deeply rooted in his priesthood in a relationship of "another Christ" to His mystical body, so that institutional religion is absorbed in his personal experience as an integrated act of worship. This is a truly appropriate foundation for his mission as Vicar of Christ.

Obviously the devotional heritage and piety of his native land are also integral to his spiritual life. With warm affection he cites Polish hymnology and the popular Polish Lenten devotions, prays the rosary, makes his Stations of the Cross, takes part in pilgrimages and other popular religious events, each replete with its own folklore.

His association with Poland's intelligentsia and the scholarly world brought him to follow St. Paul's advice that "your faith should be reasonable but firm." Thus, beneath his theological and cultural sophistication was a well-grounded faith, implicitly integrated with his religious make-up. He had no room for the usual academic skepsis,[258] but rather followed the well-known maxim of St. Augustine: *Credo ut intelligam* ("I believe that I may understand") together with the other popular theological dictum: *Fides quaerens intellectum* ("Faith seeking understanding") (cf. John Paul II, *Redemptor hominis,* March 4, 1979, note 150).

Devotion to Mary

As a result Karol kept not only the vitality of his faith, as manifested by his practice, but also the simplicity[259] of his faith. Biographers trace these qualities to the early influence of a man who has already been mentioned and whom the new Pope is said to regard also as having been his spiritual mentor, Jan Tyranowski, a humble tailor.

One must not pass over, in this connection, the new Pope's zealous devotion to the Blessed Mother, who perhaps in some way substituted for his beloved deceased mother. His Marian devotional dedication is so wholesome that not only did he always pray for, experience, and enjoy her protection, but he also placed his whole pontificate under the special protection of the Blessed Mother, as it were to verify that well-known motto: *Per Mariam ad Jesum* ("To Jesus through Mary").

In view of historical old Poland's tradition of a Marian cult, one has to say that the new Pope is in this also a true Pole. Daily recitation of the rosary, a proverbial characteristic of Polish Catholicism, for a philosopher Pope no less than for any unlettered villager, is especially typical of it.

Faith Supported by Works

Another aspect of Wojtyla's spirituality is seen in a *living faith,* one that is not only practiced but also substantially supported with good deeds. This sense of the social gospel is so well developed that he believes and urges that some social reforms be effected by it. A classical example can be seen in his trip to Latin America.[260] His compassion for the poor is completely integral with his personality owing not only to his experience of the difficult years of his childhood and his adolescence, but to the great suffering his country witnessed.

He has a good understanding of the biblical adage: "The poor you will have always with you," and of the eight beatitudes, since these are his chosen spiritual foundation (Mt 5:3ff). This is the reason he has such appeal to all kinds of people, with special attraction for the poor, who sense his sincere and compassionate feeling for them. As certain things in one's life cannot be learned but must be experienced before they can be effective, so Wojtyla had plenty of experience of poverty, difficulties, tensions, and chicaneries in his personal life. Thus, compassion is truly his natural and religious feeling and is accepted as authentic by the faithful.

The new Pope has touched several times already on the need of faith in Christ and the necessity to apply that faith in efforts to feed, clothe, and care for the needy. He speaks often and sometimes so effusively[261] that it was and is difficult to sort out the emphases. The shape of his attitudes seems, nonetheless, to surface. He asks a comprehensive approach toward mankind, one that views spiritual, social, cultural, and political matters in an ordered yet critical contingency in their relations to one another, with the aim to help the poor of the world. The frequency of his talks about the needs of the poor is clear evidence that the mind of the new Pope is preoccupied with the topic and that his spirituality is indeed socially sensitive.

An Ascetical Spirituality

This spirituality has also an ascetical[262] connotation in the sense that one's spiritual life should have a deep detachment from worldly comfort. It is imperative that one who strives for perfection should have also that spirit of internal poverty of St. Francis of Assisi with his minimal needs for one's life, reading, the evangelical simplicity. "It is witness of that surprising holiness that passed here like a great breath of the Spirit," said Pope John Paul II while visiting the Basilica of St. Francis in Assisi on November 5, 1978,

> . . . a breath in which St. Francis of Assisi participated, as well as his spiritual sister St. Clare and so many other saints born from their evangelical spirituality. The Franciscan message spread far beyond the frontiers of Italy, and soon it also reached Polish soil, from whence I come. And it still operates there with abundant fruits, as moreover in other countries of the world and in other continents.

> I will tell you that, as archbishop of Krakow, I have lived near a very ancient Franciscan church, and from time to time I went there to pray, to make the "Via Crucis" ["Way of the Cross"] and to visit the chapel of Our Lady of Sorrow. Unforgettable moments for me. One cannot fail to mention here that it was just from this magnificent trunk of Franciscan spirituality that the Blessed Maximilian Kolbe came, a special patron in our difficult times.
>
> I cannot pass over in silence furthermore the fact that just here, in Assisi, in this Basilica, in the year 1253 Pope Innocent IV proclaimed Saint the bishop of Krakow, the martyr Stanislaus, now the Patron Saint of Poland, whose unworthy successor I was until a short time ago.[263]

And overwhelmed by this historical dynamic retrospection, the Pope reaffirmed the relevance of this Franciscan spirituality:

> Today, therefore, setting foot for the first time as Pope at the sources of this great breath of the Spirit, of this marvelous revival of the Church and of Christianity in the thirteenth century, linked with the figure of St. Francis of Assisi, my heart opens to our Patron Saint and cries:
>
> "You, who brought Christ so close to your age, help us to bring Christ close to our age, to our difficult and critical times. Help us! These times are waiting for Christ with great anxiety, although many men of our age are not aware of it. We are approaching the year A.D. 2000. Will they not be times that will prepare us for a rebirth of Christ, for a new Coming?"
>
> Every day, we express in the eucharistic prayer our expectation, addressed to him alone, our Redeemer and Savior, to him who is the fulfillment of the history of man and of the world.
>
> Help us, St. Francis of Assisi, to bring Christ closer to the Church and to the world of today.
>
> You, who bore in your heart the vicissitudes of your contemporaries, help us, with our heart close to the Redeemer's heart, to embrace the events of the men of our time. The difficult social, economic and political

problems, the problems of culture and contemporary civilization, all the sufferings of the man of today, his doubts, his denials, his disorders, his tensions, his complexes, his worries. . . .

Help us to express all this in the simple and fruitful language of the Gospel. Help us to solve everything in an evangelical key, in order that Christ himself may be "the Way—the Truth—the Life" for modern man.[264]

With such an undertone of this Franciscan spirituality in the Pope's personality all his endeavors for a simplicity of outlook on the papacy as well as that of its occupant are well understood.

Defender of the Faith

There is yet another part of John Paul's spirituality—its fighting character in the sense that he is a defender of the faith. And what is more distinctive in him is that this mandate to defend the faith is accepted by him not only as an obligation and a responsibility but as a privilege to serve. His free, willing, generous, and loving mandate is to be fulfilled as his life's mission.

This again is a result of his endless struggles with the Polish Communist regime in defense of the rights of the Church and of the human rights of individuals. The new Pope expressed his readiness to defend steadfastly his Church as he mentioned in his inaugural address in a story of St. Peter's fleeing from Rome and his meeting with Christ carrying His cross and his subsequent return to Rome, as told so beautifully in the novel *Quo vadis Domine?* written by the Polish author Henryk Sienkiewicz.[265]

This fighting spirit for Church rights developed in him from his underground activities in the struggle for national survival. It is an integral part of his witnessing to Christ who is being opposed. This sense of defense of the Church was a necessary sequence of his deep sense of loyalty, which always was a distinct mark of his character—a mark which was also a basis for heroism of the Christians in the Roman catacombs.

Compassion on Oppressed Christians

From past experiences with Polish Communists Wojtyla has a special understanding for the oppressed Christians behind the Iron Curtain, a sympathy one can feel in his warm relationship with all the bishops of these countries; especially has it been so with Cardinal Frantisek Tomasek of Prague, whom he assured: "We are very close to each other and now shall be even closer, because from now on I am also entrusted with care for you. I assure you that I shall do all I can for the growth of spiritual life in your country. I shall give you a special place in my prayers. Please give my greetings to your bishops, priests, members of the Holy Orders, and all the faithful. Also I shall count on your prayers very much."

Later, he said with special emphasis: "We in Poland are especially grateful to you, the Czechs, for having introduced the Christian faith into our country. Yes, it was the first bishop of Prague of Slavonic blood, Saint Vojtech[266] and the Przemyslid Countess Dubravka who had founded it here. And you are successor to Saint Vojtech. It is therefore also thanks to you, the Czechs, that today the Church has at its head a pope of Slavonic blood."[267]

This is not only a true testimonial of the Pope's spirituality of compassion for his suffering friends, but his expression of real spiritual concern, keeping in mind its historical dimension.

An Ecumenical Spirituality

His spirituality is furthermore distinctly ecumenical for Wojtyla never misses an opportunity to remind all that every schism in the Church created a scandal and that Christian unity is desirable not only for practical reasons, that is, that all Christians form one front against their common enemy, but mainly for the theological rationale that they be "one in Christ" (cf. Jn 20:21-24). This concern for our "separated brothers" is well substantiated by the fact that the papacy in its pastoral ministry is serving as protective shield for all Christians.

The Pope evidently prefers the reunion of Eastern Churches and is desirous of ecumenical endeavor with all Protestants on the basis of a full understanding and acceptance of doctrinal and biblical truth. Well aware of the difficulties involved and the urgent need for adjustments by various Churches before any union can be effected, he is working hard toward all possible accommodations, this with a true concern, as a good shepherd's care for his scattered sheep.

With sentiments of longing that the much-desired unity will not be further delayed, the Pope stated the situation: "The journey however is not finished and we must continue it to reach the goal. Let us, therefore, renew our prayer to the Lord, so that He may give to all Christians light and strength to do everything possible to attain as soon as possible full unity in truth. . . ."[268]

Jesus as the Foundation for Humanism

Not least in importance, it should be stressed that the spirituality of this Pope is deeply rooted in biblical theology as the prime source of its orientation and ultimate inspiration.

Considering John Paul II on these points, one can see that the new Pope's spirituality is clearly marked by intellectual vigor, philosophical soundness, theological substance, humanity, concern, love, and warmth. Even more, it is a spirituality based on a faith that is unabashedly evangelical. Jesus Christ constitutes for him the foundation for a Christian humanism confident of its ability to compete successfully with any attempt to fabricate a humanism without God.

The Pope's deep concern for spirituality is evidenced by his first encyclical *Redemptor hominis*, of March 4, 1979, which deals with the spiritual nature of man.[269] Its theme is one that the Pope has discussed repeatedly in talks given since his election. In those of his Advent series given for general audiences, he said that the concepts of "God" and "man" are at the basis of all human thought, even when marked by other concepts of contemporary civilization.

A Vatican source insists that the Pope held up publication of any document related to the 1977 Synod of Bishops as well as one already completed on Catholic universities because he wished the encyclical to be the first major publication of his pontificate. The spiritual nature of man is of such importance and relevance that the Pope himself affirms that "only a holy man can stand firm."[270]

A Practical Spirituality

Perhaps as revealing the principal hallmark of his pontificate, it has to be hard for anyone to understand the spirituality of John Paul II without understanding also that, like John of the Cross, John Paul II firmly believes that a Christian's life in the world must be totally sanctified; his religion must not be relegated only to church on Sunday, but practiced in such a way as to sanctify one's marriage, work, love, all of life. It is a practical spirituality, one modern in its approach but old in its principles, based on a living faith, an intrepid hope, and a dynamic love, which he wishes to share with the world.

In accord with all this Humberto Cardinal Medeiros styles this Pope as "a man filled with Christ,"[271] and with the same sentiment John Cardinal Krol of Philadelphia says of him: "He is a very spiritual man. The Church is blessed to have him as the Holy Father."[272]

His spirituality embraces everything, even his poetical thought, as can be seen in the following lines:

A conversation with God begins

The human body in history dies more often and earlier
than the tree.
Man endures beyond the doors of death in catacombs
and crypts,
Man who departs endures in those who follow.
Man who follows endures in those departed.
Man endures beyond all coming and going
in himself and in you.

The history of men, such as I, always looks for the body
you will give them.
Each man in history loses his body and goes towards you.
In the moment of departure
each is greater than history
although but a part
(a fragment of a century or two,
merged into one life).[273]

Chapter 16

THE FISHERMAN'S APOSTOLIC VISION

Prognosis of the Future

AFTER outlining the spiritual profile of the present Pope, one is eager to know more of his policies, his thought, his program, his goals, and the course he may follow. Although a kind of prognosis of his goals can be detected to a certain extent from his personal makeup and his previous actions, we will follow with a realistic appraisal of his policies, one based on his concrete ideas, ideals, and goals rather than in speculation on them.

Holding that his program and direction are reflections of his ideas, ideals, and goals in spiritual and pastoral concerns, we will term them an apostolic vision which may include even certain dreams the Pope may have tied to his ideals. Nevertheless, since he is a realist, the apostolic vision of the new Pope appears factual in the framework of his biography.

To begin with, as with any election of a new pope, the faithful expect change, but feel, more than ever, that John Paul will effect many. A sign of these expectations is echoed, perhaps, from an event immediately after his election. As he turned from his official greeting of diplomats and world leaders assembled to congratulate him on his election, Wojtyla remarked to one of his aides: "And now after we have set the wheel in motion, I wonder how many of them will survive. And of the survivors how many will return to salute us?"

To Cardinal Wyszynski, leaving him and about to return to Poland, he said: "Old friend, pray for me. If I succeed I may not see you again. If I fail you may not see me again!"[274] Surprises began to unfold as soon as he assumed his reign.

Views on Controversial Issues

The new Pope, perhaps too quickly and without the usual diplomatic maneuvering to make himself clear, expressed his views on the most controversial issues of the day. He will not sanction married priests or women priests, and he will maintain the Catholic Church's ban on the practices of homosexuality and of contraception.[275] He is in full agreement with the attitude of John Paul I[276] as regards deviations in theology and morality that have crept into Catholic teaching and practice since Vatican Council II.

The Pope is explicit in matters of liturgical worship by ending the period of experimentation and is adamant in realizing the spirit of Vatican II and its conciliar decrees.[277] He is emphatic in his resolution to restore priestly discipline and religious faithfulness to traditions, including clerical dress and the religious habit.[278]

Thus the mind and some actions of Karol Wojtyla as Pope may be at first perplexing, for people, troubled as they are by their problems, are said to remain complacent in their assumptions. John Paul II, on the other hand, is not a complacent sort. He comes of a social, political, and humanist background that holds in little respect both the so-called European Enlightenment of the 18th century and the material betterment spawned by modern technology as propagated in Western Europe and the United States.

Approach to Christian-Marxist Dialogue

Divergence in the approach of John Paul II to a *Christian-Marxist dialogue* must be met by surprise by all its advocates, either in the manner of R. Garaudy[279] or of those who, in principle, insist that such a dialogue materialize, the renewal of the world in the spirit of Vatican II.[280] The present Pope insists that there cannot be dialogue nor political cooperation between Marxists and Christians, insofar as dialogue implies a compromise on political issues that involve articles of the Catholic faith.

He regards the political structure of the Communist State as irreconcilable with Christianity. He believes in the right to private property, one's own initiatives, and dislikes to see the State have anything to do with education, or trade on the ordinary life of citizens except to help the people in their needs. He believes that Christian-Marxist dialogue is handicapped by the atheistic nature and materialistic approach of Communism;[281] as a result it could not work.[282]

The present emphasis on Christian humanism[283] points perhaps to a direction by which Communists can find their way "from anathema to dialogue." Some modification of their atheistic humanism[284] could provide the basis for such mutual encounter. With certain changes in Communist philosophy, the dignity of human beings could again appear and the "robot" be reinstated as an "image of God" or at least as a free person.

From his previous encounters with Communists in his native Poland, the Pope knows too well that this could not happen, given the nature of Communism[285] itself, and therefore entirely distrusts any brand of Christian-Marxist dialogue, unless the Church be completely free from any Communist harassment. If, in fact, it is understood as a talk between equal and free partners, the dialogue itself demands such recognition of religious freedom and of the Church lest it become merely a monologue.

The Church as Defender of Human Rights

In this connection, logically, it is not surprising that John Paul II should be—as he is—such an unyielding and forceful spokesman for human rights. The Pope expressed this clearly and decisively himself in his recent speech at Puebla, Mexico:

> It is, therefore, not through opportunism nor thirst for novelty that the Church, "the expert in humanity" (Paul VI, address to the United Nations, October 4, 1965), defends human rights. It is through a true evangelical commitment, which, as it was with Christ, is commitment to the most needy. In fidelity to this commitment, the Church wishes to stay free with regard to the competing systems, in order to opt only for human beings. Whatever the miseries or sufferings that afflict them, it is not through violence, the interplay of power, and political systems, but through the truth concerning man that they journey toward a better future.[286]

The Pope here singles out the Church as an adequate defender of human rights with no need to affiliate itself with any other organizations to solicit motif or support from them. In fact, he safeguards the Church's right to pursue this apostolate:

> You are priests and members of religious orders. You are not social directors, political leaders, nor functionaries of a temporal power.[287]
>
> Pastoral commitments in this field must be encouraged through a correct Christian idea of liberation. The Church feels the duty to proclaim the liberation of millions of human beings, the duty to help this liberation become truly established, liberation made up of reconciliation and forgiveness, liberation springing from the reality of being children of God, whom we are able to call *Abba*, Father (Rom 8:15), a reality which makes us recognize in every man a brother of ours, capable of being transformed in his heart through God's mercy.
>
> To safeguard the originality of the Christian and the energies he is capable of releasing, one must at all costs

> avoid any form of curtailment or ambiguity, as Pope Paul VI asked. The Church would lose her fundamental meaning. Her message of liberation would no longer have any originality and would easily be open to monopolization and manipulation by ideological systems and political parties.[288]
>
> The idea of Christ as a political figure, a revolutionary, as a subversive man from Nazareth, does not tally with the Church's catechesis.[289]

Attitude toward Theology of Liberation

What alienated the activists and blinded them to what he was saying was that the Pope refused to say it as a Marxist. He refused to cast Christ in the role of a gun-toting revolutionary, as one of the guerrilla priests for whom the liberal U.S. news media has such fondness.[290] At Cuilapan, a village in Oaxaca in Mexico's heavily Indian Southeast, he said: "In light of a situation that continues to be alarming, the Pope wants to be your voice, the voice of those who cannot talk or who are silenced, in order to be the conscience of consciences, the invitation to action, in order to make up for lost time, which frequently is a time of prolonged suffering and unsatisfied hopes."[291] What more can be said if this convincing clarity in showing him as an energetic spokesman of human rights be not enough?

The Pope's stand in regard to the theology of liberation in Latin America was greatly misinterpreted by many journalists,[292] as for instance, cartoonist Tony Auth, who produced a tasteless and unfair depiction of Pope John Paul II as saying to Christ at the multiplication of the loaves and fishes: "Shouldn't you leave problems of food distribution to the authorities?"[293]

Far from stating that the Church and its members should be unconcerned with meeting human needs, the Pope did say: "The Lord outlined in the parable of the Good Samaritan the model of attention to all human needs, and He said that in the final analysis He will identify Himself with the disinherited, the sick, the imprisoned, the hungry, the lonely—who have been given a helping hand."

Pope John Paul II neither admonished nor abdicated the merciful service of the needy; rather, in discouraging violence and encouraging love, he sought fidelity to the Gospel of Christ.

New Type of Ecumenism

There is another scenario of radical change which caused a certain anxiety in some or caught others by surprise—the sincere, open ecumenism of John Paul II. It is known that, on the one hand, he regards the ecumenism of Western Europe and of America as a dead end, while on the other he is very keen for another form of ecumenism. He gave the world an early and open sign of ecumenism when, as already mentioned, he stood on the balcony of St. Peter's on the evening of October 16th and crossed his hands on his chest, his fists closed. This is the ancient gesture of Eastern Orthodoxy, repeated endlessly in its history and in its icons, heavy with the significance of unity and perseverance until death in belief in Jesus and in His salvation. Already on January 17, 1979, the Pope announced:

> I wish to mention now that the Catholic Church and the [Eastern] Churches of the Byzantine tradition are about to open a theological dialogue aimed at eliminating those difficulties which still impede Eucharistic celebration and full unity. We have been holding dialogues with our brothers in the West—Anglicans, Lutherans, Methodists, and the Reformed. On themes which in the past contributed great differences, consoling convergences have been made. The voyage is not yet finished, however, and we must speed up our pace to reach our goal.[294]

With such ecumenism in mind, it is not hard to discern policies and actions that reach far beyond his trip to Poland—policies which may finally accomplish the reunion of Eastern Orthodox Churches with Rome, for which so many efforts were made in the past in the Unionistic Congresses in Velehrad[295] (1907-47) in Czechoslovakia, organized by truly unionistic apostles such as the late Archbishop Antonin Cyril Stojan[296] of Olomouc and the saintly apostle of Church unity, none other than Metropolitan Andrew Sheptytsky,[297] Archbishop of Lwow, Cardinal Joseph Slipyj of Lwow, now in Rome, and with scholars of such world renown as Professors Josef Vajs, Josef Vasica of Prague, J. Urban, SJ, of Krakow, or the famous Byzantinist Professor Francis Dvornik, [298] originally of Charles University in Prague, later of Harvard, to name but a few.

The reunion with the Eastern Churches is reachable with much difficulty chiefly owing to the Cyrilomethodian tradition,[299] which has been the common heritage of all Slavs since 863. Against such historical background, this Polish Pope is oriented to achieve unity sooner than the sophisticated person of this modern age would dare to admit.

Behind such a policy of "doubling back" into the very heart of Communist territory and peoples behind the Iron Curtain lies a far more cold-blooded calculation than most Western observers, analysts, and commentators are either desirous or capable of accepting, much less of formulating. The vision of a strong leadership appears in John Paul II, for in a few years he will constrain Communistic countries to compromise and press for fresh and new interpretation of the material prosperity of Western Europe as well as America.

Developments in State-Church Relationships

In this connection also, and against the Pope's background of a definite stand in regard to Christian-Marxist dialogue, as mentioned above, it is interesting to note John Paul's flexibility. This he displayed in the private audience with Soviet Foreign Minister Andrei Gromyko on January 24, 1979, discussing "peace, peaceful coexistence, and international cooperation" for the sake of survival in the danger inherent in Communism that the Pope so much detests.

After having seen his brilliant performances in Latin America, reporters did not fail to note emerging in him a new talent to add to so many others—that of a skilled diplomat and politician who not only knows his goal well but the way to reach it. This is a quality certainly needed in the framework of pastoral prudence which he developed so well in Poland in his life of stress and duress and from his training in moral theology and ethics, with their subtle distinctions among pragmatism, expediency, and choice of the lesser evil as the way out of complexity without sacrifice of a principle.

In this light, it is to be understood that owing to unusual contemporary situations of State-Church relationships in countries behind the Iron Curtain, the Pope will have, at least for the time being, to make some accommodations to the existing "Communist ecclesiology,"[300] which does not alway accord with traditional canonical forms of Church-State arrangements.[301] At the same time, however, he will be trying to effect a change in their conditioning whenever and wherever possible without having any room for option or choice.

Association with the Poor and the Worker

There is another eye-opener for some accustomed to associate, with the Church, power and wealth rather than the poor. The Pope's visit to Latin America was an attempt to strike a delicate balance. While clarifying the theology of liberation, he seemed to be telling them that the Gospel itself is revolutionary enough to bring about social change while yet rejecting violence, and insisting that the priests should be catalysts rather than activists.

By taking every opportunity, during the visit to Latin America, to visit the poor as did Christ, he was showing clearly that the Church should be with the underdog. While challenging the oppressive military and dictatorial governments in Latin America in his emphasis on human rights, he challenged also wealthy Christians by stressing their need for social concern. His speech in Mexico on January 31, 1979, following the social thought of Popes John XXIII and Paul VI,[302] insisted:

> The worker has the right that the barriers of exploitation be destroyed, barriers which frequently are made of intolerable selfishness, against which the best efforts of self-improvement usually clash. He has the right to effective help which is neither charity nor the crumbs of justice—so that he may have access to the development to which his human dignity and status as a son of God give him the right.
>
> Therefore it is necessary to act quickly and with intensity. It is necessary to effect bold transformations which are profoundly innovative. It is necessary to initiate without delay urgent agricultural reforms. It cannot be forgotten that adequate means must be used. The Church does defend the legitimate right to private property, but it teaches with no less clarity that, above all, private property always carries with it a social obligation, so that material possessions may serve the general goal that God intended. And if the common good requires it, there must be no doubt about expropriation itself, carried out in the proper manner.
>
> The agricultural world has great importance and great dignity; it is that which offers society the products necessary for its nourishment. It is work that deserves the appreciation and grateful esteem of all, a recognition of the dignity of those who work the land.[303]

This must have given the scare to the Communists behind the Iron Curtain, as they read the challenge of the Pope's social vision, in their fear that their program be invalidated by a truly Christian design. Likewise, it must have been met with a great surprise by rich landowners and selfish calculators whose wealth was gained at the expense of workers' rights. That even Italian Communists were perplexed, one might gather from the action of the Italian Communist party in withdrawing support from the Christian Democratic government of Prime Minister Giulio Andreotti, only one day after the Permanent Council of the Italian Bishops Conference, held on January 22-25, urged Catholics to avoid Marxist solutions to their community problems,[304] following faithfully the social thought of the Pontiff.

Role of Peacemaker

A most interesting aspect of the Pope's apostolic vision is that of peacemaker. In a document signed by John Paul II on December 8th and released on the 21st, the theme of the 1979 World Day of Peace was described: "To arrive at Peace, educate to Peace." It was the theme chosen by Pope Paul VI shortly before his death.[305]

This document is not a pedagogical directory, but it sets out to present an overall view, a mobilizing synthesis, which explains broadly the aim to be reached, peace, in order to define clearly the nature of the education which seeks to promote this peace. Pope John Paul II adapted Paul VI's text by making the topic more concrete: "To reach peace, teach peace."[306]

The new Pope's document is divided into three parts: (I) A hard task, an irrepressible aspiration for peace. (II) Education for peace by (a) bringing visions of peace, (b) speaking a language of peace, and (c) making gestures for peace. (III) The specific contribution by Christians, with the Christian vision of peace, which the Pope spells out in the following:

Peace—Our Part as Human Beings

> Dear Brothers and Sisters in Christ, the aspiration for peace that you share with all men and women corresponds to an initial call by God to form a single family of brothers and sisters, created in the image of the same Father. Revelation insists upon our freedom and our solidarity. The difficulties that we encounter in our journey towards peace are linked partly to our weakness, as

creatures who must necessarily advance by slow and progressive steps.

These difficulties are aggravated by our selfishness, by our sins of every sort, beginning with the original sin that marked a break with God, entailing a break between brothers and sisters. The image of the Tower of Babel well describes the situation. But we believe that Jesus Christ, by giving His life on the Cross, became our Peace: He broke down the wall of hate that divided the hostile brothers (cf. Eph 4:14). Having risen and entered into the glory of the Father, He mysteriously associates us with His Life: by reconciling us with God, He heals the wounds of sin and division and enables us to produce in our societies a rough outline of the unity that He is re-establishing in us.

The most faithful disciples of Christ have been builders of peace, to the point of forgiving their enemies, sometimes even to the point of giving their lives for them. Their example marks the path for a new humanity no longer content with provisional compromises but instead achieving the deepest sort of brotherhood. We know that, without losing its natural consistency or its peculiar difficulties, our journey towards peace on earth is comprised within another journey, that of salvation, which reaches fulfillment in an eternal plentitude of grace, in total communion with God.

Thus, the Kingdom of God, the Kingdom of Peace, with its own source, means, and end, already permeates, without dilution, the whole of earthly activity. This vision of faith has a deep impact on the everyday action of Christians.

Peace—the Gift of God

It is true that we are advancing along the paths of peace with the weaknesses and the gropings of all those making the journey with us. With the latter we suffer from the tragic deficiencies of peace. We feel ourselves constrained to remedy them with even greater resolution, for the honor of God and for the honor of man. We do not claim to find in the Gospel text ready-made formulas for making today this or that advance towards peace. But on almost every page of the Gospel and of

> the history of the Church we find *a spirit*, that of brotherly love, powerfully teaching peace.
>
> We find, in the gifts of the Holy Spirit and in the sacraments, *a strength* drawn from the divine source. We find, in Christ, *a hope*. Setbacks cannot render vain the work of peace, even if the immediate results prove to be fragile, even if we are persecuted for our witness in favor of peace. Christ the Savior associates with his destiny all those who work with love for peace.
>
> Peace is our work: it calls for our courageous and united action. But it is inseparably and above all a gift of God: it requires our prayer. Christians must be in the first rank of those who pray daily for peace. They must also teach others to *pray for peace*. It will be their joy to pray with Mary, the Queen of Peace.
>
> To everyone, Christians, believers, and men and women of good will, I say: Do not be afraid to take a risk on peace, to teach peace. The aspiration for peace will not be disappointed for ever. Work, for peace inspired by charity which does not pass away, will produce its fruits. Peace will be the last word of History.[307]

The Pope's concept of peace is certainly a comfort to all peace lovers, it is realistic for those of good will, is alarming for those troublemakers who make hypocritical pretensions for peace, even while obstructing it, and is abhorrent to those with destructive designs in mind. Peace for John Paul II is a thing to be watched always, to be desired and appreciated, maintained and if necessary defended. It is for him a conditioned and dynamic thing. It is indivisible and organic, for peace abides in one's mind, in the conscience, is actualized in a person before it can be permanent in a society, a State, a nation, the world. Peace is harmony on the human and spiritual levels before it can be applied to the material.

Apostle of Peace

The present Pope's wholesome analysis of peace is an urgent call for a thorough examination of conscience, not only by statesmen, by lawmakers, by diplomats, but by each person who is a real maker of peace, for "a man can only reap what he has sown. If you sow in the field of selfishness, it will bring you a harvest of death and decay; if you sow in the field of the Spirit you will reap a harvest of life everlasting" (Gal 6:8) and "it is the Spirit that gives life, the flesh is of no avail" (Jn 6:63). Peace is entirely rooted in the spiritual wellspring before it can bear its fruit in a society at all.

In the interest of peace, this Pope has been from the beginning of his reign very busy in promoting it. Almost all his speeches and documents touch on peace. He sent a special message to the United Nations[308] to enforce it. He organized a diplomatic mediation on the territorial controversy between Chile and Argentina[309] and joined in the appeals to spare Bhutto's life in Pakistan.[310]

He is a crusader for prayers for peace and a zealous apostle in spreading the spirit of peace on the human, social, national, and international level. In this respect he is not only a builder of mutual human and social understanding but a true peacemaker in the sense of biblical emphasis,[311] with a condition that a true peacemaker can only be—and in fact is—one who is a faithful follower of Christ's beatitudes (Mt 5:3-8).[312]

The Pope is an example of the modern apostle of peace, whose firm stand on Christian principles is in harmony with one's action, based on good will even at the price of suffering and sacrifice in imitation of Christ,[313] the Prince of Peace.

On New Year's Day of 1979 he implored nations and statesmen to work for peace, while he celebrated Mass before a great crowd of 25,000 faithful in St. Peter's Basilica to mark World Peace Day (which Pope Paul VI established in 1967). He prayed: "I beseech you, as a son of a nation, which throughout history, and particularly in our own history, has been among the most sorely tested by horror, cruelty, and the cataclysm of war, to work for peace!"[314]

Emphasis on Collegiality

While these points given previously are the Pope's concern for values, they should be applied to the apostolate as the Pope sees it. He has even more concern for the Church as a functioning organism. In this respect his emphasis on the idea of collegiality comes to the fore. This idea, which crystallizes in Vatican Council II, never really came to maturity, although it was championed somewhat by Pope Paul's creation of the World Synod of Bishops, convoked irregularly in Rome to formulate guidelines for evangelization. National episcopal conferences were established, and statutes for their work were approved by Paul VI on January 10, 1977.

When on December 19, 1978, John Paul II received members of the Council of the Episcopal Conference of Europe, led by the Council president, Archbishop Roger Etchegaray of Marseilles, along with two vice presidents, Bishop John Baptist Mustj of Botmana and Archbishop Jerzy Stroba of Poznan, he said:

> It is one of the ways of incarnating collegiality in the framework in which the teaching of the Second Vatican Council can yield all its fruit. Collegiality means the mutual opening and brotherly cooperation of bishops in the service of evangelization, of the mission of the Church. An opening and cooperation of this kind are necessary, not only at the level of the local Churches and the universal Church, but also at the level of continents, as is testified by the vitality of other regional organisms—even if the statutes are a little different—such as the Latin American Episcopal Council [CELAM], and Symposium of Episcopal Conferences of Africa and Madagascar [SECAM], or the Federation of the Asian Bishops Conference [FABC] to mention only these great assemblies.
>
> The Pope and the Holy See make a point of promoting these organisms, at the various levels of collegial cooperation, its being understood that regional or continental bodies do not replace the authority of each bish-

op or of each of the episcopal conferences as regards decisions, and that their research is set in the framework of the more general orientations of the Holy See, in close liaison with Peter's successor. And in the present case, the European dimension seems to the Pope very important and even necessary. . . .

The Council of European Episcopal Conferences constitutes a special representation of the Catholic episcopates of Europe. We must hope that all episcopates are fully represented in this organization, with the possibility of taking a real part in it. It is only under these conditions that the analysis of the essential problems of the Church and of Christianity can be complete.

It is a question of the problems of the Church and of Christianity, approached also in an ecumenical perspective. For if it is true that the whole of Europe is not Catholic, it is almost all Christian. Your Council must become a kind of breeding-ground in which there is expressed, developed, and matured not only awareness of what Christianity was yesterday, but responsibility for what it must be tomorrow.[315]

The Pope's emphasis on the collegiality of bishops goes hand in hand with the historical importance of the first episcopal synods,[316] which the ancient Church placed always in them. Bishops were not only of exclusive and legitimate trust in formulating doctrine in general councils[317] but also constitutive factors of the pentarchy[318] in the administration of the Church. Thus a well-developed collegiality means not only a return to the early Church's traditions but also a kind of decentralization of papal powers into delegated jurisdictional entities to increase the effectiveness of the papacy. This would enhance the prestige of bishops and mediate the sharing of power of the Vicar of Christ.

Doctrinal Purity and Church Discipline

On November 9, 1978, the Pope received the American bishops of a certain number of dioceses led by Cardinal Cody of Chicago; among the reminders of their pastoral concerns, he reaffirmed a commitment of his pontificate to the continuation of genuine application of Vatican Council II and to fulfill its legacy, "that the sacred deposit of Christian doctrine should be more effectively guarded and taught. To present this sacred deposit of Christian faith in all its purity and integrity, with all its exigencies and in all its power, is a holy, pastoral responsibility. It is, moreover, the most sublime service we can render."[319]

In addition to his concern for a doctrinal purity and integrity, he expressed hope for the preservation of the great discipline of the Church, a hope eloquently formulated by John Paul I on the day after his election: "We wish to maintain intact the great discipline of the Church in the life of priests and of the faithful, as the history of the Church, enriched by experience, has presented it throughout the centuries, with examples of holiness and heroic perfection, both in the exercise of the evangelical virtues and in service to the poor, the humble, the defenseless."[320]

On another occasion, on November 17th, to the Canadian bishops John Paul II urged the adherence of the faithful to the sacramental discipline of the Church, guarantee of the continuity and the authenticity of Christ's saving action, guarantee of the dignity and the unity of Christian worship, and finally guarantee of the real vitality of the people of God.

Recommendation of Religious Garb

On yet another occasion to the Roman clergy, November 9, 1978, the Pope said: "Let us not deceive ourselves that we are serving the Gospel if we try to 'water down' our priestly charism through exaggerated interest in the vast field of temporal problems, if we wish to secularize our way of living and acting, if we cancel even the external signs of our priestly vocation. We must keep the sense of our singular vocation, and this 'singularity' must be expressed also in our exterior garb. Let us not be ashamed of it. Yes, we are in the world! But we are not of the world.

"Our priesthood must be clear and expressive, and if in the tradition of our Church, it is closely linked with celibacy, this is due precisely to the clarity and evangelical expressiveness referred to in Our Lord's words on celibacy, 'for to such belongs the kingdom of heaven'" (Mt 19:13).[321]

Even more concern the Pope expressed in regard to women religious. On November 10, 1978, he received 12,000 sisters resident in Rome and commended them on their generous commitment to be witnesses of sincere consistency with Gospel values and the specific charism of their institutes. On November 16th, to the annual session of the International Union of Superiors General of religious orders and congregations, he begged for their sincere observance of their Rule:

> Be true, Daughters of the Church, not only in words but in deeds. The treasure of the evangelical counsels and the commitment—taken after mature reflection and irrevocable—to make them the charter of a Christian existence cannot be relativized by public opinion, even if it were ecclesial. The Church and, let us say, the world itself needs, more than ever, men and women who sacrifice everything to follow Christ in the way of the Apostles. And if your consecration to God is really such a deep reality, it is not unimportant to bear permanently its exterior sign, which a simple and suitable religious habit constitutes: it is the means to remind yourselves constantly of your commitment which contrasts strongly with the spirit of the world; it is silent but eloquent testimony; it is a sign that our secularized world needs to find on its way, as many Christians, moreover, desire. I ask you to turn this over carefully in your mind.[322]

Re-Creating Christlike Image

On the occasion of an audience given to the male superiors general on November 24, 1978, the Pope stressed that on every religious community, on every religious weighs a particular coresponsibility for the real presence of Christ Who is meek and humble of heart in the world of today—

of the crucified and risen Christ—Christ among brothers; the spirit of evangelical maximalism which is differentiated from any socio-political radicalism. "At the same time as being a challenge to the world and to the Church herself, this silent witness of poverty and abnegation of purity and sincerity of self-sacrifice in obedience 'which religious are called to bear' can become an eloquent witness capable of touching also non-Christians who have good will and are sensitive to certain values."[323]

Considering all these concerns of the Pope, one is certain of his determination to have self-reform within the Church before any kind of reform outside the Church can be effective. The Pope, "the man filled with Christ,"[324] attempts sincerely to re-create the Christlike image of Christians in Christ's Church. Without our detailing all the spiritual needs of the Church this Fisherman's apostolic vision, in our view, includes also the central issues for the Church's future which some modern theologians have in the recently published book *Toward Vatican III* outlined as the work that needs to be done.[325]

As an antithesis to the modern corrupt and permissive world John Paul seems to be very unusual, controversial, seemingly unreal, and yet so authentic, sincere, honest, and so inspiring that crowds of people come wherever Christ's Fisherman spreads his nets for apostolic angling. Everyone feels that we have found in him a friend, a humble pastor, a leader, a man of vision and of prayer, of compassion, and of understanding, all these qualities resulting from his own spiritual maturity through suffering and adversity, hard work, dedication, love of God, zeal—a truly authentic witness to Christ. No wonder that, seen in the perspective of such a Fisherman's apostolic vision, he seems by general consensus to be God's gift to the Church and to the world, with expectations of a rich legacy to be fulfilled.

Chapter 17

A LEGACY TO BE FULFILLED

Cooperation between Church and State

THE general use and meaning of the term legacy denotes the legal, rightful, and just basis for its exercise without imposition on anyone's rights, but with an inherent and justified claim to it by all concerned.[326] When applied to the Pope's legacy, it means that which is inherent in his mission and that is expected to be fulfilled rather as a right than as a privilege.

The Pope's mandate to exercise his authority was well delineated by Jesus Christ Himself as He spoke to the Jewish authorities who questioned Him: "Render therefore to Caesar the things that are Caesar's and to God the things that are God's" (Mt 22:21). Thereby He distinguished the two powers: the secular and the spiritual, and by so doing emancipated the souls of men.[327] The position and relation of the State to the Church is the necessary result of the objective competency of both these orders: their mutual positions do not depend on the will of the people. Their relations or positions arise ontologically, that is, from their very being, and they should be recognized as such. In order that a clash between the Church and the State may be avoided, it is logically necessary that there be mutual cooperation.

The problem is not new. It has frequently recurred in history. Caesaropapism with its principle of *imperator est episcopus rerum externarum* ("the emperor is the bishop of external things"), as we already read in the Codex Encyclius[328] (and the medieval idea of *rex-sacerdos*—"king-priest"[329]) was the measure of relations between Church and State in Central Europe, and finally the foundation of the feudal system.[330] This was all taken over by the Communists who added much hostility toward the Church. On the other hand, papocaesarism as it occurred under Gregory VII (1075-88), or under Popes Innocent III and IV, or Boniface VIII, to name but a few, grew out of the defense of the Church against excessive encroachment by secular power. Equally, it should be said that in either case there was misuse of authority.

The Byzantine concept of the emperor's beneficent protectorate over the Church soon became the heritage of all countries of Eastern Europe and in time degenerated into State control of the Church.[331] This development of the crossing of lines between spiritual power *(sacerdotium)* and secular power *(imperium)*, however, called for their distinct delineation. It was effected by Pope Gelasius[332] and Emperor Anastasius I in the 5th century for the first time and ever since it has been a legacy of two distinct powers, for them to go about their business of ruling and administering human affairs accordingly.

Much effort was needed to keep this distinction alive as a valid principle during the centuries, and for it much blood was shed. With the Bolshevik Revolution of 1917 the Communists attempted first to liquidate religion and the Churches.[333] Failing in this, they reintroduced caesaropapism in a form of rigid State control of Churches and established in all satellite countries Government Bureaus for Church Affairs, through which they maintained the Churches in chains of slavery and kept them in suspense by constant terrorism.[334] The status of the persecuted Churches was known as the Church of Silence.

Two Distinct Powers

In retrospect it seems that the first legacy to be fulfilled by a new Pope is to enforce the old Gelasian doctrine of two distinct powers and to abolish effectively the monstrous structure of State Offices for Religious Affairs in all satellite countries, that the Churches may again administer their own Church affairs. Immediately after his election John Paul II reassured the Poles: "From now there will be no Church of Silence!"

Whether the Pope will succeed in abolishing the State Offices for Church Affairs in all countries of Eastern Europe remains to be seen. Owing to the centuries-long Byzantine influence there is much national feeling in all the Eastern Churches, a situation which makes it difficult to cut them from State ties; nevertheless the mandate for this change is so urgent that Communists themselves, after fifty years of cruel persecution, should know better by now. It is unnatural for any State to rule the Church and it is a great shame that an atheist should control the Church.

Furthermore, it is immoral on the part of the State to rule the Church, from any point of view, since it is totally repugnant to the biblical direction in this regard. Freedom of the Church is, moreover, a condition for the conduct of proper Christian-Marxist dialogue if a dialogue is in fact understood as a talk between equal and free partners. The dialogue itself demands such a recognition, lest it become merely a monologue—hypocritical and meaningless as it has been until now.

Since, however, a direct confrontation with the machinery of the powerful Communist State would be suicidal, with no positive outcome, an exercise of indirect pressures appears better calculated to effect some change. The Pope's drive for human rights, religious freedom, and the dignity of a free person is pushing the Communists to the wall in shame, so that some reform within the State can eventually be effected, while its monolithic body disintegrates and no room is left for any synthesis.[335] Evidently the new Pope must display a great deal of clever politics to succeed in effecting some change through various indirect pressures on government, this by following some previous tactics of the ecclesiastical politician in Poland, for which he earned respect[336] even from the Polish Marxist regime.

New Direction for Achieving Reforms

Another legacy to be fulfilled by a new Pope is to search for and find a fitting direction for a successful achievement of reforms and changes that would facilitate the task of bringing his apostolic vision to fruition. In this regard, noted and forceful Polish liberal humanist Leszek Kolakowski[337] brings into our focus a valuable suggestion, part of which is worthy of being reproduced here for the benefit of all concerned. He titled it, "Prospective Prophecies and Pious Wishes of a Layman at the Threshold of a New Pontificate concerning the Perpetual Problem of the Rights of Caesar and of God." It follows:

One Suggested Approach

> We shall ignore the understandable, but for our purposes irrelevant, euphoria of the Polish people which set in when a Pontifex Polonus sat on the Apostolic Throne. We shall also ignore the possible consequences of this event for the Church in Poland as well as its possible effects on the struggle in Poland, the struggle of the people for their rights as citizens and the struggle in defense of human rights. It is clear that this event is of universal importance and that, from the perspective of the Universal Church, it is not important that a new pope has come from Krakow to Rome.
>
> It is important, however, that the Pope has spent his pastoral life in a politically adverse but in a socially friendly environment. He knows very well the essence of confrontation between the Church and the Communist system of government; he knows it from experience and because of this struggle between the "integralistic"

and the "progressive" tendencies of Christianity. It is not necessary to prove that this struggle is a key to the fate of Christianity and the world.

In this matter I wish to voice privately my opinion based on my positive attitude toward the affairs of Christianity as I understand them. I admit that both the "integralists" and the "Progressives" have some valid arguments, especially when they voiced them in their criticisms of each other; but from my point of view, I am not trying to establish a synthesis, but simply to voice an independent, well-argued standpoint. . . .

Mission of the Church

We speak of the Church as an institution that is supposed to bring to the world the good news of Salvation and Unity, and it cannot expect from its faithful that they flee from the affairs of this world and that they develop virtues in desertlike loneliness; it can expect, however, that they should seek in contemporary thorns the Kingdom of God and that they assume responsibility, not just on an individual basis, i.e., each one for himself, but also for others. Thus arises the difficulty, unlimited and lasting, of an exact demarcation between things of God and things of Caesar.

Christianity (with the exception of some sects) does not believe that people can construct with their own strength the Kingdom on earth and eradicate evil altogether. The intention to build a paradise on earth with human hands alone may well appear as an inspiration of demonic pride, just as the building of the Tower of Babel, which yielded nothing but a warning and the confusion of human tongues. It is also not the task of the Church to formulate rules for a good political system nor to write constitutions for secular states.

On the other hand, considering what is good and what is evil, Christianity cannot properly separate—and this is of greatest importance—the judgment of the people from the judgment of institutions. It is said, for example, that the failure to pay a worker and the exploitation of orphans and widows are sins crying for revenge to heaven. Thus the Church judges not just individuals but also institutions. Therefore in everyday life moral commandments and prohibitions must be understood in terms of social thinking as a *sui generis* position in important political matters.

For this reason, an essential part of the Church's work must be subject to rules which are made by secular bodies. This duality may not be completely avoided. The head of the Church speaks, according to St. Paul, that he took as grace the Church from Christ as well as the apostolic office and bases his authority on that. But he also says, as did Peter to the centurion, "*Surge, et ego ipse homo sum* (Stand up; I too am a man)" (Acts 10: 26).

Two Extreme Positions Concerning Implementation

The various interpretations of the borders between the things of Caesar and the things of God are the basis of the extreme positions of Christianity: the "integralistic" and the "progressivistic."

Roughly speaking the Catholic "integralism" appears an anachronistic perpetuation of the situation in which the Church saw its main enemy in liberalism, that is to say, in a situation which had its classic existence under the pontificate of Pope Pius IX. Rationalism, the theory of evolution, the principle of division between Church and State were the focal points of the attacks on the Church at that time.

Today's traditionalism, although it does not demand a theocracy, continues to maintain the mentality of the Syllabus epoch, at least in the sense that it would like to make use of secular help in defense of the faith against criticism, and would like to assure the Church the right as an institution to have some say-so in individual worldly matters.

When "integralism" in its perfect form is an anachronistic negation of the autonomous sphere of the *profanum,* then "progressivism" in its perfect form is a renunciation of the autonomy of the faith and the Church and an attempt to subordinate the faith to the demands of politician and doctrinal expediency which can be understood one way or another.

The "integralists" are willing to make peace, and in the eyes of their opponents even identify themselves with those political forces which for one reason or another are able to assure the Church of certain privileges; the "progressives" are willing to make peace or even to identify with anyone who recognizes the slogan's egalitarianism, even if, according to experience, they would have to strive toward a destruction of Christianity on the basis of their own principles (at least in the sense that Christianity would have to be something different from a synopsis of political slogans). From the point of view of Christian tradition, we are dealing in both cases with the obliteration of the borders between the *sacrum* and the *profanum*.[338]

Need for Proper Balance

The advice given hereby that the Pope should strike a balance between integralists and progressives to be on the right course is a reasonable one, for everything is conditioned to different circumstances to differentiate also that balance to be taken accordingly and without being too pragmatic.

For one to be able to do this one has to be a person of principle and of conscience, and this is why the Pope is so persistent in his emphasis on the spiritual nature of man, whether he be in authority or under authority of others. Spiritual maturity influences all human actions and it is this spiritual element that makes a better person for a better society.

It is a "Christian person" who should do better than a "secular person," and it is "Christian humanism" that should be more effective than "atheistic humanism" (contrary to Kolakowski, to be sure), as a corrupted society can originate only from a corrupted person.[339] The human person has to be graced by edification of a Christian conscience and intensification in Christian faith to be able to emanate from its level of corruption to the vision of the image of God.

"Integralism" and "Progressivism"

Nevertheless some weak points of "integralism" and "progressivism" manifest themselves in varying circumstances: in military dictatorships, and (although not always totalitarian) despotic States of the Third World, especially in Latin America. In these countries "integralism" shows the tendency to identify with oppressive structures of the State if they be anti-Communist and to allow the Church all kinds of privileges under condition of political loyalty. "Progressivism" in the same situations shows a tendency to identify with the Communist opposition.

Both forms of reaction are disastrous for both the future of democracy and for Christian values, the preservation of which is most important for mankind. "Integralistic" identification is suspicious, because in the name of institutional privilege people's eyes are closed to violations of human rights; "progressivist" identification is powerless to refute the challenge it contributes to the triumph of political force, which everywhere and without exception makes inroads on Christianity, and on legal and human rights.

The assumption that in non-Communist tyrannies Christians should for the time being struggle toward common goals and discard all else that differentiates them from Communism for a hope for tomorrow, is a testimony of a total lack of memory or of mendacity, because it is generally known that under conditions of Communist power there is no tomorrow. Likewise, the readiness of some Christians to serve as manure for dictators and the naming of this readiness the "theology of liberation"[340] is no less an aberration just because it stems from good will.

Dialogue with Despotic Regimes Not Avoidable

Christianity which sides with the oppressed, the exploited, and the poor against dictatorships in non-Communist countries should not for that reason camouflage its principal opposition against totalitarianism. The Church can easily avoid suspicion of being identified with an evil power because it is not a political party. If the Church speaks not in the name of a political system, but in the name of human rights for spiritual freedom, and it discards the remnants of its own theocratical tradition, there is a possibility of ensuring itself its own position in social conflicts without its being accused that in overcoming tyranny in one form, it but fosters it in a new form. In this respect, both the "integralists" and the "progressives" to some extent are correct. This stand is reflected in all the speeches the Pope gave during the Latin American visit, and it was formulated in a document for a conference of Latin American bishops at Puebla.

In this connection it should be understood that for practical reasons there must be some dialogue with all existing dictators and with Communist despotic rulers while pressures for a change and reform are being applied. Such dialogues are simply conditioned and pressed by the circumstances, with no implication of the Church's approval of them and even less of an insinuation that the Church would agree with them. These should be interpreted existentially, i.e., in view of a given situation. They stress at the same time, however, that the Thomistic *distinguo*[341] must not be forgotten lest Christians lose their identity.

Another Rationale

Another rationale seems to be formed in Kolakowski's interpretation, nevertheless:

> That which the "progressivists'" language calls the dialogue between Christians and Communists is almost always the result of mendacity or self-delusion. Most frequently this dialogue consists in an exchange of unbinding and easily acceptable humanitarian phrases, the objective of which is to preclude the revelation of real differences and to block with verbosity the historical experience.
>
> In such cases we can expect from a Christian words like the following: "Oh, we are also for social justice and for the people's liberation." To which the Communists may reply, "We appreciate your good will and we are willing to cooperate, although we ourselves are guided by a scientific world-view." Out of expediency they re-

frain from stating that their dialogue partners are victims of superstitions surviving from the Middle Ages. Today such dialogue is a verbal screen which is supposed to cover the black realities of Christian life under a Communist regime.

Regardless of how things were in history, in today's world Christianity and representational democracy are positively connected as can be seen in all the places where these institutions are lacking, i.e., on the greater part of the globe. In all these parts Christianity is threatened, to be sure in various degrees. It can be destroyed, according to historical events, in many ways. It need not be destroyed by means of persecution and violence, but also by its own inner barrenness, by the reduction to its own organizational structure, or to its morality, or, what is even worse, to a political morality.

It is possible that even liturgical changes favor one danger or another. Maintaining unchangeable liturgical forms may produce a lack of faith in the essence of Christianity, which is found in various and mutable aspects of expression. The accelerated liquidation of the inherited devices of liturgical communication poses a similar danger; it is possible to lose the content by forsaking the form. Apparently, many Catholics ponder this in an oppressive coldness of modernized temples.[342]

In this regard it should be taken into consideration that any stagnation of old forms should and must be challenged for the new needs of the faithful and for the sake of the Church in the modern world.

Rediscovery of a Spirituality That Celebrates Life

There is yet another concrete legacy to be fulfilled, namely for post-Vatican II Catholics. Perhaps the most fitting to the spirit of the times and the actual situation is thus described by Francine Cardman:

Among Catholics, the chaotic currents of change set in motion by Vatican II seem to have settled into a number of fairly obvious channels. There is on the one hand the stream of individual renewal and spiritual growth. Its manifestations range from the charismatic movement to marriage encounter, from the search for spiritual direction or guidance in prayer to the building of satisfying liturgical community. Some of these movements certainly extend beyond the limits of personal spirituality; but insofar as they are directed principally to the inner needs of individual Christians or Christian groups, they represent a truncated expression of Christian spirituality.

On the other hand, there is a growing emphasis on social justice and the radical demands of a Christian lifestyle in a world of limited resources and a country whose affluence depends on depriving much of the rest of the world of a share in the good things of creation. Political activists and lobbyists, families trying to live simply, alternative communities, revolutionaries: all are part of this stream. Where their efforts are not grounded in prayer and centered on love of God through love of neighbor, they too represent a truncated spirituality.

The challenge facing Catholics and all Christians today is to rediscover a spirituality that lives and prays justly, that unites flesh and spirit, that celebrates life even as it confronts the powers of death and destruction in the world and in ourselves. This new yet old spirituality is ecumenical in the most profound sense: reconciling and uniting sisters and brothers everywhere, and so extending the body of Christ throughout the *oikumene* —the whole world. To live this spirituality is to actively expect the resurrection, to look forward to the restoration of all Creation, and to celebrate and share that future hope now in the Eucharist, the sacrament of the new community that exists not for itself but for the world and for God.[343]

In this sense she is speaking out the mind of John Paul II, who right after his election took upon himself the faithful execution of all decrees of Vatican II[344] as a priority legacy of his pontificate.

Relationship with Bishops and Priests

Among priority tasks is the Pope's anxious concern for a consolidation of a situation resulting from the aftermath of Vatican II, namely, to insure doctrinal authenticity, to ameliorate relationship of the Pope to the Bishops, and to reaffirm the need and the value of Catholic education in the schools. How serious the Pope is on these points can be seen in the circumstance that the book of Father Jacques Pohier, *Quand je dis Dieu* [*When I Say God*], was put on the Index, a practice almost abandoned in the post-Vatican II period and by many received rather as a surprise.[345]

More emphatically, the Pope touched on the betterment of Pope-Bishop relationship by singling out the Post-Vatican topic of collegiality: "We must express the wish, today especially, that everything that the Second Vatican Council so wonderfully renewed in our awareness should take on an ever more mature character of collegiality, both as the principle of our collaboration *(collegialitas effectiva)* and as the character of a cordial fraternal bond *(collegialitas affectiva)*, in order to build up the Mystical Body of Christ and to deepen the unity of the whole people of God."[346]

In his spirited letter to all the priests, the Pope reminds them that they are stewards and witnesses, and inspires them to the observance of law and order, with discipline, in the spirit of the traditions. The Pope insists that "the priestly life is built upon the foundation of the sacrament of Orders, which imprints on our soul the mark of an indelible character. This mark, impressed in the depths of our being, has its 'personalistic' dynamism. The *priestly personality* must be *for others* a clear and plain *sign and indication*. This is the first condition of our pastoral service."[347]

He warns priests against getting embroiled in secular affairs. "Those who call for the secularization of priestly life and applaud its various manifestations will undoubtedly abandon us when we succumb to temptation. We shall then cease to be necessary and popular. The only priest who will always prove necessary to people is the priest who is conscious of the full meaning of priesthood; the priest who believes profoundly, who professes his faith with courage, who prays fervently, who teaches with deep conviction, who serves."[348]

The Role of Catholic Education

Perhaps the greatest concern the Pope expresses is in regard to Catholic education and Catholic schools, for teaching is one of the fundamental missions of the Church. Let us hear what he says in this regard.[349]

"Praised be Jesus Christ.

"It is a joy for me to address the members of the National Catholic Educational Association of the United States, as you assemble in the great cause of Catholic Education. Through you I would hope that my message of encouragement and blessing would also reach the numerous Catholic schools of your country, all the students and teachers of these institutions and all those generously committed to Catholic education. With the Apostle Peter I send you my greeting in the faith of our Lord Jesus Christ: 'Peace to all of you who are in Christ' (1 Pt 5:14).

"As Catholic educators assembled in the communion of the universal Church and in prayer, you will certainly share with one another insights of value that will assist you in your important work, in your ecclesial mission. The Holy Spirit is with you and the Church is deeply grateful for your dedication. The Pope speaks to you in order to confirm you in your lofty role as Catholic educators, to assist you, to direct you, to support you.

Value of Catholic Schools, Teachers, and Education

"Among the many reflections that could be made at this time there are three points in particular to which I would like to make a brief reference at the beginning of my pontificate. These are: the value of Catholic schools, the importance of Catholic teachers and educators, and the nature of Catholic education itself. These are themes that have been developed at length by my predecessors. At this time, however, it is important that I add my own testimony to theirs, in the special hope of giving a new impulse to Catholic education throughout the vast area of the United States of America.

"With profound conviction I ratify and reaffirm the words that Paul VI spoke originally to the bishops of your country: 'Brethren, we know the difficulties involved in preserving Catholic schools, and the uncertainties of the future, and yet we rely on the help of God and on your zealous collaboration and untiring efforts, so that Catholic schools can continue, despite grave obstacles, to fulfill their providential role at the service of genuine Catholic education, and at the service of your country' (Address of September 15, 1975).

"Yes, the Catholic school must remain a privileged means of Catholic education in America. As an instrument of the apostolate it is worthy of the greatest sacrifices. But no Catholic school can be effective without dedicated Catholic teachers, convinced of the great ideal of Catholic education. The Church needs men and women who are intent on teaching by word and example—intent on helping to permeate the whole education milieu with the spirit of Christ. This is a great vocation, and the Lord Himself will reward all who serve in it as educators in the cause of the word of God.

"A Question of Communicating Christ"

"In order that the Catholic school and the Catholic teachers may truly make their irreplaceable contribution to the Church and to the world, the goal of Catholic education itself must be crystal clear. Beloved sons and daughters of the Catholic Church, brothers and sisters in the faith: Catholic education is above all a question of communicating Christ, of helping to form Christ in the lives of others. In the expression of the Second Vatican Council, those who have been baptized must be made ever more aware of the gift of faith that they have received, they must learn to adore the Father in spirit and in truth, and they must be trained to live the newness of Christian life in justice and in the holiness of truth.

"These are indeed essential aims of Catholic education. To foster and promote them gives meaning to the Catholic school; it spells out the dignity of the vocation of Catholic educators.

"Yes, it is above all a question of communicating Christ, and helping his uplifting Gospel to take root in the hearts of the faithful. Be strong, therefore, in pursuing these goals. The cause of Catholic education is the cause of Jesus Christ and of his Gospel at the service of man.

"And be assured of the solidarity of the entire Church, and of the sustaining grace of our Lord Jesus Christ. In His name, I send you all my Apostolic Blessing: in the name of the Father, and of the Son, and of the Holy Spirit. Amen."[350]

To this emphasis on Catholic education and need of Catholic schools, the Pope added another reminder, namely, that such a teaching must be free from any kind of coercion. "Nobody can be forced to embrace faith against one's will," he said. "The act of faith is by its nature a free act." On the other hand, "the government cannot force citizens to reject religion, just as the Church cannot coerce religious belief."[351]

To one reflecting on these several papal documents, it is clear that the Pope is serious about his Father's business,[352] to cleanse the Church of corrupting modern influences and yet to bring the Church with her holy mission into step with modern times, as legacies he will fulfill.

A New Kind of Papacy

Concomitantly with hopes raised, a new kind of papacy emerges, one with a new Pope's reassurance: "Don't be afraid. Throw wide open the doors to Christ. Open the borders of States, economic and political systems, the immense areas of culture, civilization, development. Don't be afraid!"[353]

There is clear-cut evidence that this Pope intends to fulfill all these legacies[354] placed on him, with a love and ecumenical openness of John XXIII and with determined efforts for the Christian orthodoxy and authenticity of Paul VI, whose inheritance is to be executed in faithfulness to John Paul I's dedicated manner, as he chose both their names as hallmark of his pontificate.

With such reassurances we are indeed comforted to know that these and all legacies to be fulfilled are in good hands, those of John Paul II, for they are an integral part of this Fisherman's apostolic vision.

CONCLUSION

PRESENTING a festive profile of John Paul II has been my pleasurable task, for I sensed that the people placed their hopes in him immediately. We have learned from former times, and since Vatican II especially, the dangers of setting our hopes too high, but is it too much to hope that the moral center of the world, in both the religious and the secular sense, may once again be Rome?

Catholics and all Christians want a good Pope. They wish a Pope to be proud of: a strong, pastoral, brave, compassionate Christian capable as an evangelist of attracting, as an apostle of inspiring, as the Vicar of Christ of leading, the while keeping everyone confident, alert, and faithful, all feeling good to be included in this Fisherman's apostolic vision.

Is it too much to require? Certainly one can ask from the Pope the qualities of a leader and some signs of it: that he know leadership must be learned, respect earned, and assent and consent won. What we get from Pope John Paul II may depend as much on our expectations as on his delivery and on his expectations of us. Most important in his legacy will certainly stand out his presentation of the authority and the magisterium that concern the very essentials of the Christian faith, the Christian life, and the Christian heritage to which we must hold on.

Certain comforting signs of such leadership are evident already. This Pope appears to us no prisoner of the Vatican, not one boxed in by the Roman Curia, nor yet one in a hurry to make false moves or mistakes. He will make changes, to be sure, in his own time. Until then, observers will read, be constrained even to construe every move and every statement howsoever they choose.

As young as he is, John Paul II could be Pope for the rest of this century. As young as he is, too, he has the time and the energy to plan a new kind of papacy for a changing Church in a modern world. It is the Catholic faith that he, as Vicar of Christ, has in his trust, the Kingdom of Christ which is not of this world (cf. Jn 15:19), and as it is in this world (cf. 2 Cor 5:19). It is understandable then that the faithful expect of him so much. It is imperative that he recognize the unbounded trust the faithful put in him. Thus with the Pope I say: "Don't be afraid!"

NOTES

CHAPTER 1

1. Francis Dvornik, *The Idea of Apostolicity in Byzantium and the Legend of the Apostle Andrew* (Cambridge, Mass., 1958), pp. 1-41 and *passim*.

2. Felix Mikula, "Neitalsti papezi," *Nový svet* (Cleveland) Dec. 8, 1978; NC News Release, Oct. 17, 1978; Joseph Brusher, SJ, *Popes through the Ages* (Princeton: Van Nostrand Co., Inc., 1956).

3. Francis Dvornik, *Byzance et la Primauté Romaine* (Paris, 1964); *idem,* "Eastern Churches and Roman Primacy," *Diakonia* 1 (1966), pp. 3-6.

4. Thomas P. Neill and Raymond H. Schmandt, *History of the Catholic Church* (Milwaukee: Bruce, 1937), pp. 624-626; Wilfrid Parsons, *The Pope and Italy* (New York, 1929); Philip Hughes, *Pope Pius the Eleventh* (New York, 1937); James H. Ryan, ed., *Encyclicals of Pius XI* (St. Louis, 1927).

5. John Meyendorff, *The Orthodox Church* (New York: Pantheon Books, 1962), pp. 39-60.

6. NC News Release, Washington D.C., Oct. 18, 1978.

7. Joseph X. Dever, "Cardinal Krol talks to Society," *Philadelphia Bulletin,* Nov. 1, 1978.

8. Ludvik Nemec, "The Communist Ecclesiology during the Church-State Relationship in Czechoslovakia, 1945-67," *Proceedings of the American Philosophical Society* 112, no. 4 (Aug. 1968), pp. 245-276. Analogous Communist ecclesiology was pressed in all satellite countries behind the Iron Curtain.

9. József Cardinal Mindzenty, *Memoirs,* trans. Richard and Clara Vinston (New York: Macmillan Pub. Co., 1974), pp. 232-246 and *passim.*

10. George J. Prpic, "New Era in Yugoslavia," *America* 116 (April 8, 1967), pp. 528-530; Peter Segvic, "Positive Development of Relations between Yugoslavia and the Vatican," *RCDA* 17 (N.Y., 1978), pp. 81-83.

11. "Materials of the Visit Paid by Eduard Gierek to the Pontiff, Pope Paul VI," *Information Bulletin of Christian Social Association* no. 12 (Warsaw, Dec. 1977), pp. 25-35; Bohuslav Hruby, "First Visit of a Communist Leader to Vatican," *RCDA* 17 (New York, 1977), pp. 77-80.

12. "In Memoriam: Pope John Paul I. After 34 Days, a Lasting Impression," *News World,* Oct. 22, 1978; see *The Message of John Paul I* (Boston: Daughters of St. Paul, 1979).

13. David A. Andelman, "New Pope Stirs Czech Church's Hopes," *New York Times,* Feb. 16, 1979.

14. "Young: Pope Can Help Detente," *Impact* 8 (Dec. 1978), p. 7.

15. *Pastoral Constitution on the Church in the Modern World,* Walter M. Abbott, ed., Joseph Gallagher, trans., *Documents of Vatican II* (Herder and Herder, 1966), pp. 199-308.

16. *Declaration on Religious Freedom,* Abbott, *Vatican II,* pp. 672-700, on the right of the person and of communities to social and civil freedom in matters religious; Pius Augustin, *Religious Freedom in Church and State* (Baltimore: Helicon, 1966), pp. 269-312; Floyd Anderson, ed. *Council Daybook: Vatican II* (Washington, D.C.: NCWC, 1966), pp. 35-40 and *passim.*

17. Malachi Martin, "John Paul II—How He Will Surprise Us—and the Reds," *New York Daily News,* Nov. 12, 1978; *idem, Final Conclave* (New York, 1975).

18. Martin, "John Paul II."

19. Richard McBrien, "Author's Writings Imply Pope Will Favor East over West," *Byzantine Catholic World,* Feb. 25, 1979.

20. "Homily of His Holiness, Pope John Paul II, at the Mass Marking the Beginning of His Pastoral Ministry, Sunday, Oct. 22, 1978," *Osservatore Romano,* English ed., Nov. 2, 1978.

21. John Jay Hughes, "A New Era, Exorcising the Demons of History," *Commonweal* 105, no. 22 (Nov. 10, 1978), pp. 708-710.

CHAPTER 2

22. "Chaos Marked Reign of Last Non-Italian Pope," *News World,* Oct. 2, 1978.

23. Jean Potin, *La Croix,* Oct. 18, 1978.

24. Milan J. Reban, "John Paul's Church," *Dallas Morning News* reprinted in *Hlas Naroda* (Chicago), Jan. 6, 1979.

25. André Geraud, "An Historic Choice," *La Croix,* Oct. 18, 1978.

26. "An Historic Choice," *Osservatore Romano,* Eng. ed., Nov. 18, 1978.

27. "Bless the Pope from Poland," *Tablet* (London), Oct. 19, 1978.

28. "Pope John Paul II, First Polish—Third Slavic Pontiff of the Catholic Church," *American Ethnic* 6 (Winter 1978), p. 3.

29. David A. Andelman, "A Popular Catholic Weekly in Poland Mirrors Church-State Conflict," *New York Times,* Jan. 5, 1979, p. A4.

30. "A Witness to the Gospel in a Changing World," *Osservatore Romano,* Nov. 16, 1978.

31. Published in *Il Giornale,* Oct. 18, 1978.

32. Richard Kenyon, "Archbishop's [Weakland] Comments on the Pope Draw Fire from Polish Community," *National Catholic Reporter,* Jan. 12, 1979, concerning an interview with Archbishop Rembert Weakland in Wilwaukee, Wis., that was reported in the *Milwaukee Journal.* Archbishop Weakland insisted that his comments were taken out of context and explained the whole interview in the *Catholic Herald Citizen,* Jan. 1, 1979.

33. NC News Release, Oct. 17, 1978.

34. "Pope John Paul I (1912-78)," *The Pope Speaks* 23, no. 4 (Winter 1978), pp. 291-384; the entire issue is dedicated to the active, short life of this Pope; "A Swift Stunning Choice," and "Compassionate Shepherd," *Time,* Sept. 4, 1978; Maria Leonhauser, "The Warm Wisdom of the First John Paul," *Philadelphia Bulletin,* Feb. 3, 1979; Albino Luciani, *Illustrissimi: Letters from Pope John Paul I* (New

York: Little, Brown, 1979); Edward P. Spurgiacz "New Pope's Tribute to His Predecessor," *Tablet* (London), Oct. 19, 1978.

CHAPTER 3

35. Especially expressed by the *Constitution on the Church*, promulgated Nov. 21, 1964, by the Second Vatican Council; see Abbott; *Vatican II*, pp. 9-102.

36. Eleanor M. Gates, *Encyclopedic Dictionary of Religion* (1979), s. v. "Tiara." He gave it really to the poor. In fulfillment of this, visitors contribute to the work of Mother Teresa of Calcutta for the poor.

37. Robert I. Gannon, *The Cardinal Spellman Story* (New York: Doubleday, 1962), *passim*.

38. "Homily of His Holiness, Pope John Paul II at the Mass Marking the Beginning of His Pastoral Ministry, Sunday 22 October," *Osservatore Romano*, Eng. ed., Nov. 2, 1978.

39. *Encyclopedia Britannica*, 22:176, s. v. "Tiara."

40. Donald Attwater, *A Catholic Dictionary*, 3d ed. 1958, s. v. "Tiara." This formula was introduced in 1596.

41. Costly tiaras were made especially in the pontificates of Paul II (d. 1464), Sixtus IV (d. 1484), and above all in that of Julius II (d. 1513), whose tiara was valued at 200,000 ducats and made by the jeweller Caradosso of Milan.

42. *Enciclopedia Cattolica*, 12:69-71, s. v. "Tiara."

43. Francis Dvornik, *Early Christian and Byzantine Political Philosophy* 2 vols. (Washington, D.C.: The Dumbarton Oaks, 1966), vol. 1, pp. 24, 114, 115, 118-119.

44. *Idem, The Conflict between Sacerdotium and Imperium in the Middle Ages: East and West* (Washington, D.C.: Catholic Univ. of America Press, 1979).

45. *Idem, Byzantium and Roman Primacy* (New York: Fordham Univ. Press, 1966), pp. 85-166.

46. Since the Lateran Treaty of Feb. 11, 1929; see Thomas P. Neill and R. H. Schmandt, *History of the Catholic Church* (Milwaukee, 1939), pp. 624-626. This can also be understood as an historical prolongation of the old idea of Rome as *caput totius orbis terrarum* [capital of the whole world]; see F. Dvornik, *Early Christian and Byzantine Political Philosophy* (Washington, D.C., 1966), vol. 1, pp. 27-35.

CHAPTER 4

47. Francis Dvornik, *The Slavs, Their Early History and Civilization* (Boston, 1956), pp. 107-115.

48. *Idem, The Conflict between Sacerdotium and Imperium in the Middle Ages: East and West* (Washington, D.C. 1979).

49. J. W. Thompson, *Feudal Germany* (Chicago, 1926); M. Z. Zedlicki, "Les rapports entre la Pologne et l'empire Germanique," *La Pologne au VIIe Congres inter. des sciences historiques* (Varsavie, 1933), p. 3; T. Sulimirski, *Poland and Germany, Past and Future* (London, 1942).

50. B.B. Szezesniak, *New Catholic Encyclopedia*, 13:692-3, s. v. "Stanislaus of Cracow."

51. J. Zathey, "O kilku przepadlych zabytkach rekopismiennych Biblioteki narodomej w Warzzavie" [Remnants of some lost manuscripts in the National Library in Warsaw], *Studia z dziejow kultury polskiej* (Warsaw, 1949), pp. 73-86.

52. The country remained divided into several hereditary dukedoms—Great Poland with Gniezno (Gnesen); Little Poland with Krakow, Mazovia, Sandomierz, and Silesia, which were often subdivided into small territories given to the members of the reigning families.

53. Josef Šusta, Soumrak Prèmyslovcu a jejich dĕditví (Prague, 1935), pp. 45ff.; B. Bendl, "Les derniers Prĕmyslides," *Revue historique* 129 (1937), pp. 34-62.

54. Oswald Balzer, *Krolewstwo Polskie, 1295-1370* 2 vols. (Lwow, 1919), *passim.*

55. J. Kaczmarczyk, Kazimierz Wielki (Warsaw, 1948), pp. 388-394; J. Sieradzki, *Polska wieku XIV, Studium z czasow Kazimierza Wielkiego* (Warsaw, 1959).

56. O. Balzer, *Les statuts de Casimir le Grand* (Poznań, 1947), *passim.*

57. F. M. Bartoš, "Nejstarší polský kronikár a jeho céský původ," *Vestnik* on the Czech Academy 61 (1952); M. Plezia, *Kronika Galla* (Krakow, 1947).

58. J. Poś, *Poczatki pišmiennictwa polskiego* (Lwow, 1922), pp. 3-98.

59. Bruce A. Boswell, "Poland and Lithuania in the Fourteenth and Fifteenth Centuries," *CMH,* vol. 8, pp. 556-586; H. Paskiewicz, *Regesta Lithuaniae ab origine usque ad magni Ducatus cum Regni Poloniae unione* (Warsaw, 1930); St. Kutrzeba, *Unijz Polski z Litwa* (Krakow, 1914).

60. S. Zempicki, *Renesans i humanism w Polsce* (Warsaw, 1951).

61. *Annales seu cronica inclyti regni Poloniae* and *Historiae Poloniae Libri XII.*

62. *A History of Devotio Moderna* by Albert Flyma (Flamden: Archon Books, 1965).

63. J. Krzyžanowski, *Mikolaj Rej i Stăs Caska* (Warsaw, 1958).

64. John Paul II chose to mention the Polish 19th-century historical fiction writer Henryk Sienkiewicz in the homily of his inaugural Mass (see text in ch. 13). Jeremiah Curtin, who translated *Quo Vadis: A Narrative of the Time of Nero,* wrote that the classic "gives us pictures of the opening scenes in the conflict of moral ideas with the Roman Empire." ("Only authorized edition" New York: Grosset and Dunlap, 1925; the translator's copyright of 1896 was renewed in 1925 by Alma M. Curtin.)

65. Francis Dvornik, *The Slavs in European History and Civilization* (Rutgers Univ. Press, 1902), p. 306.

66. S. Kot, *Humanizm i Reformacja w Polsce* (Lwow, Warsaw, 1927).

67. I. Grabowski, *Literatura luterska w Polsce wieku XVI, 1530-1630* (Poznań, 1920).

68. R. H. Lord, *The Second Partition of Poland: A Study in Diplomatic History* (Cambridge, Mass., 1915); *idem*, "The Third Partition of Poland," *Slavonic Review* 3 (1925), *passim*.

69. K. Lutoslanski, *Les Partages de la Pologne et la lutte pour l'indépendance* (Paris, 1918).

70. Arlene Swidler, "Jews and Poles Fight Cold War," *National Catholic Reporter*, Feb. 2, 1979; "Exhibit To Help Kill the 'Big Lie'," *Polish American Journal* (Feb. 1979), p. 7, Professor Zajaczkowski insists that Poles' relations toward Jews were fair; *Sacrum Poloniae millennium*, 10 vols. (Rome, 1954-64).

71. O. Halecki, *A History of Poland* (3d ed., New York, 1961); W. F. Reddaway, ed., *Cambridge History of Poland* 2 vols. (Cambridge, 1941-50); J. Umiushi, *Historia Kosciola*, ed. W. Urban, 4th ed., 2 vols. (Opole, 1959-60); W. Markert, ed. *Polen* (Cologne, 1959); W. Meystowitz, *L'Église Catholique en Pologne entre deux guerres 1919-1939* (Rome, 1944).

72. B. Stasiewski, *New Catholic Encyclopedia* (New York: McGraw Hill, 1968), s. v. "Poland."

73. J. K. Zawodny, *Death in the Forest: The Story of the Katyn Forest Massacre* (Univ. of Notre Dame Press, 1962), pp. 49-73 and *passim;* see also Kazimierz Skarzynski, "Katyn Polski Czerćony Krzyz" [Katyn and the Polish Red Cross], *Kultura* no. 9/51 (May 1955), pp. 140ff; Jack Anderson, "Voice of America Censors Item of Katyn Massacre," *Philadelphia Bulletin*, Feb. 17, 1979.

74. Jan M. Ciechanowski, *The Warsaw Rising of 1944* (Cambridge Univ. Press, 1974), pp. 69-243; see Nemec's review in *Slavic Review* (1975) and in *Narod Supplement* (Chicago, July 21, 1974).

75. Maria Winowska, *The Death Camp Proved Him Real: The Life of Father Maximilian Kolbe, Franciscan* (Kenosha, Wisconsin Prow, 1971).

76. P. Lenert, *L'Église Catholique en Pologne* (Paris, 1962); W. Zylinski and B. Wierzbianski, eds., *White Paper on the Persecution of the Church in Poland* (London, 1954).

77. Bohuslav Hruby, "First Visit of a Communist Leader in Vatican," *RCDA* 17, nos. 4, 5, 6 (New York, 1978), pp. 77-80; both speeches, i.e., of Prime Minister Gierek and Pope Paul VI, can be found in *Information Bulletin* of Christian Social Association, May 12 (Warsaw, Dec. 1977), pp. 25-35; these Eng. texts were reprinted in *RCDA*.

CHAPTER 5

78. Paul Hofmann, "Small Town in Poland, Pope's Birthplace, Glows in Reflected Glory," *New York Times*, Jan. 14, 1979.

79. *Tomus* IV c. 1920 *Liber natorum*, p. 549: "18 May Carolus Joseph, filius legitimi tori Wojtyla (pater) oficialis militum, filius Matiae et Annae Przeczka. Mater—Kaczorowska Emilia (died 13. IV. 1929 r. Corka Feliksa i Marii Scholc) Chrzesni rodzice: Josephus Kuczmierczyk mercator Maria Wiatrowska. Ochr zcil Franciszek Zak, Kaplan."

80. *Ibid.*

81. *Philadelphia Bulletin*, Nov. 8, 1978.

82. Jef De Roeck, *L'Uomo dalla Polonia* (Marietti, 1978), pp. 77ff.

83. "A Pope from Poland," *Newsweek*, Oct. 18, 1978, pp. 78-87, especially p. 83.

84. Malachi Martin, "John Paul II," *Winnipeg Free Press*, Dec. 2, 1978.

85. Otakar Odlozilik, *The Way of Light: The Glory and Martyrdom of Czechoslovak Schools* (Chicago: Czechoslovak National Council, 1942).

CHAPTER 6

86. *Osservatore Romano*, Dec. 28, 1978.

87. Michal Radgowski, Marta Wesolowska, and Wojciech Gielzynski, "Pope an Ordinary Boy, Stood Out from Others," *Polityka;* repr. in *Philadelphia Sunday Bulletin*, Nov. 5, 1978, interview with M. Kydrynski.

88. *Ibid.*

89. Andres Barriales, "Papa Wojtyla: Dramaturgo y poeta," *Ecclesia* 33 (Madrid, Nov. 25, 1978), pp. 27-29.

90. Morris West, "John Paul II: A Pope for All the People," *Reader's Digest*, vol. 114 (Feb. 1979), pp. 129-135.

91. Gene Wright, ed., *Four Popes, Keepers of the Faith since 1958* (New York: Ideal Publishing Corp., 1978), p. 13.

92. Random House, New York, 1979.

93. Hugh T. Henry, *Poems, Charades, Inscriptions of Pope Leo XIII . . . with English Translation and Notes* (New York-Philadelphia: Dolphin Press, 1902); see Sister Margaret Rose, SSJ, *Encyclopedic Dictionary of Religion* (1979), s. v. "Henry, Hugh Thomas" which gives details of Msgr. Henry as a distinguished hymnologist and educator.

94. *Osservatore Romano*, Dec. 1, 1978.

CHAPTER 7

95. Janko Mlynar, "Svǎty Otec—so Slovakmi" *Jednota*, Feb. 21, 1979, p. 11.

96. Anna M. Cienciala, *Poland and the Western Powers 1938-1939* (Univ. of Toronto Press, 1968).

97. Stefan Korbowski, *The Polish Underground State: A Guide to the Underground 1939-1945* (Denver: East European Monograph, 1978).

98. *Newsweek*, Oct. 8, 1978, pp. 78-87.

99. See notes 100 and 101.

100. P. Arturo D'Onofrio, *Luminosi Albori di un Pontificato Giovanni Paulo II* (Naples-Rome: 2d ed. 1979), pp. 25-26.

101. "Dr. Josef Lichten (interview of Nov. 3, 1978), *Kultura* (Warsaw, Dec. 1978), pp. 29-31.

CHAPTER 8

102. Francis X. Murphy and Norman Shaifer, *John Paul II: A Son from Poland* (N.J.: Shepherd Press, 1978), pp. 10-12.

103. Jef de Roeck, *L'Uomo dalla Polonia*, p. 86.

104. *Ibid.*

105. Leopold Tyrmand, "Poland, Marxism and John Paul II," *Hlas Naroda,* Feb. 17, 1978, p. 16.

106. *Ibid.*

107. Walter M. Abbott, ed., Joseph Gallagher, trans., *Documents of Vatican II* (Herder and Herder, 1966), pp. 199-308.

108. *Ibid.*

109. D'Onofrio, *Giovanni Paulo II,* p. 39 and *passim.*

110. Published in Polish as *Milosc i odpowiedzialnosc* (Krakow: Wydawnictwo Znak, 1964); it was translated by Ambretta Betti Milanoli (1968) with a 2d ed. (1978) by Marietti Publishers House.

111. Wright, *Four Popes,* p. 15.

CHAPTER 9

112. "To the Archdiocese of Krakow, 'I Offer to the Lord This So Beloved Land'," letter of Pope John Paul II and cosigned by Auxiliary Bishop Julian Groblicki of Krakow, *Osservatore Romano,* Eng. ed., Nov. 9, 1978. It is a beautiful and emotional farewell to his former Archdiocesan See. It is full of patriotism and memories.

113. Oscar Halecki, *The Millennium of Europe* (Univ. of Notre Dame Press, 1964); cf. *idem, A History of Poland,* 3d ed. (New York, 1961), *passim.*

114. This is the partial text of a leaflet distributed on the occasion to the pilgrims. It addresses some bitter sarcasm to the Polish Communists who denied the Pope a visa.

115. This was practical advice for a new apostolate of the Church for extending herself to the people. It reveals also Wojtyla's sharp grasp of the psychological moment to increase his appeal to the people.

116. Sister Margaret Rose Brown, SSJ, *Encyclopedic Dictionary of Religion* (1979), s. v. "Black Madonna"; J. Blair, *ibid.,* s. v. "Czestochowa, Our Lady of."

117. Donald Attwater, *A Dictionary of Mary* (New York: P. J. Kenedy, 1914), pp. 60-61.

118. Howard H. Kaminsky, *A History of the Hussite Revolution* (Berkeley: Univ. of California Press, 1967), *passim;* see review by L. Nemec in *Theological Studies* 29 (1968), pp. 128-130.

119. F. E. Kissling, "President of the U.S. Gives Black Madonna's Replica to Texas Church: Our Lady of Jasna Gora," *Crusaders Almanac,* July 1, 1966.

120. D'Onofrio, *Giovanni Paulo II,* pp. 62-63.

121. *Ibid.*

122. On Aug. 21, 1969, the Russian Army invaded Czechoslovakia to suppress Dubcek's movement for a "socialism with a human face," Josef Kalvoda, *Czechoslovakia's Role in Soviet Strategy* (Washington, D.C.: Univ. Press of America, 1978), pp. 258-277.

123. Jerzy Turowicz, "Dnia 16 Pazdziernika 1978 arcybiskup- metropolita Krakowski Karol Kardynal Wojtyla wybrany zostal papiezem Kosciola Powszechnego i przybral imie Jana Pawla II," *Tygodnik Powszechny,* Oct. 21, 1978.

124. *Rzeczpospolita,* Nov. 26, 1946.

125. Jacek M. Majchrowski, "The Origin and Early Activities of the Pax Movement in Poland," *East European Quarterly* 12, no. 4 (Winter 1978), pp. 385-397.

126. *Ibid.*

127. Peter Hebblethwaite, *The Year of Three Popes* (Cleveland: William Collins, 1979), *passim;* see John Jay Hughes' review in *America* (March 3, 1979), pp. 164-165.

128. *Ibid.*

129. Richard W. Daw, *Nights of Sorrow, Days of Joy* (Washington, D.C.: NC News Service, 1978), p. 126.

130. Karol Wojtyla, *Il Buon pastore: Scritti, discorsi e lettere pastorali,* trans. Elzbieta Cywiak and Renzo Panzone (Rome: Edizioni Logos, 1978), pp. 147-155.

131. *Ibid.*

132. "Wahrt Christus, seinem Kreuz und der Kirche die Treue," *Osservatore Romano,* German ed., Nov. 3, 1978.

133. D'Onofrio, *Giovanni Paulo II,* pp. 57-58: "Nowa Huta Strenua lotta per la Chiesa" (author's translation) *(paragraphing added).*

134. NC News Service, *Nights of Sorrow,* p. 136.

135. *Ibid.*

136. This synthesis is by the author on the basis of a report from this Synod; see "Sulla Collegialità" in D'Onofrio, *op. cit.,* pp. 44-46.

137. *Ibid.,* pp. 46-47.

138. *Ibid.,* pp. 52-53.

139. *Ibid.,* pp. 48-49.

140. *Ibid. (paragraphing added).*

141. *Nový Zivot* 30 (1978), p. 222.

142. Josef Korbel, *Poland between East and West: Soviet and German Diplomacy toward Poland* (Princeton, N.J.: Princeton Univ. Press, 1963), pp. 68-93.

CHAPTER 10

143. D'Onofrio, *Giovanni Paulo II,* p. 55.

144. Karol Wojtyla, *Segno di contraddizione: Meditazioni* (Milan: Catholic Univ. Press, 1977), Eng. trans. *Sign of Contradiction* (New York: Seabury Press, 1979).

145. From Stefan Cardinal Wyszynski's preface to Wojtyla's book *Segno di Contraddizione,* written in Warsaw on Nov. 16, 1976, to Polish ed., *Znak, ktoremu sprzeciwiac sie beda,* ed. Pallotinum (Poznan-Warsaw, 1976).

146. An essential index of Wojtyla's writings appeared as "Bibliografia essenziale di Karol Wojtyla" in Jef de Roeck's *L'uomo dalla Polonia* (Marietti, 1978), pp. 121-123; see also *Osservatore Romano,* Nov. 12, 1978.

147. Leo D. Rudnytsky, "Past Encounters with a Future Pope," *La Salle Quarterly* (Winter 1978-79), pp. 17-19; Pam Robbins, "Wojtyla at Harvard," *Sign* (Feb. 1979), pp. 19-20.

148. It was published in book form as Karol Wojtyla, *Fruitful and Responsible Love* (New York: Seabury Press, 1979), pp. 11-35, together with comments by other participants.

149. Karol Wojtyla (Andrzej Jawien), *Easter Vigil and Other Poems* (New York: Random House, 1979).

150. NC News Service, *Nights of Sorrow,* pp. 144-145.

151. Murphy and Shaifer, *John Paul II,* p. 14.

152. Abbott, *Vatican II,* pp. 341-367.

153. *Ibid.,* pp. 675-697.

154. *Ibid.,* pp. 199-308.

155. Dominik Horodynski, "Jan Pawel II," *Kultura,* Oct. 29, 1978.

156. Ludvik Nemec, "Stephen Cardinal Trochta, an Educator, a Churchman, and an Ecumenist," *Bohemia,* Jahrbuch des Collegium Carolinum 17 (Munich, 1976), pp. 282-324.

157. *Ibid.*

158. This was a complaint, as reported in the press, to Cardinal Alfred Bengsch of Berlin, who too was surprised by these same tactics of the Czechoslovakian Communists, *Nový Zivot* 30 (Rome, 1978), p. 205.

159. *"Urbi et Orbi"* of Pope John Paul II *(paragraphing added).*

160. *Newsweek,* Oct. 30, 1978, pp. 83-84.

161. *Ibid.*

162. Marx is not the original author of this slogan; for the first time it was used by Charles Kingsley (1819-75). See Fulton J. Sheen, *Communism and the Conscience of the West* (Indianapolis, 1948), p. 62; Henri de Lubac, *The Un-Marxian Socialist: A Study of Proudhon* (New York, 1948), *passim. Der Grosse Herder* 6: 1384-85.

163. *Newsweek,* Oct. 30, 1978, p. 84.

164. *Ibid.,* p. 85.

165. Ludvik Nemec, *The Communist Ecclesiology during the Church-State Relationship in Czechoslovakia 1945-1967,* PROCEEDINGS OF THE AMERICAN PHILOSOPHICAL SOCIETY vol. 112, no. 4 (Aug. 1968), pp. 245-276.

166. Radgowski et al., "Pope an Ordinary Boy."

CHAPTER 11

167. Daughters of St. Paul, pamphlet ed. (1978) *(subheads added).*

168. Resolution on the religious situation in Czechoslovakia was published in the *Congressional Record* of Sept. 2, 1976; see text also in Czech *Catholics at the 41st International Eucharistic Congress Held August 1-8, 1976 in Philadelphia, USA* (New York-Philadelphia, 1977), pp. 98-103; note the photo of Cardinal Wojtyla at the Congress, p. 31E; James M. Talley, ed., *Jesus, the Living Bread: A Chronicle of the Forty-First International Eucharistic Congress, Phila., Pa., August 1976* (Plainfield, N.J.: Logos International, 1976), *passim.*

169. NC News Service, *Nights of Sorrow,* pp. 129-130.

170. See Luke 16:1-14; consult also, for both Old Testament and New Testament references, the biblical concordances of Cruden; Fuller; Thompson and Stock; and the *Jerome Biblical Commentary.*

171. John Paul II, *Talks of John Paul II,* ed. Daughters of St. Paul (Boston: St. Paul Editions, 1979), pp. 39, 44-46.

172. *Tygodnik Powszechny* (Krakow, Oct. 8, 1978), p. 1; complete English trans. "New Pope's Tribute to His Predecessor," may be found in the *Tablet* (Brookyn) Oct. 19, 1978.

173. *The Message of John Paul I* (Boston: St. Paul Editions, Daughters of St. Paul, 1979), *passim:* Petr Ovecka, "Naplnil casy mnohe" [He fulfilled much], *Nový Zivot* 30 (Rome, 1978), pp. 208-210.

174. Karol Wojtyla, *Il Buon pastore: Scritti, discorsi e lettere pastorali,* trans. Elzbieta Cywiak and Renzo Panzone (Rome: Edizioni Logos, 1978).

CHAPTER 12

175. Remo Bezmalinovich-Gianni Merlin, *Un anno: tre papi* (Udine: I D edizioni, 1978), *passim.*

176. *Ibid.,* pp. 54-114; "Pope John Paul I (1912-1978)," *The Pope Speaks* 23, no. 4 (Winter 1978). The whole issue is dedicated to his life and thought.

177. "John Paul II—Poland's Gift to the World," *Polish American Journal* 67, no. 11 (Scranton, Nov. 13, 1978), pp. 1-2.

178. Richard W. Daw, ed., *Nights of Sorrows, Days of Joy: Papal Transition: Paul VI, John Paul I, John Paul II.* (Washington, D.C.: The National Catholic News Service, 1978), p. 136.

179. Francis X. Murphy and Norman Shaifer, "The Conclave and the Voting Process," *John Paul II: A Son from Poland* (South Hackensack, N.J.: Shepherd Press, 1978), pp. 17-19, 20-24.

180. Thomas P. Neill and Raymond H. Schmandt, *History of the Catholic Church* (Milwaukee: Bruce, 1957), pp. 560-561; Igino Giordani, *Pius X: A Country Priest* (Milwaukee, 1959), pp. 155-194.

181. Stefano de Andreis and Marcella Leone, *Il Pastore venuto da Lontano* (Milan: Editrice Magna, 1979), pp. 91-100; Robert I. Gannon, SJ, *The Cardinal Spellman Story* (New York, 1962), *passim.*

182. "Four Popes, Keepers of the Faith since 1958," souvenir issue of *Ideal Magazine* 12 (1978), pp. 64-65 and *passim.*

183. *Osservatore Romano,* Oct. 1, 1975; AAS 57 (1975), *passim.*

184. "Four Popes," p. 24; Peter Hebblethwaite, "Papal vote deduced," *National Catholic Reporter* (Nov. 3, 1978), p. 3.

185. Cf. *Osservatore Romano,* Oct. 16, 1978.

186. Winston S. Churchill and editors of *Life, The Second World War* 2 vols. (New York: Time, 1960), vol 2, pp. 523-526, zone accepted pp. 535, 559.

187. Ernest Cuneo, "Pontiff Personifies Strength of the Poles," *Polish American Journal* 58 (Scranton, Jan. 15, 1979), p. 1.

188. *Nový Zivot* 30 (Rome, 1978), p. 205; Patrick D. McCarthy, "Church, State, and Italy," *America,* Dec. 30, 1978, pp. 490-492.

189. Latin American Bishops Conference at Puebla. Held Jan. 29-

Feb. 7, 1979; Arthur Jones, "John Paul Faces Marxism in Puebla," *National Catholic Reporter* (Jan. 26. 1979), p. 12.

190. Henry Tanner, "Gromyko received by Pope Paul," *New York Times* (Jan. 25, 1979), p. A3.

191. *Ibid.*, "Vatican and Poland compromise on Form and Time of Papal Visit," (March 3, 1979), p. 2.

192. David A. Andelman, "New Pope stirs Czech Church's Hopes," *New York Times* (Feb. 16, 1979), p. A3.

193. Rudolf Otto, *Das Heilige* (Vienna, 1914), *passim.*

194. *Osservatore Romano* (Oct. 22, 1978).

195. *Ibid.* (Oct. 18, 1978). About the universality of the Church.

196. *Ibid.* (Oct. 20, 1978). On "the Church's service to humanity."

197. *Ibid.* (Oct. 21, 1978). Regarding "the freedom of information in the Service of Truth."

198. Andrew Greeley, "Defending Pope Paul," Newark *Advocate* (Feb. 7, 1979).

199. "Coat of Arms of Pope John Paul II," *Talks of John Paul II, op. cit.*, p. 47.

200. From the Homily of John Paul II at his Inauguration Mass October 22, 1978. Cf. *Osservatore Romano* (Oct. 22, 1978).

CHAPTER 13

201. "Kardynal Karol Wojtyla 264 papiezem," *Polityka* 22, no. 42 (Warsaw, Oct. 21, 1978); Dominik Horodynski, "Jan Pawell II," *Kultura* 16 (Warsaw, Oct. 29, 1978).

202. See especially Francis X. Murphy and Norman Shaifer, *John Paul II, A Son from Poland* (N.J.: Shepherd Press, 1978), pp. 25-42.

203. "Homily of His Holiness, Pope John Paul II at the Mass marking the Beginning of His Pastoral Ministry, Sunday, 22 October," *Osservatore Romano,* English ed., Nov. 1978 *(paragraphing and subheads added).*

204. This designation appears frequently in several journals; the term was coined in *Commonweal* (1979) and used elsewhere; see Donald McGuire, "A Pope for Our Times," *Tablet* (Brooklyn) Oct. 19, 1978.

205. Henry Tanner, "John Paul II Determined To Assert His Leadership," *International Herald Tribune,* Jan. 9, 1979; Peter Hebblethwaite, "How the Pope Will Change the World," *Esquire* (May 8, 1979), pp. 25-36.

CHAPTER 14

206. Paul Hofmann, "Pope with a Style All His Own," *New York Times,* Jan. 26, 1976, p. A4.

207. Alan Riding, "Over a Million in Mexico City Excitedly Greet the Pope," *New York Times,* Jan. 27, 1976, p. 14.

208. "Mobs, Quake Greet Pope in Mexico," *Philadelphia Bulletin,* Jan. 27, 1979.

209. David B. Richardson, "Behind Pope John Paul's Pilgrimage," *U.S. News and World Report,* Jan. 29, 1979, pp. 34-35.

210. *Ibid.*, p. 35; "Pope Visits Slum, Urges Aid to Poor," *Philadelphia Bulletin,* Jan. 26, 1979.

211. *Osservatore Romano* (Eng. ed.), Oct. 23, 1978.

212. Richard W. Daw, ed., *Nights of Sorrow, Days of Joy: Papal Transition: Paul VI, John Paul I, John Paul II* (Washington, D.C.: NC News Service, 1979), p. 144.

213. *Ibid.*, pp. 44-46.

214. Jerry Filteau, "John Paul II Brings New Style to Papacy," *Catholic Standard and Times,* Nov. 16, 1978.

215. Louis Bouyer, "Liturgical and non-Liturgical: The Spirit of Liturgy and of Devotion," *Life and Liturgy* (London and New York: Sheed and Ward, 1962), pp. 243-256; Donald J. Wolf and James V. Schall, *Current Trends in Theology* (New York: Doubleday, 1968), pp. 97-116 and *passim.*

216. "In Memoriam: Pope John Paul I: after 34 days, a Lasting Impression," special supplement to *News World,* Oct. 22, 1978.

217. "Letter of Pope John Paul II Nominating Secretary of State," Oct. 24, 1978, *Osservatore Romano* (Eng. ed.), Nov. 2, 1978.

218. Leszek Kolakowski, "Pomyslne proroctwa i pobozne zyczenia i laika na progu Nowego Pontyfikatu w wiecznej sprawie praw cesarskich i Boskich," *Kultura* (Paris, Dec. 1978), pp. 5-13.

219. "Pope Visited Harvard in '76," *Harvard Crimson,* Oct. 27, 1978.

220. James R. Brockman, "Seventeen Days in Puebla," *America* 140, no. 9 (March 1979), pp. 180-183.

221. "Liberation Theology Involves 'That Truth Which Made Us Free'," *Osservatore Romano* (Eng. ed.) Feb. 26, 1979.

222. Jan de Oris, "Argentina and Chile Ask Pope To Mediate Border Dispute," *New York Times,* Jan. 10, 1979, p. A3; "Pope's Appeal to Presidents of Argentina and of Chile," *Osserv. Romano,* Jan. 1, 1979.

223. *Ibid.,* Dec. 25, 1978.

224. Henry Tanner, "Vatican and Poland Compromise on Form and Time of Papal Visit," *New York Times,* March 3, 1979.

225. Arthur Jones, "John Paul Faces Marxism in Puebla," *National Catholic Reporter,* Jan. 26, 1979.

226. Igino Giordani, *Le Enciccliche sociali dei Papi (da Pio IX a Pio XII—1864-1946)*, 3d ed. (Rome: Ed Studium, 1946), *passim;* John Maher, "Pope Shows Concern for Social Services," *Catholic Standard and Times,* Feb. 22, 1979.

227. "Puebla Conference Expresses Collegiality," *Osservatore Romano,* Eng. ed., Feb. 12, 1979.

228. This interview was given to Robert Holton, editor of *Common Sense,* Memphis diocesan newspaper, during the recent meeting of Latin American bishops in Puebla, Mexico. It was recorded in the press and carried as "John Paul II—Administrator Who Gets to the Crux of Problems," *Byzantine Catholic World* 24, no. 9 (March 11, 1979), here reproduced in part *(subheads added).*

229. " 'Help Us Preach Love,' Pope asks in prayer," *Philadelphia Bulletin,* Jan. 8, 1978.

230. From the prayer of the Pope in the basilica of Our Lady of Guadalupe (Jan. 28, 1979), dedicated to the Indian Blessed Virgin. This basilica is the center of Mexican Catholicism; see "A Pilgrim to Guadalupe," *Osservatore Romano,* Eng. ed., Jan. 29, 1979.

231. Hofmann, "Pope with a Style," *New York Times,* Jan. 26, 1979, p. A4.

232. Pierre Teilhard de Chardin, *The Divine Milieu* (New York: Harper, 1960), *passim.*

233. Paul F. Healy, "Brzezinski Talks about the Pope and the President," *Catholic Digest* 43, no. 6 (April 1979), pp. 55-59.

234. Balfour Brickner, "Impressions of John Paul II," *America,* April 7, 1979, pp. 279-280. Rabbi Brickner, as director of the Department of Interreligious Affairs of the Union of American Hebrew Congregations, took part in an audience on March 12, 1979, at the Vatican.

CHAPTER 15

235. These remarks were made by Cardinal Wyszynski after the surprise election of Wojtyla. They appeared in several journals and were reprinted because of the importance of their coming from the Cardinal Primate of Poland.

236. This is the author's translation from the Polish; the entire text appeared also in Czech in *Nový Život* 30 (Rome, Dec. 1978), pp. 214-216 *(subheads added).*

237. Hansjakob Stehle, "Wohin steuert der neue Papst?" *Die Zeit,* Oct. 27, 1978.

238. Ronald Modras, "The Spirituality of John Paul II," *America,* Dec. 30, 1978, pp. 492-495.

239. Emmanuel Mounier (1905-50) wrote this 2-vol. book while he was still at the Sorbonne.

240. Gabriel Marcel, *The Mystery of Being* 2 vols. (Chicago: Regnery, 1951); *idem, Homo Viator* (New York: Harper, 1962).

241. Martin Buber (1878-1967) wrote, among others, a book entitled *I-Thou* (1945).

242. Jacques Maritain, *The Person and the Common Good* (London: Geoffrey Blenn, 1978).

243. Walter M. Abbott, ed., Joseph Gallagher, trans., *Documents of Vatican II* (Herder and Herder, 1966), pp. 199-308.

244. *Ibid.,* pp. 210-222.

245. Leszek Kolakowski, "Pomyslne Proroctwa i Pobozne Zyczenia laika na progu Nowego Pontyfikatu w wiecznej Sprawie Praw Cesarskich i Boskich," *Kultura* (Paris, Dec. 1978), pp. 5-13.

246. Andrew C. Varga, *On Being Human: Principles of Ethics* (Paulist Press, 1976).

247. Pam Robbins, "Wojtyla at Harvard," *Sign* (Feb. 1979), pp. 19-21.

248. *Ibid.*

249. Walter Kasper, *Jesus the Christ* (New York: Paulist Press, 1970); Hans Küng, *On Being a Christian,* trans. Edward Quinn (Simon and Schuster, Pocket Books, 1978).

250. Karol Wojtyla, "Denial of God and Contemporary Anthropocentrism," *Osservatore Romano,* Nov. 24, 1978 (from *Segno di contraddizione: Meditazioni,*, ed. Vita e Pensiero, Milan: Università Cattolica, 1977).

251. Keith R. Bridson, "A Christian Critique of Secular Anthropologies," *Conflicting Images of Man,* ed. William Nicholls (New York: Seabury Press, 1966), pp. 71-108.

252. Rudolph Otto, *The Idea of the Holy* (New York: Harper, 1962); C. J. Bleeker, *The Sacred Bridge: Researches into the Nature and Structure of Religion* (Leiden: E. J. Brill, 1963).

253. Henri de Lubac, *The Drama of Atheist Humanism* (Cleveland: World Publishing, Meridian Books, 1967), pp. 61-72.

254. *Osservatore Romano,* Dec. 25, 1978 *(subheads added).*

255. Modras, "John Paul II," p. 298.

256. Hans Urs von Balthasar, *Theology of History* (New York: Sheed and Ward, 1963), *passim.*

257. "Liberation Theology Involves 'That Truth Which Makes Us Free,'" from the Pope's discourse in general audience of Feb. 21, 1979, *Osservatore Romano,* Feb. 26, 1979.

258. As is usual with some intellectuals, as the afore-mentioned Czech philosopher Jan Blahoslav Kozak, *Jezis ve vírě a skepsi* [Jesus of the faith and skepsis] (Prague, 1939); *idem, Uboji o duchovní hvdnoty* [Struggle for spiritual values] (Prague, 1930).

259. Tadeuz Zychiewicz, "Janowi Pawlowi," *Tygodnik Powszechny, Oct.* 22, 1978).

260. Kenneth A. Briggs, "Papal Journey: New Guideline," *New York Times,* Feb. 2, 1979, p. A2.

261. Only the first volume of *Talks of John Paul II* (Boston. St. Paul ed., 1979) edited by Daughters of St. Paul contains the full text of the 109 talks given from Oct. 16, 1978, to Dec. 27, 1978.

262. Pascal P Parente, *The Ascetical Life* (St. Louis: Herder, 1951), *passim;* cf. Reginald Garrigou-Lagrange, *Christian Perfection and Contemplation* (Herder, 1937), *passim.*

263. "Pope John Paul II at Assisi," *Osserv. Romano,* Nov. 16, 1978.

264. *Ibid.*

265. "Homily of His Holiness, Pope John Paul II at the Mass Marking the Beginning of His Pastoral Ministry, Sunday 22 October 1978," *Osservatore Romano,* Nov. 2, 1978.

266. Ludvik Nemec, "The New Historical Perspective of St. Adalbert," *Polish Review* 7 (New York, 1962), pp. 21-64; *idem,* "Czech Role in the Christianization of Poland," *The Central European Federalist* 14 (New York, 1966), pp. 6-15.

267. "Close to Us," Cardinal Tomásek delivers the Pope's message to the Czechoslovak faithful, *Voice of the Nation* (Chicago: Dec. 22, 1979), pp. 23-24.

268. Pope's speech on Jan. 17, 1979, on the eve of the world Week of Prayer for Christian Unity, *Osserv. Romano,* Eng. ed., Jan. 22, 1979. The topic of ecumenism is a frequent subject of the Pope's talks.

269. *Catholic Standard and Times,* March 15, 1979, has entire text, in English and with notes. See also John Maher, "Pope Preparing Encyclical on Spiritual Nature of Man," *ibid.,* Feb. 15, 1979; Henry Tanner, "An Encyclical That Stresses Church Religious Freedom, Cites Threat in Injustice, Decline in Moral Issues," *New York Times,* March 16, 1979, pp. A1, A12.

270. Eamon Andrews, "A Holy Man Can Stand Firm," *Catholic Herald,* London, Oct. 20, 1978.

271. "A Man Filled with Christ," homily of thanksgiving for the Pope, by Humberto Cardinal Medeiros of Boston in *Talks of John Paul II* (Boston: St. Paul ed., 1979), pp. 31-36.

272. "Pope John Paul II Invites Cardinal Krol To Preach in Krakow," *Soul* 20 (Jan.-Feb. 1979), pp. 5-6.

273. Karol Wojtyla, *Easter Vigil and Other Poems,* trans. Jerzy Peterkiewicz (New York: Random House, 1979), p. 75; cf. David A. Andelman, "Poetry of the Pope, Published as Book," *New York Times,* March 25, 1979, p. A4.

CHAPTER 16

274. Malachi Martin, "John Paul II," *Winnipeg Free Press,* Dec. 2, 1978.

275. Morris West, "John Paul II: A Pope for All the People. I. The Man. II. The Burden," *Reader's Digest,* Feb. 1979, pp. 129-134.

276. "A Swift Stunning Choice: In an 'Instant Conclave.' the Cardinals Elect a New Pope: John Paul I, a Compassionate Shepherd," *Time,* Sept. 4, 1978, pp. 60-66.

277. Pope John Paul II, "Urbi et Orbi Message on Oct. 17, 1978, Pledges Fidelity to Vatican II," *Osservatore Romano,* Eng. ed., Oct. 26, 1978.

278. Paula Herbert, "Some Nuns Balk at Papal Request To Don Habits Again," *Philadelphia Bulletin,* Nov. 20, 1978.

279. Roger Garaudy, "Christian-Marxist Dialogue," *Journal of Ecumenical Studies* 4, no. 2 (Spring 1967), pp. 207-222; cf. Markus Barth, Developing Dialogue between Marxists and Christians," *Journal of Ecumenical Studies* 4, no. 3 (Summer 1967), pp. 385-405; Oliva Blanchette, SJ *Initiative in History: A Christian Marxist Exchange* (Cambridge, Mass, An occasional paper by the Church Society for College Work, 1967), pp. 1-27; here is a detailed account of the dialogue, held at Harvard Divinity School in 1967, sponsored by the Church Society for College Work in the United States; cf. Bernard Haring, *Road to Renewal* (New York: Doubleday, 1967), *passim;* Nels F. S. Ferrer, "The Church, Communism or Christ Community," *Journal of Religious Thought* 22, no. 1 (Washington, D.C. 1965-66), pp. 51-71.

280. Pope Paul VI's *Decree on Ecumenism* of Nov. 21, 1964; see its Eng. trans. in Walter M. Abbott, ed., Joseph Gallagher, trans., *Documents of Vatican II* (Herder and Herder, 1966), pp. 341-366; cf. Pope Paul VI's *Declaration on the Relationship of the Church to non-Christian Religions* of Oct. 28, 1965; see Abbott, *Vatican II,* pp. 660-668; see also *Pastoral Constitution on the Church in the Modern World* of Dec. 7, 1965; see Abbott, *Vatican II,* pp. 199-308.

281. A. Z. Jordan, *Philosophy and Ideology: The Development of Philosophy and Marxism-Leninism in Poland since the Second World War* (Dordrecht, 1963); a very interesting book on this subject is Milan Machovec, *Marxismus und Dialektische Theologie* (Zurich: EVZ-Verlag, 1965), Czech original (Prague, 1961). The first dialogue was sponsored by Paulus-Geselleschaft, directed by Father Erich Kellner of Germany and by the Sociological Institute of the Czechoslovak Academy of Sciences in Prague, directed by Dr. Erika Kadlecova, with the approval of government and ecclesiastical authorities.

282. Dale Vree, *On Synthesizing Marxism and Christianity* (New York: John Wiley and Sons, 1976); see review by Francis X. Maier, "Curious Bed Fellows: Marxism and Christianity," *National Catholic Reporter,* Feb. 18, 1979.

283. Karl Rahner, "Christian Humanism," *Journal of Ecumenical Studies* 4, no. 3 (Summer 1967), pp. 309-384.

284. Henri de Lubac,. *The Drama of Atheist Humanism* (Cleveland: The World Publishing Co., 1963), pp. 188-213; cf. "Marxist Sociology of Religion," *Herder Correspondence* 4, no. 2 (Feb. 1967), pp. 57-60; Olof Klohr, *Religion and Atheism Today* (Jena, 1966); H. Lilje, *Atheismus-Humanismus-Christentum* (Hamburg, 1962).

285. N. Lenin, *Socijalism i religya,* Polnoe sobranie socineny, 10; cf. Leonard Shapiro and Peter Reddaway, ed., *Lenin: The Man, the Theorist, the Leader* (Stanford Univ. Press, 1967); Mark Frankland, *Khrushchev* (New York: Stein and Day, 1967); A. Doak Barnett, *China after Mao* (Princeton Univ. Press, 1967).

286. The author's English translation from Latin address of John Paul II to the American bishops at Puebla, Mexico, on Jan. 28, 1979, *Osservatore Romano,* Jan. 29, 1979.

287. Jerry Filteau, "Priests Should Stay Out of Factional Politics," *The Catholic Standard and Times,* Feb. 8, 1979, an address to Mexican priests and religious men at the Basilica of Our Lady of Guadalupe, Mexico City, Jan. 27, 1979.

288. From the apostolic exhortation, *Evangelii nuntiandi,* of Paul VI, who prepared it for the opening of the Conference and its theme: "The present and the future of evangelization in Latin America," par. 9, 15, 30, 32, and *passim.* See "Liberation Theology Involves 'That Truth Which Made Us Free,'" by Pope in general audience of Feb. 21, 1979, *Osservatore Romano,* Eng. trans. Feb. 26, 1979.

289. "John Paul versus Liberation Theology," *Time,* Feb. 12, 1979; "The Pope and Theologies of Liberation," *America,* Feb. 10, 1979; Penny Lernoux, "Puebla: Will the Latin American Church Remain with the People?" *National Catholic Reporter,* Feb. 9, 1979.

290. Adrian Lee, "For Faith, the Pope Took His Lumps," *Philadelphia Bulletin* Feb. 8, 1979.

291. Jaime Fonseca, "'Let Me Be Your Voice' Pope Tells Peasants," *Catholic Standard and Times,* Feb. 8, 1979.

292. Andrew M. Greeley, "The Pope Has Been Getting Bad Press," *Philadelphia Inquirer,* Feb. 23, 1979.

293. *Philadelphia Inquirer,* Jan. 31, 1979.

294. *Byzantine Catholic World* (Pittsburgh), Feb. 11, 1979; see full text in *Osservatore Romano,* Jan. 22, 1979. The Pope spoke in general audience on the theme, "Charity Is a Gift of God."

295. Maurice Gordillo, "Velehrad e i suoi Congressi unionistici," *Civilta Cattolica,* anno 108 (1957), vol. 2, p. 577; Peter Esterka, "Toward Union: The Congresses at Velehrad," *Journal of Ecumenical Studies* 8 (Winter 1971), pp. 10-51; Francis Cinek, *Velehrad* (Olomouc, 1936). These were published in *Acta conventus Velehradensis* after each Congress, held periodically from 1907 to 1947.

296. Frantisek Cinek, *Antonin Cyril Stojan, arcibiskup Olomoncky* (Olomouc, 1933), *passim;* Josef Olšr, *Antonin Cyril Stojan* (Rome, 1961).

297. George J. Perejda, CSSR, Apostle of Church Unity: Metropolitan Andrew Sheptytsky (Yorkton, Sask., Canada: The Redeemer's Voice Press, 1960), *passim.*

298. Ludvik Nemec, "The Festive Profile of Francis Dvornik, the Scholar, the Historian, and the Ecumenist," *The Catholic Historical Review* 59, no. 2 (July 1973), pp. 185-224.

299. Francis Dvornik, *Byzantine Missions among the Slavs* (New Brunswick: Rutgers Univ. Press, 1970); *idem, Byzantske Misie u Slovanu* (Prague: Vysehrad, 1971).

300. Ludvik Nemec, "The Communist Ecclesiology during the Church-State Relationship in Czechoslovakia, 1945-1967," *Proceedings of the American Philosophical Society,* 112, no. 4 (Aug. 1968), pp. 245f.

301. Alaphidus Ottaviani, *Institutiones juris publici ecclesiastici,* 2 vols. (Rome, 1952), vol. 2; for other forms see John Courtney Murray, "Separation of Church and State," *America* 76 (Dec. 7, 1946), pp. 261ff; *idem, We Hold These Truths* (New York: Newman, 1960); cf. *idem,* "On Religious Freedom," *Theological Studies* 10 (Sept. 1949), pp. 22-23; Joseph C. Fenton, "Principles Underlying Traditional Church-State Doctrine," *American Ecclesiastical Review* 126 (June 1952), pp. 452-462; Donald J. Wolf, "American Catholic Theories of Church-State Relationship," *Current Trends in Theology,* ed. D. J. Wolf (New York: Doubleday, 1965), pp. 197-220; for their historical perspective, see E. A. Goerner, *Peter and Caesar: Political Authority and the Catholic Church* (New York: Herder and Herder, 1965); cf. its critical review by Patricia Barret in *Theological Studies* 27 (March 1966), pp. 138-141.

302. John XXIII, *Mater et magistra,* encyclical of May 15, 1961, in Lawrence Elliott, *I Will Be Called John: A Biography of Pope John XXIII* (New York: E. P. Dutton and Co., 1973), pp. 294-295; and encyclical, *Progressio populorum* of Paul VI, 1965; Philip S. Laud, "The Social Theology of Paul VI," *America,* May 12, 1979, pp. 392-394.

303. NC News Release of Jan. 31, 1979.

304. John Maher, "'Avoid Marxist Solutions' Say Italian Bishops," NC News Release, Jan. 31, 1979.

305. Presentation of the theme: "To Arrive at Peace, Educate to Peace," for World Day of Peace, 1979, *Osservatore Romano,* Eng. ed., Dec. 21, 1978, document initiated by Pope Paul VI and announced in the press office by Pope on July 18, 1978.

306. Pope's message for World Day of Peace, Jan 1, 1979, "To Reach Peace, Teach Peace," *Osservatore Romano,* Dec. 28, 1978.

307. "Pope John Paul Calls for a 'True Spirit of Peace,'" *Wanderer,* Jan. 4, 1979 *(paragraphing and subheads added).*

308. "Pope's Message on 30th Anniversary of Declaration of Human Rights: Recognition of Inherent Dignity of Each Person Is the Foundation of Freedom, Justice, and Peace," *Osservatore Romano,* Dec. 21, 1978.

309. "Argentina and Chile Ask Pope To Mediate Border Debate," *New York Times,* Jan. 10, 1979, p. A3.

310. "Brezhnev, Pope Join in Appeals To Spare Bhutto," *New York Times,* Feb. 10, 1979, pp. 1, 5.

311. Beatitudes; cf. Mt 5, 3-8; cf. John E. Steinmueller and Kathryn Sullivan, *Catholic Biblical Encyclopedia: New Testament* (New York, 1950), pp. 67-88; Roland H. Bainton, *Christian Attitudes toward War and Peace* (New York, 1960); cf. Dietrich Bonhoeffer, *The Cost of Discipleship* 12th printing (New York, 1970); cf. Rollo May, *Power and Innocence* (New York, 1972); cf. Thomas Merton, *Faith and Violence* (1968); cf. Helder Camara, *Spiral of Violence* (Denville, N.Y., 1971); James W. Douglass, *The Non-Violent Cross* (New York, 1970); Ralph B. Potter, *War and Moral Discourse* (Richmond, Va., 1970); P. Régamey, OP, *Non-Violence and the Christian Conscience* (New York, 1966); Arturo Paoli, *Freedom To Be Free* (New York, 1973), *passim;* Jose de Broucker, Dom Helder, *The Violence of a Peacemaker* (New York, 1973).

312. Louis A. Rongione, *Conference on the Beatitudes* (Philadelphia: Peter Reilly Co., 1959), pp. 127-142.

313. Thomas à Kempis, *The Imitation of Christ,* ed. J. M. Lelen (New York, 1941), pp. 145-148.

314. "Pope Prays for Peace in Mass Attended by 25,000," *New York Times,* Jan 2, 1979, p. A6.

315. John Paul II, *Talks of John Paul II,* ed. Daughters of St. Paul (Boston: St. Paul Edition, 1979), pp. 499-502 *(paragraph. added).*

316. Francis Dvornik, "Origins of Episcopal Synods," *The Once and Future Church,* ed. James H. Coriden (N.Y. 1971), pp. 26-56.

317. Francis Dvornik, *The General Councils of the Church* (London, 1960); *idem,* "Emperors, Popes and the General Councils," *Dumbarton Oaks Papers* 6 (1951), pp. 1-23.

318. Francis Dvornik, *The Idea of Apostolicity in Byzantium and the Legend of the Apostolic Andrew* (Cambridge, Mass., 1958), pp. 1-40; *idem, Byzantium and the Roman Primacy* (New York: Fordham Univ. Press, 1966), pp. 1-176.

319. John Paul II, *Talks,* pp. 197-204.

320. *The Message of John Paul I,* comp. Daughters of St. Paul (Boston: St. Paul Edition, 1979), p. 31; Pope's speech to cardinals on Aug. 27, 1978.

321. John Paul II, *Talks,* pp. 193-195.

322. *Ibid.,* pp. 257-262.

323. Apostolic exhortation, *Evangelii nuntiandi,* no. 69, 2, in *Talks of John Paul II,* pp. 305-312; also in *Osservatore Romano,* Nov. 24, 1978.

324. "A Man Filled with Christ," homily of Humberto Cardinal Medeiros of Boston, to be found in *Talks of John Paul II*, pp. 31-36.

325. David Tracy, *Toward Vatican III: The Work That Needs To Be Done* (New York: Gill-Macmillan, 1978), *passim;* see review by John Harriot under title "Central Issues for Church's Future," *Catholic Herald*, Oct. 20, 1978.

CHAPTER 17

326. *Roget's International Thesaurus*, new ed. (New York: Thomas Y. Crowell Co.) no. 270.3 (transference), 284.6 (bequest), 775.4 (inheritance), and 780.3 (estate).

327. Jacques Maritain, *The Things That Are Not Caesar's* (trans. *of Primauté du Spirituel* by J. F. Scanlan (London: Sheed and Ward, 1939), pp. 6-10 and *passim; idem., Man and the State* (Chicago Univ. Press, 1951), *passim.*

328. Theodor Schnitzler, *Im Kampfe un Chalcedon: Geschichte und Inhalt des Codex Encyclius von 458* (Rome: Gregorian Univ. Press, 1938), pp. 104-108.

329. Francis Dvornik, "Church and State in Central Europe," *The Soviet Union: A Symposium*, ed. W. Guricu (Univ. of Notre Dame Press, 1951), pp. 195-216.

330. *Idem, The Making of Central and Eastern Europe* (London: Polish Research Center, 1949), pp. 44-47 and *passim.*

331. *Idem*, "Byzantium, Muscovite Autocracy and the Church," *Rediscovering Eastern Christendom, Essays in Commemoration of Dom Bede Winslow*, ed. A. H. Armstrong and E. B. Fry (London, 1903), pp. 106-118.

332. *Idem*, "Pope Gelasius and Emperor Anastasius I," *Byzantinische Zeitschrift* 44 (1951), pp. 111-116.

333. James Zatko, *Descent into Darkness: The Destruction of the Roman Catholic Church in Russia*, 1917-1923 (Univ. of Notre Dame Press, 1966), *passim.*

334. Ludvik Nemec, "The Ruthenian Uniate Church in Its Historical Perspective," *Church History* 37, no. 4 (Dec. 1968), pp. 1-24.

335. Dale Vree, *On Synthesizing Marxism and Christianity* (New York: John Wiley and Sons, 1976); see review by Francis H. Maier, "Curious Bed Fellows: Marxism and Christianity," *National Catholic Reporter*, Feb. 18, 1979.

336. Peter Hebblethwaite, *The Year of Three Popes* (Cleveland: William Collins, 1979); review by Francis X. Murphy, *National Catholic Reporter*, March 16, 1979.

337. Leszek Kolakowski, "Pomyslne proroctwa i pobozne zyczenia laika na Progu Nowiego Pontyfikatu w wiecznej Sprawie Praw Cesarskich i Boskich" [Prospective Prophecies and pious wishes of a layman at the threshold of a new pontificate concerning the Perpetual Problem of the Rights of Caesar and of God] *Kultura* (Paris, Dec. 1978), pp. 5-13; see also Michael Freeden, *The New Liberalism: An Ideology of Social Reform* (New York: Oxford Univ. Press 1978) of which a positive review by Paul Barton Johnson is in *American Catholic Historical Review* 84, no. 1 (Feb. 1979), pp. 166-169.

338. Translated and adapted by author and provided by Professor Leo Rudnytsky of La Salle College, Philadelphia, Pa. *(paragraphing and subheads added).*

339. Karol Wojtyla, "Denial of God and Contemporary Anthropocentrism," *Osservatore Romano,* Nov. 23, 1978, from *Segno di contraddizione,* ed. Vita e Pensiero (Milan Università Cattolica, 1977); see also *Sign of Contradiction* (New York: Seabury Press, 1979).

340. Karol Wojtyla, "O la identidad cristiana," *Ecclesia* (Madrid, Feb. 10, 1979); the whole issue is dedicated to "El Papa estuvo en Puebla"; "Compromisos pastorales, en una concepción cristiana de la evangelización," pp. 4-9.

341. *Duchovní Pastýr* 17, no. 1 (Prague, Jan. 1967), pp. 16-17.

342. Kolakowski, *Kultura,* pp. 12-13.

343. Francine Cardman, "A Lightning Look at the History of Christian Spirituality," *The Wind is Rising,* ed. William R. Callahan, SJ, and Francine Cardman, 2d ed. (Mount Rainier, Md.: Quixote Center, 1979), pp. 37-40.

344. Editorial, "The Hope: A New Kind of Papacy," *National Catholic Reporter,* Dec. 8, 1978.

345. Sacred Congregation for the Doctrine of the Faith, Declaration concerning the book 'Quand je dis Dieu' by Fr. Pohier and in *l'Osservatore Romano* No. 16 (April 17, 1979), in Declaration of April 3, 1979, signed by Franjo Cardinal Seper, prefect and Jermie Hamer, O.P., titular archbishop of Lorium, a secretary, with the Pope's approval.

346. Letter of the Supreme Pontiff John Paul II to all the bishops of the Church on the occasion of Holy Thursday, 1979. *l'Osservatore Romano* No. 16, (April 17, 1979) p. 5.

347. Letter of the Supreme Pontiff John Paul II to all the priests on the occasion of Holy Thursday, 1979. *l'Osservatore Romano* No. 16, (April 17, 1979) pp. 6-9.

348. Paul Hofmann, "Pope in Letter to Priests reaffirms celibacy rule as holy commitment." *New York Times,* April 10, 1979, pp. A1, A6.

349. Pope to *NCEA* Delegates: "The Church is grateful for your dedication." *The Catholic Standard and Times* of April 19, 1979, p. 3.

350. This is the complete text of the address of Pope John Paul II to the delegates to the National Catholic Education Association Convention, held in Philadelphia, April 15-19, 1979. The message was recorded on videotape and shown at the Civic Center in Philadelphia; it also appeared on television. See *The Catholic Standard and Times* of April 19, 1979, p. 3.

351. "Pope says officials can't force rejection of Church." *Philadelphia Bulletin* of April 23, 1979.

352. Reference to Christ's cleansing the temple (Lk 19:45-46) and to His Mission (Lk 2:41-50).

353. *Osservatore Romano,* Nov. 2, 1978.

354. The first encyclical of His Holiness Pope John Paul II, *Redemptor hominis* of March 4, 1979. The complete Eng. authorized text is to be found in *Osservatore Romano,* March 19, 1979, pp. 3-14.

SUPPLEMENTARY BIBLIOGRAPHY

(in addition to already mentioned articles, translated works, and studies in the notes)

Bezmalinovich, Remo and Merlin, Gianni, *Un anno: tre papi* (Udine: I D Edizioni, 1978).

Baum, Gregory, *Religion and Alienation* (New York: Paulist-Newman Press, 1976).

Bourdeaux, Michael, *Religious Ferment in the Soviet Union* (New York: St. Martin, 1960).

Churchill, Winston S. and eds. of *Life, The Second World War,* 2 vols. (New York: Time Inc., 1960).

Ciechanowski, Jan M., *The Warsaw Rising of 1944* (Cambridge Univ. Press, 1974).

Cienciela, Anna M., *Poland and the Western Powers, 1938-1939* (Univ. of Toronto Press, 1968).

Daw, Richard W., ed., *Nights of Sorrow, Days of Joy: Papal Transition: Paul VI, John Paul I, John Paul II* (Washington, D.C.: National Catholic News Service, 1978).

De Andreis, Stefano and Leone, Marcella, *Il Pastore venuto da Lontano* (Milan: Editrice Magna, 1978).

De Roeck, Jef, *L'Uomo dalla Polonia* (Turin: Marietti Edition, 1978) (in German, English, French, Spanish, and Italian).

D'Onofrio, Arturo, *Luminosi albori di un pontificato Giovanni Paulo II:—Profile biografico—discorsi, scritti ed omelie del Card. Karol Wojtyla,* 2d ed. (Naples-Rome: Libreria Editrice Redenzione, 1978).

Dooley, N, "A Foreign Pope," *Time* (Oct. 30, 1978), pp. 87-100).

Dunn, Dennis J., *The Catholic Church and the Soviet Government, 1939-1949* (Denver: East European Monograph, 1978).

Dvornik, Francis, *The Slavs: Their Early History and Civilization* (Boston: American Academy, 1956).

———, *The Slavs in European History and Civilization* (New Brunswick, N.J.: Rutgers Univ. Press, 1962).

———, *Byzantine Missions among the Slavs* (New Brunswick, N.J.: Rutgers Univ. Press, 1970).

Eine neue Ara hat begonnen: Johannes Paul II, a special issue of *Weltbild,* Oct. 30, 1978.

Elliott, Lawrence, *I Will Be Called John: A Biography of Pope John XXIII* (New York: E. P. Dutton & Co., 1973).

Gannon, Robert I, SJ, *The Cardinal Spellman Story* (New York: Doubleday and Co., 1962).

Giordani, Igino, *Le Enciccliche sociali dei Papi (da Pio IX a Pio XII 1864-1946)*, 3d ed. (Rome: Editrice Studium, 1946).

Greeley, Andrew M., *A Making of the Popes 1978: The Politics of Intrigue at the Vatican* (Chicago: Andrews & McMeel, 1979).

Gross, John Tomasz, *Polish Society under German Occupation: The General Government, 1939-1944* (Princeton: Princeton Univ. Press, 1979.

Halecki, Oscar, *A History of Poland,* 3d ed. (New York: Fordham Univ. Press, 1961).

———, *The Millennium of Europe* (Univ. of Notre Dame Press, 1963).

Hatch, Alden and Walshe, Seamus, *Crown of Glory: The Life of Pope Pius XII* (New York, Hawthorn, 1957).

Hebblethwaite, Peter, *The Year of Three Popes* (Cleveland: William Collins, 1979).

———,"Wojtyla at Krakow," *Sign* 58, no. 7 (April, 1979), pp. 13-20, 48-52.

Henry, Hugh T., *Poems, Charades, Inscriptions of Pope Leo XIII,* with Eng. trans. and note (New York-Philadelphia: The Dolphin Press, 1902).

Hughes, Philip, *Pope Pius the Eleventh* (New York, 1937).

John Paul I, *The Message of John Paul I,* ed. Daughters of St. Paul (Boston: St. Paul Editions, 1978).

John Paul II, encyclical, *Redemptor hominis,* of March 4, 1979, Eng. text, *Osservatore Romano* March 19, 1979.

———, *Talks of John Paul II,* ed. Daughters of St. Paul, foreword by John Cardinal Krol (Boston: St. Paul Editions, 1979).

Jordan, A. Z., *Philosophy and Ideology: The Development of Philosophy and Marxism-Leninism in Poland since the Second World War* (Dordrecht, 1963).

Kolakowski, Leszek, *Pomyslne Proroctwa i Pobożne życzenia Laika na Progu Nowego Pontyfikatu w wiecznej Sprawie Praw Cesarskich i Boskich* [Prospective prophecies and pious wishes of a layman at the threshold of a new pontificate concerning the perpetual problem of the rights of Caesar and of God] (Paris-Grudzin: Kultura, 1978).

Korbel, Josef, *Poland between East and West: Soviet and German Diplomacy toward Poland* 1919-1933 (Princeton Univ. Press, 1963).

Korbowski, Stefan, *The Polish Underground State: A Guide to the Underground, 1939-1945* (Denver: East European Monograph, 1978).

Korolevskji, Cyrille, *Metropolite Andre Szeptyckyj 1865-1955* (Rome, 1964).

Kosinski, Leszek A., ed. *Demographic Developments in Eastern Europe* (New York: Prager Publishers & Co., 1977).

Krol, John Cardinal, *The Church: Life-giving Union with Christ* (Boston: St. Paul Editions, 1978).

Lauer, Quentin, SJ, "The Philosopher Pope," *America* 140, no. 15 (April 21, 1979), p. 337.

Locigno, Joseph R., *We Have a Pope* (Rockville Center, N.Y.: Manor Books Inc., 1978).

Luciani, Albino, *Illustrissimi: Letters from Pope John Paul I* (New York: Little, Brown, 1979).

McEoin, Garry, *The Inner Elite: Dossiers of Papal Candidates* (Washington, D.C., 1978).

Majchrowski, Jacek M., *The Origin and Early Activities of the Pax Movement in Poland* (Denver: East European Monograph, 1978).

Malinski, Mieczyslaw, *Pope John Paul II: The Life of Karol Wojtyla* (New York: The Seabury Press, a Crossroad Book, 1979).

Marcel, Gabriel, ed., *Fresh Hope for the World* (London: Longmans, 1960).

Maritain, Jacques, *The Things That Are Not Caesar's,* trans. of *Primauté du spirituel* by J. F. Scanlon (London: Sheed and Ward, 1939).

Markert, W., ed., *Polen* (Cologne, 1959).

Martin, Malachi, *The Final Conclave* (New York: Pocket Book, 1977).

Meystowicz, W. *L'Eglise Catholique en Pologne entre deux guerres, 1919-1939* (Vatican City, 1944).

Mikolajczyk, Stanislav, *The Rape of Poland* (New York: Wittlesey House, 1948).

Mindszenty, Jozsef Cardinal, *Memoirs,* trans. Richard and Clara Winston (New York: Macmillan Publishing Co., 1974).

Murphy, Francis X. and Shaifer, Norman, *John Paul II: A Son from Poland* (South Hackensack, N.J.: Shepherd Press, 1978).

Nemec, Ludvik, *The Communist Ecclesiology during the Church-State Relationship in Czechoslovakia,* PROCEEDINGS OF THE AMERICAN PHILOSOPHICAL SOCIETY (Philadelphia, 1976).

———, *Czech Catholics at the 41st International Eucharistic Congress,* Held August 1-8, 1976, in Philadelphia, USA (New York-Philadelphia, 1977).

———, *Stephen Cardinal Trochta, an Educator, a Churchman and an Ecumenist,* special offprint of *Bohemia,* vol. 17 (Munich-Vienna, 1976).

Neill, Thomas P. and Schmandt, Raymond H., *History of the Catholic Church* (Milwaukee: Bruce, 1937).

The New Pope: John Paul I, special issue *Time* (Sept. 4, 1978).

O'Brien, Thomas C., "John Paul II. Pope," *Encyclopedic Dictionary of Religion* (Chicago: SSJ and Corpus, 1979), II: p. 1904.

O'Hare, Joseph, "John Paul II: A Pope from the East," *America* (Oct. 28, 1978), pp. 278-280.

Oram, James, *The People's Pope, the Story of Karol Wojtyla of Poland* (Sydney and London: Bay Books, 1979). See review, *Osservatore Romano,* May 7, 1979), pp. 11.

Ottaviani, Alaphridus, *Institutiones juris publici ecclesiastici,* 2 vols., ed., tertia typis (Polyglottis Vaticanis, 1947).

Parsons, Wilfrid, SJ, *The Pope and Italy* (New York, 1929).

"Pope John Paul I (1912-1978)," *The Pope Speaks,* special Winter issue of 1978.

Ringelblum, Emmanuel, *Polish-Jewish Relations during the Second World War,* ed. and with footnotes by Joseph Kermish and Shmuel Krakowski, trans. from the Polish by Dafna Allon, Danuta Dabrowska, and Dana Keren (New York: Howard Fertig Inc., 1976) (biased), see review by Professor George J. Lerski of the Univ. of San Francisco, *The Catholic Historical Review* 65, no. 1 (Jan. 1979), pp. 96-99.

Ryan, James H., *Encyclicals of Pius XI* (St. Louis: Herder, 1927).

Sacrum Poloniae millennium, 10 vols. Rome, 1954-64.

Tillard, J. M. R., OP, "The Jurisdiction of the Bishop of Rome," *Theological Studies* 40 (March, 1979).

Tracy, David, *Toward Vatican III: The Work That Needs To Be Done* (New York: Gill-Macmillan, 1978).

Uninski, J., *Historical Kosciola,* ed. W. Urban, 2 vols. 4th ed. (Opole, 1959-60).

Vree, Dale, *On Synthesizing Marxism and Christianity* (New York: John Wiley and Sons, 1976).

Winowska, Maria, *The Death Camp Proved Him Real: The Life of Father Maximilian Kolbe, Franciscan* (Kenosha, Wis.: Prow Press 1971).

Woodward, Kenneth, "Boy Called Lolek," *Newsweek* (Oct. 30, 1978), pp. 78-81.

Wojtyla, Karol, *Segno di contraddizione: Meditazioni,* ed. Vita e Pensiero (Milan: Publicazioni della Universita Cattolica, 1977).

———, *The Eucharist and Man's Hunger for Freedom* (Boston: Pamphlet Edition, Daughters of St. Paul, 1978).

———, *Amore e responsabilità: Morale sessuale e vita interpersonale* (Turin: Marietti, 1978).

———, *Il Buon pastore: Scritti, discorsi e lettere pastorali,* trans. by Elzbieta Cywiak and Renzo Panzone (Rome: Edizioni Logos, 1978).

———, *Sign of Contradiction* (New York: The Seabury Press, a Crossroad Book, 1978).

———, *The Acting Person,* trans. Andrzej Potocki (Reidel, Analecta Husserliana, 1979).

———, *Fruitful and Responsible Love* (New York: The Seabury Press, a Crossroad Book, 1979).

——— (Andrzej Jawien), *Easter Vigil and Other Poems,* trans. from Polish by Jerzy Peterkiewicz (New York: Random House, 1979).

Wright, Gene, ed., *Four Popes, Keepers of the Faith since 1958* (New York: a memorial ed., Ideal Publishing Corp., 1978).

Zawodny, J. K., *Death in the Forest: The Story of the Katyn Forest Massacre* (Univ. of Notre Dame Press, 1962).

Zylinski, W. and Wierzbianski, B., eds., *White Paper on the Persecution of the Church in Poland* (London, 1954).

INDEX